P9-CKV-408

McClain, Alva J.
ROMANS: THE GOSPEL OF GOD'S GRACE

CORBAN
COLLEGE

5000 DEER PARK DRIVE, S. E.
SALEM, OREGON 97302

The Author

Before his death in 1968, DR. ALVA J. MCCLAIN, past president and professor of Christian theology at Grace Theological Seminary, taught also at the Philadelphia School of the Bible, the Bible Institute of Los Angeles, Ashland College, and Ashland Theological Seminary, serving as dean in the last-named school. In 1937 he directed the founding of Grace Theological Seminary, and after that time served continuously as president and professor of Christian theology until his retirement. He also served as president of Grace College from its organization as a four-year school of liberal arts in 1953.

Dr. McClain served as a member of the Scofield Reference Bible Revision Committee, was a member of Phi Beta Kappa, and was a charter member of the Evangelical Theological Society. He authored *The Greatness of the Kingdom.*

HERMAN A. HOYT, Editor, is president of Grace College and Grace Theological Seminary, having served there in various capacities since 1937. He received a Th.M. and Th.D. from Grace Theological Seminary, a B.Th. from Ashland Theological Seminary, and an A.B. from Ashland College. He has authored several books including *The End Times*

Romans: The Gospel of God's Grace

Romans: The Gospel of God's Grace

The Lectures of
ALVA J. McCLAIN

Compiled and edited by
HERMAN A. HOYT

MOODY PRESS

CHICAGO

© 1973 by
THE MOODY BIBLE INSTITUTE
OF CHICAGO

Library of Congress Catalog Card Number: 72-95027

ISBN: 0-8024-7373-3

Printed in the United States of America

Contents

Foreword

THE LATE Dr. Alva J. McClain was a master teacher, whether in the pulpit or in the classroom. In the closing year of a five-year ministry at the First Brethren Church of Philadelphia, Pennsylvania, he delivered a series of expository messages on the epistle to the Romans. For more than forty years he delivered this same series of messages to his students. In the providence of God they are now being put into print.

These messages were stenographically recorded by Mrs. Alice Longaker Andrews (then Miss Longaker), who was a member of Dr. McClain's congregation. In 1942 she presented the manuscript to Dr. O. D. Jobson, who in turn made it available for publication.

After consultation with the widow of Dr. McClain, the manuscript was given to me for editing and publication. I had been one of Dr. McClain's students who enjoyed the privilege of hearing this remarkable and soul-searching series of messages. I later served as colleague with him for more than thirty years and succeeded him as the second president of Grace Schools in Winona Lake, Indiana. More than anything else, the years of close association with Dr. McClain have enabled me to edit this material.

To prepare his series of messages, Dr. McClain used the American Standard Version almost exclusively. This will be apparent in the frequent reference to that translation. There were also times when he referred to the King James Version, the version of his parishioners. This, too, will be obvious to the reader.

I must also acknowledge the painstaking and efficient assistance given by Mrs. Agnes N. Derr, secretary to the president, in the several typings of this manuscript and her vigilance in noticing areas that needed further clarification.

This manuscript is now being put into print with the prayer and the expectation that the blessing it has brought to hundreds of students will become available for multitudes more.

HERMAN A. HOYT

Outline of the Epistle of Paul to the Romans

TEXT—"The just shall live by faith"
THEME—"The gospel of God"

INTRODUCTION (1:1-17)

1. Salutation (vv. 1-7)
2. Personal communication (vv. 8-15)
3. Transition to the main theme (vv. 16-17)

I. CONDEMNATION—THE WRATH OF GOD REVEALED
    (1:18—3:20)

Question—Is the world lost?
Answer—"All the world . . . guilty before God" (3:19)

1. The heathen condemned (1:18-32)
2. The moralist condemned (2:1-16)
3. The Jew condemned (2:17—3:8)
4. The world condemned (3:9-20)

II. SALVATION—THE RIGHTEOUSNESS OF GOD REVEALED
    (3:21—8:39)

Question—How does God save sinners?
Answer—"In Christ Jesus" (8:1)

1. Justification—declared righteous in Christ (3:21—5:21)
2. Sanctification—made holy in Christ (chap. 6 and 7)
3. Preservation—kept securely in Christ (chap. 8)

III. VINDICATION—THE WISDOM OF GOD REVEALED
    (9:1—11:36)

Question—Why has Israel been set aside?
Answer—"That He might have mercy upon all" (11:32)

IV. EXHORTATION—THE WILL OF GOD REVEALED

(12:1—15:33)

Question—How should a saved man walk?

Answer—"Be ye transformed" (12:2)

1. Recommendation (vv. 1-2)

2. Salutations (vv. 3-16, 21-24)

3. Warning (vv. 17-20)

4. Doxology (vv. 25-27)

Introduction

IN THIS INTRODUCTION we will examine some preliminary facts about the book of Romans: the writer, the church to which it was written, and his purpose in writing. All of these will be amplified in the exposition of the book.

First, notice this is the epistle of Paul to the Romans. The apostle Paul was the writer, under God, of this great book.

While the date of his birth is unknown, it must have been somewhere near the birth of Jesus Christ. A short time after the death of Jesus Christ, Stephen was stoned, and the executioners laid their apparel at the feet of a young man named Paul (Ac 7:58). It is fairly certain that Paul was a member of the Sanhedrin (Ac 6:12; 7:58; 8:1), and led the persecution against the church (Ac 8:1, 3). To belong to the Sanhedrin, a man must be at least thirty years of age; so, as a young man but a member of the Sanhedrin, he was probably near thirty.

It is well known that Paul was born at Tarsus, a city about seven hundred miles north of Jerusalem, and capital of the Roman province of Cilicia (Ac 22:3). Tarsus was a very important city in the ancient world and ranked with Athens and Alexandria in culture and learning. It was not only noted as one of the three university centers, but it was also noted for its corruption. When confronting the chief captain of the Roman guard, Paul insisted that he was a citizen of Tarsus, no mean city (Ac 21:39). All the records confirm this.

His father, according to his own testimony, was a Pharisee (Ac 23:6). In addition, Paul claimed Roman citizenship. When facing the threat of scourging at the hands of Romans, he appealed to the Roman captain on the basis of this citizenship. The captain marveled, "With a great sum obtained I this freedom," and Paul replied, "But I was free born" (Ac 22: 25-28). So his father was not only a Jew who had gone up

11

to Tarsus and settled there, he was a Roman citizen; therefore, Paul was a free-born, not a naturalized, Roman citizen.

There is reason to believe his father was a well-to-do man. Paul may intimate this in Philippians, where he says he lost everything (Phil 3:7-9). When he was struck down on the way to Damascus, called Jesus "Lord," and from that time on acknowledged Him and preached Him, he may at that instant have lost his family, his inheritance—everything. The tense of the Greek word in Philippians suggests the possibility of an instantaneous catastrophe—lost, all at once.

The advantages he enjoyed are those bestowed by wealth. He undoubtedly had access to the excellent education available in Tarsus, and there became acquainted with Greek philosophy. It was in the university of the city that he had intimate touch with the various schools of Greek thought. From there he was undoubtedly sent down to Jerusalem, where he sat at the feet of the greatest of all ancient Hebrew teachers, Gamaliel, the man who made the Pharisaical teaching so great (Ac 22:3).

Then, after all his learning in philosophy and in the lore of the Old Testament, in addition to the education given him by the Lord Himself when He took him to the desert, on top of all that, he had been taught a trade. He knew how to weave tent cloth. What a practical thing this was, and what a fine thing it would be today if every man, whether he starts out to be a doctor, a teacher, or a lawyer, would be taught a trade. Then, if something happens to his profession, he need not be at the mercy of the world. When Paul went out to preach the gospel, he could start to ply his trade if he needed money, and make it. This was undoubtedly one of the practical things learned by the Jews in the midst of a hostile Gentile world. The course of the Russian revolution confirms the wisdom of this policy: one of the most pitiful things about this revolution was that the aristocrats and statesmen, the men who held high place in the Russian nation, were literally at the mercy of hunger and need when they were turned out.

Paul was chosen of God to write the greatest book of the Bible. Consider how well fitted he was for his work. As a Greek he was learned in all the philosophy of Greece; as a Hebrew, he knew the Old Testament, the law, the traditions; on top of all that, he was a Roman citizen, a member of the greatest empire of ancient days. Greek culture, Hebrew culture, Roman culture—all were summed up in this one man. Even then he was not ready to write this book, but God Himself took him in hand, off by himself, away from all human teachers, and taught him things he could not learn from flesh and blood. All this formed the background for the writing of this great epistle. As with Moses and John the Baptist, God took Paul off in the desert, and there schooled him so he might fulfill his ministry.

There is a time in the life of the young man who is preparing to preach the gospel, when he can afford to shut himself up and neglect, if need be, some of the things the world needs done. A great many things needed doing while Paul was in the Arabian desert; a thousand things needed to be done while Moses was forty years in the wilderness. But God needs a man, and He needs him by himself. There is nothing better in all the world than for a man to be alone with God for three, or four, or five years—alone with God! Then he is prepared to go out into the harvest fields of ministry. Do not imagine that this preparation is too long. Reflect on the years Paul spent in preparation.

Now, let's look at the church at Rome and at the purpose and occasion for this epistle.

The Roman Catholic church believes Peter founded the church at Rome and was the first pope. I do not believe this for several reasons. First, in the salutation in the last chapter, Paul salutes twenty-seven men by name. It would have been astounding if Peter had been there and Paul had not saluted him also. Second, Paul states that it is the aim of his life to preach the gospel where it has never been preached before, "lest I should build on another man's foundation" (Ro 15:20). But he wanted to go to Rome, and he did go to Rome. If the apostle Peter had been there, the apostle Paul would not have turned his eyes in that direction.

Third, Luke was a careful historian, but he did not record in the book of Acts Peter as the founder of the church at Rome. If a man as prominent as Peter had founded this church, surely Luke would have said so.

How was it founded? On the day of Pentecost, the Holy

Spirit fell on the followers of Jesus, and they all began to speak other languages. Those that stood by were amazed and said, "Behold, are not all these which speak Galilaeans? And how hear we every man in our own tongue, wherein we were born? Parthians, and Medes, . . . and *strangers of Rome*, Jews and proselytes, Cretes and Arabians, we do hear them speak in our tongues the wonderful works of God" (Ac 2:7-11).

On the day of Pentecost there were godly Jews from practically every country under heaven who had come down for the Passover. Christ had died at the time of the Passover in Jerusalem. They remained for the day of Pentecost, exactly fifty days after that, and were there to hear what happened then, including the sermon of Peter. That is very likely how the church was founded at Rome: those from Rome who were converted at Jerusalem carried their new religion back home.

Other Christians also went to Rome; chief among them were Aquila and Priscilla. We first meet these two in Ephesus in the eighteenth chapter of Acts, where they took aside that great orator Apollos and taught him more perfectly the way of God. But in the salutation in the last chapter of Romans, we find Aquila and Priscilla up at Rome. Paul salutes them in a remarkable way: "Greet Priscilla and Aquila my helpers in Christ Jesus: who have for my life laid down their own necks: unto whom not only I give thanks, but also all the churches of the Gentiles. Likewise greet the church that is in their house" (Ro 16:3-5).

Probably the church at Rome was not at this time a completely organized body, but merely a collection of believers meeting in different places throughout the city, such as the home of Priscilla and Aquila. There may have been many little groups of believers all over Rome.

Why did Paul write to Rome from Corinth? He had made two missionary journeys and had already written five other epistles: 1 and 2 Thessalonians, 1 and 2 Corinthians, and Galatians. He had written to these churches to correct existing defects. When he hears that in Rome there are saints, a little colony of believers, and that the church is not really organized, not planted by an apostle, Paul is filled with a desire to visit this church. He knows this is the chief city of the world, the logical place to do a great work for God. In order to prepare the way for his coming, he writes them. This epistle also sets forth the gospel he preached. So for the first time, and for the only time in all the epistles of the New Testament, the great doctrines, the system of Christianity, are set forth in logical discourse. There is order all the way through. Every time I read this book, I thank God that those few Christians were at Rome, providing the occasion for Paul to write this mighty treatise. God used the human occasion as the means to this end. Paul wrote the epistle to set forth the gospel of the grace of God to the believers in Rome.

The bearer of this epistle was a woman. She is mentioned in the first verse of the sixteenth chapter: "I commend unto you Phoebe our sister, who is a servant of the church that is at Cenchreae: that ye receive her in the Lord, worthily of the saints, and that ye assist her in whatsoever matter she may have need of you: for she herself also hath been a helper of many, and of mine own self" (16:1-2, ASV). It does not say in so many words that she carried the letter, but it is undoubtedly true that she did bear it from Cenchrea.

I want to say something about the place of this epistle in the Word of God. The four gospels (Matthew, Mark, Luke, and John) are all biographical history; then the book of Acts, is history. These five books are followed by the first of the epistles, Romans. Romans was not the first epistle written. Paul wrote five others before it. Why are these books not placed in the Bible chronologically? Why is 1 Thessalonians, if it was written first, not put after the book of Acts, then 2 Thessalonians, 1 and 2 Corinthians, Galatians, and finally Romans?

Romans is the first epistle in the reading of the Word of God. I believe it was placed there by the Holy Spirit, because the canon of the New Testament would not be in proper order otherwise. It stands there much as the brazen altar stood in the tabernacle: when the worshiper started to approach the holy place, the first thing he came to was the brazen altar on which the sacrifice was placed. He could not pass; he could not enter the tabernacle until he came to that. The book of Romans in the New Testament corresponds to the brazen altar. It is the place where we find Christ set forth as the propitiation which justifies us and enables us, through faith in his blood, to go on in Christian truth.

Romans tells us what Christianity is; Ephesians, Colossians, and Philippians tell us about the body of Christ, the mystery which was never known in past ages; and 1 and 2 Thessalonians deal with the coming of the Lord and the translation of the church. In the epistles to the seven churches, Romans comes first and Thessalonians last, because one is the introduction to Christianity and the gospel, and the other points to the consummation of Christianity when Christ takes the church out of the world.

Finally, let us look at the way Romans begins. Notice the statement in the first two verses of chapter one, "the gospel of God, which he had promised afore through his prophets in the holy scriptures." The gospel that is going to be set forth in this book has been known before. Romans begins with a gospel that has always been known.

The fifty-third chapter of Isaiah and Psalm 22 speak of the suffering of the Messiah. They taught that Christ would bear our sins: "He was wounded for our transgressions, he was bruised for our iniquities; the chastisement of our peace was upon him; and with his stripes we are healed . . . The Lord hath laid on him the iniquity of us all" (Is 53:5, 6, ASV). That is the gospel that was promised beforehand, and it is that gospel that is spoken of and unfolded in Romans.

This book has a text: "The just shall live by his faith" (Hab 2:4). Paul went back to the Old Testament for a text which must be unfolded. This text occurs in Hebrews and in Galatians too (Heb 10:38; Gal 3:11). Romans emphasizes the first two words, *the just*; Galatians, the second two, *shall live*; Hebrews the last two, *by faith*. But the book of Romans gathers about this text in a peculiar way: first, justification; second, faith; third, life.

This book also has a theme: "I am not ashamed of the gospel of Christ" (Ro 1:16, KJV).

Around those two things, the text and the theme, the book is written, and the exposition will unfold from these two focal points.

ALVA J. MCCLAIN

1

Introductory Message on the Epistle to the Romans

AT LEAST THREE significant questions should be asked at the very outset: first, why is there an epistle to the Romans? second, why does this epistle stand first in the order of all the epistles? and third, why does it head the list of the Pauline epistles?

It is my conviction that even the arrangement of the books of the Bible as set forth in the King James Version was ordered of God. The facts of Christianity as centered in Christ are presented in the four gospels, while the force of those facts are recorded in the Acts of the Apostles. These five books are followed by the Pauline epistles, then the general epistles, and the New Testament is concluded with the Revelation.

The facts of the Christian faith without inspired interpretation can be misinterpreted and misused. The importance of the book of Romans is that it is an inspired interpretation of the Christian faith. It presents the most comprehensive and outstanding interpretation of the facts of the gospels and Acts.

Herein may lie the answers to why this book exists, stands at the head of all the epistles, and comes first in the arrangement of the Pauline epistles. The reader of the New Testament, after completing the record of the facts of Christianity, is confronted immediately with this inspired, comprehensive treatment of the facts.

To safeguard the believers against the clever attacks of the evil one, the Holy Spirit buttressed the New Testament record with this bulwark of inspired interpretation. The Spirit knew that men claiming to represent Christ would appear within the professing church and would seek to undermine Pauline theol-

17

ogy by taking men back to the gospels where they would have freedom to interpret loosely the facts without definite limitations.

Great Bible scholars have paid tribute to Romans across the centuries of the Christian era. Such men as Augustine, Luther, and Calvin were profoundly influenced by this book. Many Bible scholars have remarked on never seeing a man tangled up in the false theories of cult religions who knew accurately the book of Romans.

This book carries with it the blessings of salvation, security, and spiritual strength, which attend a right and thorough knowledge of the grace which God has manifested to us in Jesus Christ His Son. This information is comprehended in a message called "the gospel of Christ" (Ro 1:16). Men believed this message of good news to the saving of their souls. The Book of Romans was written that men might understand what they believed.

The gospel is spoken about using three different expressions in the book of Romans: (1) The apostle speaks in the first verse of being "separated unto the gospel of God"; (2) In verse 16 of the first chapter, he says that he "is not ashamed of the gospel of Christ"; (3) Then in verse 16 of the second chapter, he says that God in the day of judgment, "shall judge men . . . according to my gospel."

The gospel of God; the gospel of Christ; and "my" gospel. What do they mean? Simply this: the gospel is of God because God gave it; the gospel is of Christ because it is about Christ; and it is the gospel of Paul because Paul preached it.

FORMAL STATEMENT OF THE THEME

The formal statement of the theme (which is the gospel of Christ) is found in verses 16 and 17 of the first chapter, and those are the key verses of the whole book. Mark them in your Bible and memorize them: "For I am not ashamed of the gospel of Christ; for it is the power of God unto salvation to every one that believeth; to the Jew first, and also to the Greek. For therein is the righteousness of God revealed from faith to faith: as it is written, The just shall live by faith."

Those two verses sum up the whole book of Romans. I was

pulling down commentaries looking up these verses, and was astounded that not one commentary dealt with the entire passage. Some covered the statement, "I am not ashamed of the gospel of Christ" and then stopped. Others dwelled on the words, "For it is the power of God unto salvation," and still others moved to another portion.

Furthermore, one thing is the heart of the whole discussion: "for therein is the righteousness of God revealed." Take out that statement and you have nothing. The very reason the gospel is the power of God unto salvation is that the righteousness of God is revealed. The righteousness from God is a reality, whereas man is totally without righteousness.

PAUL'S TEXT FOR HIS EPISTLE

Now to the text: "The just shall live by his faith" (Hab 2:4). Paul takes a text. In this respect he is a good preacher. First the theme, then the text. "As it is written, 'The just shall live by faith.'" The whole book of Romans is based on this text from the Old Testament. It is not a very large text: six words in the English; six in the Greek; three words in the Hebrew.

First of all, *the just*. What does the word *just* mean? It means righteous and is so translated in the ASV. Is that not the problem of the ages—righteousness? Job, in the utter depths of his grief and sorrow, expressed the question of the human heart. He cried out, "How should a man be just with God?" (Job 9:2).

Then second, *shall live*. Expressed in one word, it is *life!* What will a man not give for life, and how terrible not to have life! Job talked about that, too. "If a man die, shall he live again?" (Job 14:14). The four words put together say, "the just shall live." Righteousness and life are inseparable. God is holy; He lives forever. An unrighteous man cannot live, "for the wages of sin is death" (Ro 6:23); "The soul that sinneth, it shall die" (Eze 18:4); "Sin . . . bringeth forth death" (Ja 1:15). No man is righteous, but if there is a man in all the world that is righteous, he cannot die. When the lawyer came to Jesus and asked what he should do to inherit eternal life, Jesus in turn asked him what the law had to say. "And he, answering, said, Thou shalt love the Lord thy God with all thy heart, and with all thy soul, and with all thy strength, and with all thy mind; and thy neighbor as thyself" (Lk 10:27). If a man did that he was certainly righteous. Then Christ turned to him and said, "Thou has answered right: this do and thou shalt live" (Lk 10:28). The man who could do these things would have life!

Righteousness and life go together, but the problem is how we can get them. Note the phrase *by faith*. The righteous shall live by faith; that is the way to righteousness and life. The book of Romans, from beginning to end, is simply an expansion of that little text. These six words contain four of the mightiest truths in the world.

The first truth of the text is the requirement of righteousness. The word *righteous* appears ninety-one times in the twenty-seven books of the New Testament. And thirty-five of the ninety-one occur in the book of Romans. Righteousness runs through the whole book, and four great divisions can be seen in the light of that idea: righteousness needed, righteousness supplied, righteousness unattained and righteousness applied in the life.

The second truth concerns the source of life. In the first chapter, after Paul finishes talking about the pagan world, he says, "They . . . are worthy of death" (1:32). Later, "The wages of sin is death" (6:23); and finally, Paul talks about the reception of Israel, and he says, "What shall the receiving of them be, but life from the dead?" (11:15). He also speaks of "a *living* sacrifice" (12:1). The idea of life runs through the book. First, they do not have life and God supplies it; then Israel is to have life sometime; and last of all, the Christian is to be a living sacrifice.

The third idea is that righteousness and life are inseparably bound together, expressed by "the just shall live." "The gift of righteousness shall reign in life" (5:17). In verse 18 life and righteousness are again associated. The climax comes in verse 21: "that as sin hath reigned unto death, even so might grace reign unto eternal life through righteousness by Jesus Christ our Lord." Grace cannot reign to eternal life unless it is through righteousness. When I remember that, it makes me tremble, knowing what I am! But, it was God's righteousness that provided a way that God's grace might reign with the outcome of eternal life! In the following chapter Paul again links life and righteousness (6:13). "The Spirit is life," he says, "because of righteousness" (8:10). And whose righteousness is it? Christ's!

Some people have said hard things about Paul. They have accused Paul of wrenching apart righteousness and life and saying a man could have life no matter how he lived. This criticism is not valid. Paul says that first a man must be given righteousness, and after he gets it he can live right. He is alive from the dead and able to present his members as instruments of righteousness.

We have had the three truths—first righteousness, then life, and then the two of them together. The final truth is the necessity of faith. "By faith," says the text. The words *faith* and *belief* occur fifty-five times in sixteen chapters. The first few verses of Romans start out with faith (1:5); the last chapter contains the same words, "obedience to the faith" (16:26). The Greek in both passages is exactly the same. The epistle begins and ends with faith.

Every blessing of Romans must be received by faith. There is no other way—certainly not by works. We are justified by faith (3:28). We have access to grace by faith (5:2). In reference to confusing choices, "whatsoever is not of faith is sin" (Ro 14:23). In fact, the idea of faith permeates every section of the epistle. Paul thus demonstrated that he was a good preacher; he stayed by his text. He took his little text of three Hebrew words and preached the mightiest epistle in the Word of God. Amazing treasures are hidden in the Scriptures. How many Christians are there who know what is in the book of Habakkuk? Some cannot even pronounce its name, yet the apostle Paul finds the basis of Romans in three words from that little book of the prophet Habakkuk.

Four Main Divisions

The four main divisions of the book are *condemnation, salvation, vindication,* and *exhortation.* Each main division answers a great question.

The first division (1:18-3:20) answers the question, "Is the world lost?" We can't discuss salvation until we know whether the world needs it. All the world is divided on this subject. There are three positions: man is well, man is sick, and man is dead. The Bible says he is dead.

The other day a man came to convert me to New Thought. He gave me a book which he said would show me everything I needed, *Divine Science.* Of course, it was familiar to me, though the author was not. I opened the book, looked into it, and found some exercises to go through each day. The first day one starts out reciting, "I am good. I am well. I am holy." And that is the first position. Christian Science, New Thought, and many of the cults take this position: the world is well!

The other answer is just as bad. "The world is only sick. All man needs is a physician, a little help. He has the means within himself for recovery."

The truth of the matter is that man is dead!

2. The second division (3:21-8:39) answers the question, "How does God save sinners?" When we know that man is dead, then we are ready to learn how God saves him. There are a great many different ideas on that subject. Legalism commands, "Keep the law." Asceticism says, "Scourge the body." Gnosticism urges, "Find the key to superior and secret knowledge." There is Evolutionism: "Salvation consists in a gradual development." Ritualism declares, "We are saved by the performance of ceremonies." Rationalism says, "All you need to do is to be good here and do good, and the next world will take care of itself."

It is necessary for us to find out how God saves sinners.

3. The third division (9:1-11:36) answers the question, "Why is Israel rejected?" It doesn't look as if this section belongs in the letter. It appears as if chapters 9-11 could drop out and never be missed. Did Paul get sidetracked from his subject?

On the contrary, before he can explain completely how God saves sinners, Paul has to explain the Jews. Paul said that Christ was the Messiah; thus the Jew had a right to go to Paul and ask, "If Christ is the Messiah, why is not Israel enjoying those promised Messianic blessings?" Logically, then, this section is a parenthesis inserted at this point for the Jewish reader. But it is of importance to the Christian, too; for unless the

divine promises to the Jew are fulfilled, how can the Christian
trust Christ to fulfill His promises to the believer?

4. The final section answers the question (12:1-15:33),
"How shall a saved man walk?" Some say, "Keep the Ten Commandments." Others say, "It doesn't matter how he lives, so
long as he is saved." But it does matter, and Paul discusses the
question as the concluding section of his epistle.

Those are the four questions Paul answers in the four divisions. The introduction covers the first seventeen verses of
chapter 1. Then follow the four main divisions:

1. *Condemnation, or the wrath of God revealed* (1:18-
3:20). Each main division of Romans has a distinct beginning
and ending, plainly indicated. He starts in verse 18 of chapter 1 with the wrath of God revealed! And in verses 19 to 20
of chapter 3 he closes with the world condemned.

2. *Salvation, or the righteousness of God revealed* (3:21-
8:39). Note the righteousness of God beginning this new
division. He concludes with a statement of God's love. "Now
is the righteousness of God revealed"—justification, sanctification, preservation—and he closes with the assertion that not a
thing in this world can ever separate a saved man from the
love of God!

3. *Vindication, or the wisdom of God revealed* (9:1-11:36).
Paul could wish he were accursed for the sake of his brethren.
This is a change in thought. "Why is Israel rejected?" is the
new thought Paul explains in the ninth chapter. Israel was
God's elected people; and the promises of God are not vain.
But Israel is rejected temporarily because the people rejected
God (chap. 10). In the eleventh chapter comes a promise of
reception, "life from the dead" (Ro 11:15), when "all Israel
shall be saved" (Ro 11:26). Paul explained why God has set
Israel aside: the Jews are "enemies for your sakes," that is, for
Gentile Christians. "The gifts and calling of God are without
repentance" (Ro 11:29). God has set aside Israel as a nation,
but God has not changed His mind. He has shut Israel up in
unbelief in order that He might reach the entire Gentile world.
With this explanation, Paul vindicates God.

4. *Exhortation, or the will of God revealed* (12:1-15:33).
Paul starts with the words, "I beseech you," and proceeds to

tell them how to "walk," to live their doctrine. The first three words of 16:17 are also "I beseech you." An outline of this section could be stated this way:

Chapter 12—transformation in the individual life
Chapter 13—subjection to the nation and its rulers
Chapter 14—consideration of the weaker brother within the
    Christian community
Chapter 15—exemplification of daily conduct in the life of
    Paul as he faced the changing conditions of life

Every one of these four divisions deals with a specific subject, answers a great question, and at the end makes a revelation of God: the wrath of God revealed; the righteousness of God revealed; the wisdom of God revealed; and the will of God revealed.

Paul's dealing with these great subjects led him to exclaim (in essence). "What a wise God He is! To Him belongs the glory through Jesus Christ forever" (Ro 16:27).

2

A General Survey of the Epistle

SOMETIMES when studying a book, one becomes so engrossed with the details that the great comprehensive argument is lost from view. Or, in the tour of a city, one may concentrate on one location and not experience the city as a whole. But if an airplane ride is taken over the city, a view emerges of the entire city. This chapter will be a quick tour of Romans, viewing the major divisions.

INTRODUCTION

The opening seventeen verses of the book contain three aspects.

First Paul saluted them (1-7). This salutation is longer and more lofty than those in the other epistles of Paul. But there was a reason. The Roman church was the only church to which Paul wrote that he had neither founded nor visited. This letter required more dignity, a little more claim to his apostolic authority. Second, Paul expressed his personal feelings for the church (8-15) and revealed his heart. Third, Paul stated his theme (16-17). A skillful transition from the personal element to the formal, dogmatic discussion. Paul now was ready to discuss the gospel. "So, as much as in me is, I am ready to preach the gospel to you that are at Rome also" (v. 15). Without stopping he says, "For I am not ashamed of the gospel." (Perhaps someone had insinuated that Paul would be ashamed of the gospel in that great city of Rome.) Then he launched into his dogmatic treatise. That is the last of anything personal at all until the end of the book.

Some say this book of Romans is a letter; others say it is a treatise. But it is both; it is a letter that contains a treatise. Paul writes in a personal manner up to the fifteenth verse. At the sixteenth and seventeenth verses Paul shifts over to the treatise. In chapter 15 he again takes up the personal element. By joining the two sections (1:1-15 with 15:14-16:27), one can see a letter. When the other section (1:16-15:13) is put in, the result is a treatise inside a letter. So much then for the introduction.

CONDEMNATION

The second division begins at verse 18 and extends to 3:20. It begins with the wrath of God and ends with "every mouth closed and the whole world guilty before God." There is no more distinct section in any book that Paul ever wrote than this one. There are four assertions in this section:

THE HEATHEN WORLD CONDEMNED (1:18-32)

Paul starts out with condemnation for the heathen world, one of the most terrible sections in all the Bible, in the deepest sense of the word *terrible*. In fact, there are items in that section not pleasant to read in public. But this description of godless man at his worst is not an exaggeration. When the first chapter of Romans was read at a gathering in India, an educated Indian commented, "The man that wrote that book certainly knew India." The fact is that the God who gave this Book knows men!

THE MORAL MAN CONDEMNED (2:1-16)

Paul turns to another category of man: "Thou that judgest." That is exactly what the moral man does. He sets up his standard of morality and says, "It may be true that these heathen are lost, but I am not lost. I don't do what they do." Paul turns to him and condemns him: "For wherein thou judgest another, thou condemnest thyself; for thou that judgest doest the same things." It may be that the moral man does not practice *all* the things that the heathen man does, but that awful catalog at the end of the first chapter describes things which are in every man. Even the moral man practices some of them.

THE JEW CONDEMNED (2:17-3:8)

"Behold, thou art called a Jew." Paul goes from the moral man to the Jew and condemns him also. The Jew has the law and is proud of his position as one of God's chosen people, taking confidence in his circumcision; yet Paul accuses him of not keeping the whole law.

THE WHOLE WORLD CONDEMNED (3:9-20)

"What then? are we better than they? No, in no wise; for we have before proved both Jews and Gentiles, that they are all under sin" (3:9). Paul sums up his case, leaving no one out of the general condemnation.

Paul could not discuss salvation until he demonstrated that the whole world is under condemnation. Now he is ready for the next movement of thought.

SALVATION

Three aspects of salvation appear in this very logical section of the book.

JUSTIFICATION

The first aspect is the basic doctrine of justification which has four movements of thought:

The divine method of justification (3:21-31). At this point the world is condemned and every mouth silenced—not a man saying a word, nobody answering back to God—and it looks as if the whole world is lost. "But now the righteousness of God . . . is manifested" (man has none). Then Paul explains the divine method of justification: "Being justified freely by his grace through the redemption that is in Christ Jesus" (3:24).

The Old Testament illustration of justification (4:1-12). Immediately this question would arise in the mind of the Jew: "How about Father Abraham?" So Paul discusses Abraham. "What saith the Scriptures? Abraham believed God, and it was counted unto him for righteousness" (4:3). Paul used Abraham as an illustration of the doctrine he is teaching.

The results of justification (5:1-11). "Being therefore justified by faith, we have peace with God through our Lord Jesus

Christ," Paul explains that we have peace with God, access to grace, and rejoicing because of hope.

The comparison between justification and condemnation (5:12-21). Paul makes a comparison between justification and condemnation. The contrast is between Christ and Adam: we were condemned in Adam; we are justified in Christ.

In studying this last movement of thought, notice that what God has done in Christ far exceeds what happened in Adam. Paul explains, "For as through one man," and then he makes his comparison: God has done much more through the second man or last Adam, Jesus Christ His Son. The last verse in the fifth chapter is a great summary of the two preceding sections: "Even as sin reigned unto death"—condemnation—"even so might grace reign"—justification.

SANCTIFICATION

Paul begins by anticipating the very thing that would come into some men's minds. Being justified apart from any works (that is, men do not need any works or character, which means that God saves men by their faith—right in their sin), they do not need to "clean up" and "be good." A man can stop right where he is, look up into the face of God, accept Christ, and have righteousness. This poses a real problem to some people, who say, "If that is the case, it doesn't matter how he lives." To meet that objection Paul begins his discussion: "What shall we say then? Shall we continue in sin, that grace may abound?" (6:1). He comes then to the practical section, how the justified man is sanctified and made holy in his life. This section contains chapters 6 and 7 and each chapter is a division: chapter 6 contains the right way of sanctification; and chapter 7, the wrong way.

The right way. Believe to be true what God says is true—that we died, were buried, and were raised from the dead with Christ. "Even so reckon ye also yourselves to be dead unto sin, but alive unto God in Christ Jesus. Let not sin therefore reign in your mortal body" (6:11-12, ASV). That is the way it is done—not by fighting, not by trying—just by looking at Jesus and saying, "God, you told me that I died with Christ, that I was buried with Him, that I was raised with Him." Paul points to our identity with Christ in His work. He says, "Now the way to do this is to believe what God says is true, whether you feel that way or not." This is the right way of sanctification.

The wrong way. "Or are ye ignorant, brethren (for I speak to men who know the law), that the law hath dominion over a man for so long a time as he liveth?" (7:1, ASV). All through the seventh chapter, Paul explains that the wrong way to sanctification is by the law. People try to keep the law to be sanctified, to make themselves holy. In the section on justification, Paul declared that no man could be righteous or justified by keeping the law. Stay out of the seventh chapter. Study it, but stay out of it. Folks say, "That's right, get out of it. Go over into the eighth chapter." That is not right either; get out of the seventh into the sixth chapter. If you are ever troubled by the seventh chapter, remember that it is the experience of a man who is trying to be sanctified by keeping the law. It is useless for folks to lay down rules and say, "You must do this" and "You cannot do that." I do not believe in preaching against sin in the abstract, but in dealing with the concrete things. It is no good saying, "Thou shalt not dance, or go to movies." Sanctification cannot come that way. There is only one way— reckoning the self dead to sin but alive in Christ Jesus. Then will come clean lives—lives that are not worldly. That is God's way to get what He wants in the life.

PRESERVATION

The third aspect of salvation in experience, as set forth in chapter 8, starts with "no condemnation" and ends with "no separation." Everything in between sounds forth over and over again the security of the man who believes in Christ. If the Holy Bible were likened to a beautiful ring set with jewels, the book of Romans would be the most beautiful jewel in the ring, and the eighth chapter the most beautiful facet in the jewel. Romans shows me first that I am lost, then it shows me that I am saved. God first shows men that they are condemned, then gives them righteousness, and also assures them that He is going to keep them right through to the end. There are nine aspects of preservation in this chapter: (1) preserved in the Son of God (8:1-4), (2) preserved in the Spirit of God (8:5-13), (3) preserved in the family of God (8:14-23), (4) preserved in the promises of God (8:24-25), (5) preserved in the prayer of God (8:26-27), (6) preserved in the providence of God (8:28), (7) preserved in the purpose of God (8:29-30), (8) preserved in the power of God (8:31-34), and (9) preserved in the love of God (8:35-39).

Notice that it is all in Christ Jesus. "There is therefore now no condemnation to them that are in Christ Jesus" (8:1). Even the worst calamities cannot separate us "from the love of God that is in Christ Jesus" (8:39). He begins with "in Christ Jesus" and closes with "in Christ Jesus." Chapters 5, 6, 7, and 8 all end with "in Christ Jesus" or "through Christ Jesus," emphasizing that everything God has for us is in Him and through Him.

VINDICATION

In relation to the Jew (chaps. 9-11), three movements of thought unfold Paul's discussion to them.

ELECTION

The twelfth chapter starts, "I beesech you therefore, brethren, by the mercies of God." Paul had just finished speaking of those mercies in chapter 8. Romans could have been a beautiful epistle with chapters 9-11 dropped out. But Paul had to deal with the Jew, for the Jew would immediately ask, "What about the national promises, if Christ is the Messiah who had come?" The ninth chapter, dealing with election, shows God being vindicated before the Jew.

REJECTION

The Jew might say at this point, "If I am not elected, I cannot help it. The fault is not mine." So Paul, in the tenth chapter, shows that it is not God's fault they are rejected. Every last one could believe if he wanted to, but the nation rejected the Son of God. (Don't let anybody drag election into his case. I thank God that He chose me before the foundation of the world! Election is a doctrine for the saint to enjoy, but not to teach to sinners to hide behind.)

They did not subject themselves to the righteousness of God. That is the reason they are rejected. Men are lost not because of God's election, but because they refused to believe Jesus. "Whosoever believeth on Him shall not be ashamed." There is no difference between the Jew and the Gentile; "whosoever" means salvation is offered to all. "But they did not all hearken to the glad tidings." Just a few, the remnant, received. They did not all accept. Paul quotes their own Scripture against them, closing the chapter by saying, "As to Israel, he saith, All the day long did I spread out my hands unto a disobedient and gainsaying people" (10:21). So the responsibility for their rejection rests upon the Jew himself, not upon God.

RECEPTION

Paul anticipates the next question: "I say then, Did God cast off His people?" (11:1). What is his answer? "God forbid!" The nation has been merely set aside, not cast off for good. Paul points to himself as proof that the nation is not totally rejected. "For I also am an Israelite" (11:1).

"What shall the receiving of them be, but life from the dead?" (11:15). Israel sometime is going to be received back into God's favor. That marvelous illustration of the olive tree —from which some people foolishly teach that a man can be lost after he is saved—applies to Israel. "He grafted you in." Paul does not say that to the individual Christian but to the Gentiles as a whole. Israel was the real tree, but God cast off Israel as a nation, grafting in the Gentiles as a body. Paul warns, "Don't you Gentiles be high minded, for God can cut you out and put back the Jewish nation." Paul looks forward to a time when her "blindness" shall be removed and "All Israel shall be saved," nationally brought back into favor.

Paul closes this whole section with a wonderful inscription of praise to God for His mercy, that He has rejected Israel in order to save the Gentiles.

EXHORTATION

Paul turns to the believer (chaps. 12-15). In this division four areas of personal conduct are treated.

TRANSFORMATION

Paul returns in the twelfth chapter now to the thought of the eighth chapter which had been interrupted. "I beseech you therefore, brethren, by the mercies of God [these mercies that I have been telling you about], to present your bodies . . . be not conformed to this world." Here is the end product of looking at Jesus. "But be ye transformed." Look at the end of the chapter: "If thine enemy hunger, feed him; if he thirst, give him to drink." There is need for transformation to occur so a man will act mercifully and not react vengefully to the person who hurt him. God has no place in the heart of a Christian for revenge, anger, or malice. Perhaps the worst sin is for a person to hold malice and spite; maybe more heinous in God's sight than being a drunkard, because it indicates a terrible state of heart.

SUBJECTION

This means subjection to political and governmental powers. The Christian needs to know how he ought to live in relation to the state. "Put on the Lord Jesus Christ" (13:14). What does that mean? It means to adopt His attitude toward human government. He was subject to it. Pharisees sent disciples to Christ who asked, "Teacher, is it lawful to give tribute to Caesar, or not?" (See Mt 22:15-17). He asked for a coin: "Whose is this image and superscription? . . . Render therefore unto Caesar the things that are Caesar's" (See Mt 22:19-21). In our attitude toward the government, we ought to "put on the Lord Jesus Christ" and act as He did.

CONSIDERATION

Paul indicates that we have a responsibility to the "weaker brethren" (chap. 14). "Him that is weak in the faith, receive ye" (Ro 14:1). Don't cast him out. This chapter is important for a Christian to read. There are many things that may be permissible for one person, but which might cause somebody else to stumble, especially the man that is spiritually weak. This chapter was written for that purpose. "Now we that are strong ought to bear the infirmities of the weak" (15:1).

Paul was trying to pay a compliment to those folks. He was saying, "Do you feel strong? Well then, you ought to help out with the shortcomings of the weak. That is the reason God gave you the strength."

EXEMPLIFICATION

Paul refers to his own life and labors as an example.

CONCLUSION

The final division of the book is contained in chapter 16. Four items form the conclusion: (1) a commendation (1-2), (2) a salutation (3-16) and greetings (21-23), (3) exhortations (17-20), (4) and a benediction (25-27).

Paul began his book by referring to a gospel that had always been known; and he closes by referring to a mystery that had never been known. This mystery he mentions is not discussed in the letter to the Romans but in the letter to the Ephesians. He begins by saluting all the saints that are at Rome, and then he closes by saluting particular saints that are at Rome.

3

A Declaration of Paul's Official Relation

THE FIRST SENTENCE of the book of Romans extends through
seven verses, contains 126 words, and includes the whole of
the salutation. Packed with truth, it is worth considering by
itself. The sentence consists of a simple greeting split into two
parts by a "parenthesis." This greeting is in the first and the
seventh verses: "Paul, a servant of Jesus Christ, called to be an
apostle, separated unto the gospel of God, . . . to all that are in
Rome, beloved of God, called to be saints: Grace to you and
peace from God our Father, and the Lord Jesus Christ." The
parenthesis begins at the second verse and is introduced by the
pronoun *which*. What calls for the parenthesis is the mention
of the "gospel of God."

The literary construction of this sentence is very beautiful,
and the unfolding of the ideas exquisite! It is almost like the
unfolding of a flower—first the stalk, then the bud, then the
full bloom, then the heart of it! It begins with Paul. What
about Paul? Paul is a servant of Jesus Christ; he is called to
be an apostle; he is separated unto the gospel of God. We have
been looking at the gospel, and suddenly we see Jesus. What
about the gospel? It was promised a long time ago, Paul says,
and it concerns God's Son, Jesus Christ our Lord. We have
been looking at the gospel, and suddenly we see Jesus. What
about Him? He was descended from the line of David physi-
cally, and He was shown to be the Son of God with power, according to the Spirit of holiness, by being resurrected from the
dead. Anything else? "Through Him," Paul says, "I received
grace and apostleship." And one more thing: "He called the
saints that are at Rome." We had been looking at the Son of
God, and suddenly we are introduced to the saints at Rome!

34

What about the saints at Rome? Just three things: They are called of Jesus Christ, beloved of God, called to be saints. And that is the unfolding of the first sentence.

There are just four divisions in this sentence: (1) the messenger of God, Paul, (2) the gospel of God, (3) the Son of God, and (4) the saints of God.

THE MESSENGER OF GOD, PAUL

Concerning himself, Paul makes three definite statements: (1) he is a servant of Jesus Christ, (2) he is called to be an apostle, and (3) he is separated to the gospel of God.

SERVANT OF JESUS CHRIST

There were no less than six Greek words denoting servitude, and from all these Greek words Paul might have chosen any one to express the idea of servitude to Jesus Christ. But he deliberately passed over the weakest of them and chose the very strongest word to describe the most absolute servitude. Picture a slave market: a slave is placed upon the block; the auctioneer stands up and auctions him off; somebody buys him, and he becomes a bondslave. Such a slave is called a *doulos*. Paul says, "I am a *doulos* of Jesus Christ. I am a bondslave." In other words, Jesus has purchased Paul out of the market, and now all that he is and has—his time, his strength, his talents, even life itself—no longer belongs to Paul but belongs to Him. Paul loved to call himself a bondslave; that is the word he used over and over again in his epistles. It meant a great deal to him. He put it in the catalog even before his apostleship. It is a greater thing to be a bondslave of Christ than to be an apostle of Christ. So he is a bondslave first and afterward an apostle.

We too are the *douloi* of the Lord—the bondservants. That term ought to be precious to us; it not only expresses the idea of our servitude to Christ, but reminds us that our servitude is based on purchase. I am a bondslave of the Lord because He bought me with His own precious blood. If you remember that, you will love to be called a servant of the Lord. I am not only obliged to serve Him, but I am His possession! He is responsible for me—to take care of me and provide for me.

CALLED AN APOSTLE

There are two words in italics: "to be." Those italicized words were supplied by the translators to make a smooth translation. They ought to be left out here: "called an apostle." Or, to put it another way, he was "a called apostle." It was not a future role; but Paul was an apostle the moment God called him.

Two things were necessary to qualify a man for apostleship. The first was that he must have seen the Lord. Paul had that qualification. "Am I not an apostle? Have I not seen Jesus Christ our Lord?" (1 Co 9:1). Paul connects his apostleship with having seen the Lord. "Last of all, as the child untimely born, he appeared to me also, for I am the least of the apostles" (1 Co 15:8-9). So that is the first test of an apostle—he must have seen the Lord.

The other was that his call must come directly from the Lord Himself. They did not make apostles in the early days like they do today. Today they are made by succession, by election, by self-assumption; but Paul was a called apostle, and when he says that, our minds go back to that memorable day on the road to Damascus, when God struck him down. The Lord's language when He spoke about Paul to Ananias was, "He is a chosen vessel" (Ac 9:15). It is almost identical to the words of Jesus to the twelve, for He said to them, "Did not I choose you the twelve?" (Jn 6:70). So Paul, like the twelve, was a chosen vessel—called directly.

SEPARATED TO THE GOSPEL

There were three distinct separations that took place in the life of Paul. The first was God's hand on his life even from its beginning, "Separated me from my mother's womb" (Gal 1:15). The second separation came on the way to Damascus, when God separated him from the world (Acts 9). The third occurred at Antioch, when the Holy Spirit said, "Separate unto me Paul and Barnabas for the work" (Ac 13:1-2). Three separations were in his life.

Paul was a purchased slave, a called apostle, a separated preacher. We can't all be apostles, for there never was another apostle after those first ones. There is not any succession to that office. Yet in the true sense, we can apply those three terms to ourselves: *purchased, called,* and *separated.* He purchased us with His own blood. He called us and now we are separated. Paul says that He foreordained, predestinated, called, justified, and glorified us (Ro 8:29-30). If you are a Christian, whether you live a separated life or not, you are separated nevertheless; and because God has called you, you ought to live a separated life. He bases saintliness on a fact. He says, in effect, "You are separated, now live up to it!"

THE GOSPEL OF GOD

Of this gospel he says two things: it was promised previously by His prophets, and this promise was recorded in the Holy Scriptures (1:2). This is a statement of inspiration; the source of inspiration: God. He promises the channel: the prophets, through His provision. And the object of inspiration: the Scripture.

This statement would be of special interest to the Jews, for when a man came to a Jew and preached the gospel, the first thing the Jew asked would be, "How old is it? Is it new, or can it be found in the Scriptures?" And you have to settle that question before you get any place with the Jew. Paul, on the first mention of the gospel of God in that book of Romans, hastens to add that this gospel is no novelty. It is as old as the universe, "promised before," long before the apostle sat down to explain it. Paul demonstrates this to be a fact throughout the Roman epistle by quoting constantly from the Old Testament, sixty-one times altogether. He quotes from Genesis five times; Exodus, four times; Leviticus twice; Deuteronomy, five times: 1 Kings, twice; Psalms, fifteen times; Proverbs, twice; Isaiah, nineteen times; Ezekiel, once; Hosea, twice; Joel, once; Nahum, once; Habakkuk, once; Malachi, once. Besides these sixty-one quotations, the book is full of indirect allusions to Old Testament history, type, and doctrine. Truly the gospel of God was "promised afore in the Holy Scriptures"! Only eyes closed by willful blindness could fail to see this. To take just one instance: "All we like sheep have gone astray; we have turned every one to his own way" (Is 53:6). The world appears lost even back in Isaiah. To finish the verse: "Jehovah hath laid on Him the iniquity of us all"; salvation is also prescribed. Eight chapters of the book of Romans are packed in one little verse in the Old Testament. No wonder Paul could say to the Jews, "This gospel is nothing new!" Paul confounded the Jews, showing from the Old Testament Scriptures that Jesus is the Christ of God.

The gospel was not only promised, it was "promised afore." The gospel then is not an afterthought of God. It was promised *before!* The gospel we preach is the "old gospel"; it is not some new thing that God hastily threw together as a remedy after the ruin and wreck of humanity. It is the old gospel. It is the gospel that anticipates and antedates human sin and human ruin. It goes way back before the fall. It points to the Lamb slain "before the foundation of the world" (1 Pe 1:19-20; Rev 13:8).

Second, the gospel is "concerning His Son Jesus Christ our Lord" (1:3). That is a definition which may sound like the ABCs, but a great part of Christendom seems uninformed that the gospel is "concerning God's Son"; and men are preaching today almost anything, calling it the gospel. The true gospel, God's gospel, is the gospel that has to do with Jesus. Anything not centered in Him is not the gospel of God.

THE SON OF GOD

He is the keystone of the arch, so to speak. Of Him, four things are affirmed: (1) His name, (2) His humanity, (3) His deity, and (4) His authority to dispense offices.

HIS NAME

First, He is named: "God's Son, Jesus Christ our Lord." The way He is named is worthy of your attention. Those four names and titles are rich and suggestive of meaning! "Son" defines His unique relationship to the Father. "Jesus" speaks of His humanity; He is the man Jesus. "Christ" speaks of His Messianic office; He is the Anointed One. "Lord" speaks of His exalted position and person; He is the Lord Jehovah.

Not only are the words themselves suggestive, but the very order in which they occur is significant. He is first the Son of

God, and as the Son of God He existed from all eternity. In the fullness of time, the eternal Son of God humbled Himself to be born of a virgin, and then the angelic announcement was "His name shall be called Jesus." And then Jesus lived for thirty years on the earth. He finally came to the day when He went down to the Jordan and was baptized; and the Spirit of God anointed Him, which is what "Christ" means. Then He began His Messianic ministry. First the disciples confessed Him to be the Christ of God. Christ offered Himself as the Messiah, but the Anointed One to Israel was rejected. "He humbled Himself, and became obedient even unto death, yea the death of the cross. Wherefore also God highly exalted him, and gave unto him a name which is above every name: that in the name of Jesus . . . every tongue should confess that Jesus Christ is Lord" (Phil 2:8-11). His name, as given by Paul, encompasses these four things: the Son of God from all eternity; then the man Jesus; then entering into the office of the Christ; and finally confession that He is God. "God's Son, Jesus Christ our Lord."

HIS HUMANITY

He is fully human: "Which was made of the seed of David according to the flesh." This is a marvelously accurate statement of His humanity. The ordinary word for "born" is not used. He does not say, "He was *born* of the seed of David," but "He was *made*." Paul repeats this word usage in another letter, "But when the fulness of the time was come, God sent forth His Son, *made* of a woman, *made* under the law" (Gal 4:4). John used the same expression, "made flesh" (Jn 1:14). Not "born flesh" but "made flesh." Ordinary men are born flesh, but the eternal Son of God was made flesh. This is Paul's testimony to the virgin birth. It was the creative act of God that made Him flesh. God in some way took the eternal Spirit of His Son, joined it in the seed of the woman in the womb of the virgin, and out of that He brought the man Jesus.

Our Lord's humanity, or "flesh," came from the seed of David. "According to the flesh he was made of the seed of David." In the last epistle Paul wrote, he would have us remember "Jesus Christ of the seed of David" (2 Ti 2:8). When

you open the book of Matthew, the opening sentence refers to
"Jesus Christ, the son of David." And when we come to the
closing chapter of the New Testament, we hear the voice of
the Lord in glory declaring in His final message, "I, Jesus . . .
I am the root and the offspring of David" (Rev 22:16). They
picture Him as connected with David, the great king of the
Old Testament. What is the idea of this emphasis? God would
have us never forget that Jesus is the King, and that someday
He will come and sit on the throne of his father David. This
world needs a king; it needs *the* King! Democracy is perhaps
the best government that we could have under existing circumstances, but it is weak, and it has failed. We need the King
today. Men who stand at the helm of nations would be de-
lighted to surrender all the perplexities to the Son of God and
let Him settle them.

HIS DEITY

He is "declared to be the Son of God with power, according
to the spirit of holiness, by the resurrection from the dead"
(1:4, KJV). This is the statement of His deity in contrast with
His humanity. First came the statement about His humanity,
"the seed of David," and now is presented His deity. Notice
the contrasting phrases: "According to the flesh" He is "the
seed of David"; "According to the spirit of holiness" He is "the
Son of God." That expression "spirit of holiness" is certainly
not a reference to the Holy Spirit, although the Holy Spirit
might be called "the Spirit of Holiness." It is an expression
used to designate the being or essence of God, for God is first
of all spirit. Jesus taught that God is Spirit and God is holy
(Jn 4:24; 17:11). Therefore, that divine essence of which the
Father, the Son, and the Holy Spirit all partake is "the Spirit
of Holiness." "According to the flesh" He is human, "the seed
of David," but "according to the spirit of holiness," or His
divine nature, He is "the Son of God."
    There is a striking contrast between the verbs used. As to
His humanity, He was made of the seed of David, but as to
His deity, He was declared. Humanity is a created thing but
deity is uncreated. The human nature, or flesh of Christ, was
made at a definite point in human history, but His divine nature

was existing from eternity and needed only to be declared that men might see it.

The word *declared* means literally "to mark out by sure signs." He was declared deity by the resurrection. There was need for such a sign. John said, "He was in the world, and the world was made by him, and the world knew him not. He came unto his own and his own received him not" (Jn 1:10-11). One day the Jews came to Him and said, "What sign showest thou?" (Jn 2:18). Here you are, they were saying, doing the works and teaching the teachings that belong to the Messianic office. What sign do you have? He said, "Destroy this temple, and in three days I will raise it up" (Jn 2:19). The sign of the resurrection declared Him to be what He truly was: "the Son of God."

In speaking of the resurrection, the apostle uses a rather puzzling expression: not *His* resurrection, but "resurrection." The literal translation is this: "by resurrection of the dead," not "from the dead." We have always loved the idea, "from among the dead," but Paul does not say that here. Jesus is "declared to be the son of God with power, by resurrection." Paul is not speaking merely of the personal resurrection of Jesus; but he is saying to us that the resurrection of Christ potentially involved and included the resurrection of all other men. Paul said in another place, "For as in Adam all die, even so in Christ shall all be made alive" (1 Co 15:22). The same argument arises in the fifth chapter of John, when Jesus comes to the Jews and they seek to kill Him because He called Himself the Son of God. He said God was His Father, thus making himself equal with God. His answer to that accusation: "As the Father raiseth up the dead, and quickeneth them; even so the Son quickeneth whom He will" (Jn 5:21). Concerning His life, He further asserted, "I have power to lay it down, and I have power to take it again" (Jn 10:18). Christ is the Son of God, and not only is He going to rise from the dead, but potentially everyone shall. Not only is *His* resurrection accomplished through His power, but also He is going to raise everyone someday. So, He is "declared to be the Son of God with power by the resurrection of the dead." The resurrection of all mankind will be a confirming sign of His deity.

HIS AUTHORITY

Last, Christ is said to be the channel of grace and apostle-ship. Paul says, "By whom we have received grace and apostle-ship" (1:5). Nobody but a risen Christ can dispense the of-fice of the apostleship. "He that descended is the same also that ascended . . . and He gave some, apostles; and some, prophets; and some, evangelists; and some, pastors and teachers" (Eph 4:10-11). Apostleship comes after the resurrection, properly speaking.

The grace that he links up with the apostleship is not the grace that saves men. There is a grace of God that brings salvation. But this grace is God's favor toward Paul in giving him the marvelous privilege of preaching "the unsearchable riches of Christ" (Eph 3:8). Preaching the unsearchable riches of Christ is not a hard, disagreeable duty that is placed upon us. *It is a grace!* "Grace" means God's undeserved, unmerited favor.

This division closes with the *purpose,* the *scope,* and the *motive* of Paul's apostleship (1:5). The *purpose* is to promote "obedience to the faith." The *scope* is "among all nations." The *motive* is "for His name." This statement of motive echoes the original commission of Paul. "He is a chosen vessel unto me, to bear my name before the Gentiles" (Ac 9:15). Paul goes out "for His name." Speaking of certain missionaries that went out, John said, "For his name's sake they went forth" (3 Jn 7). That is the missionary motive par excellence. It towers above all others. In the presence of this motive, all other motives fade away and disappear. That is what we ought to work for: "His name's sake."

THE SAINTS OF GOD

The transition to "the saints at Rome" is beautiful. Paul has stated his commission to be an apostle to all nations. Since they are included in his apostleship to all nations, he easily makes the transition to them: "Among whom are ye also." By means of this, he justifies the writing of this letter to Rome, because his field is the world. Note three things about "the saints."

CALLED OF JESUS CHRIST

The meaning includes the idea of possession. You might read it like this: "They are called Jesus Christ's." They are the called ones belonging to Jesus Christ. Jesus Christ called them, but He also called them to be His own.

BELOVED OF GOD

Christ is His beloved Son, and if we are His, then we are beloved, because He is beloved. We are "accepted in the beloved" (Eph 1:6).

CALLED TO BE SAINTS

The words "to be" are italicized because they were added by the translators. Excluding them, it reads: "Called saints." Paul does not say, "called to be saints," as if sainthood were some goal to be attained in the future. They are not *to be* saints— they *are* saints. They are "called saints." If the present church at Rome believed that doctrine, it would sweep away and destroy forever that awful, unscriptural doctrine of special sainthood to be attained. Not only could the Roman church learn at this point, but also the Protestant churches. If we believe what Paul teaches here, there would be more saintly lives among the saints. A Christian whose life is not what it ought to be often gives this excuse: "I don't pretend to be a saint!" It doesn't matter what you pretend to be—if you are a Christian, *you are a saint!* It is not an evidence of humility to refuse to be called a saint. It is not humility to refuse to take that name that God has given us but unbelief, masquerading in the role of humility. Does the world expect anything of a sinner? Not a thing. Does the world expect anything of a saint? It certainly does. If a man that has taken this position falls, every man will jeer at him, saying, "There is your saint!" To accept the position of saint demands living in conformity with the position. Those who do not want to take that position know that they do not intend to live in accordance with that position, and therefore they refuse to take it.

God never goes to a sinner and tells him to try to attain to sainthood. He picks us out of the mud, and He says, "You are a saint." We are not making believe. We are holy and must live in accordance with our position. This is never attained by striving, but by taking possession of sainthood, remembering our position, and living in accordance with it.

The salutation closes with "grace and peace," which can never be separated. They flow together from two persons who can never be separated—God the Father and His Son.

The words of Dr. Beet conclude the discussion of Paul's first sentence:

> Paul's opening sentence is a crystal arch spanning the gulf between the Jew of Tarsus and the Christians at Rome. Paul begins by giving his name; he rises to the dignity of his office, and then to the Gospel he proclaims. From the Gospel he ascends to its great Subject Matter, to Him Who is the Son of David and Son of God. From this summit of his arch he passes on to his apostleship again, and to the nations for whose good he received it. Among these nations he finds the Christians at Rome. He began to build by laying down his own claims; he finishes by acknowledging theirs. The gulf is spanned. Across the waters of national separation Paul has flung an arch whose firmly knit segments are living truths, and whose Keystone is the Incarnate Son of God. Over this arch he hastens with words of greeting from his Father and their Father, from his Lord and their Lord.*

---

*Beet, J. Agar, *A Commentary on St. Paul's Epistle to the Romans,* 10th ed. (London: Hodder & Stoughton, 1902), p. 38.

4

An Expression of Paul's Personal Feelings

IN THE FIRST SEVEN VERSES of the epistle, Paul established an official relation between himself and the church at Rome. The official gap is bridged. The average ecclesiastic would be satisfied with this. Paul never shrinks from declaring his official position as an apostle, but that is not enough for him. He continues beyond to establish a more intimate relation—a heart relation. There are occasions and times in our lives when, under the stress of circumstances, we unconsciously reveal our souls; and sometimes, perhaps, the revelation may be shameful. At other times, it may be glorious. If it is glorious, then we are like Moses who "wist not that . . . his face shone" (Ex 34:29). It is so here with the apostle Paul, and these verses are a glorious unconscious revelation of his great and tender heart: "I thank my God" (v. 8), "I serve with my spirit" (v. 9), "I long to see you" (v. 11), "I purposed to come unto you" (v. 13), "I am [a] debtor" (v. 14), and "I am ready" (v. 15).

These personal statements reveal seven characteristics in the life of the apostle Paul: (1) his thanksgiving, (2) his service, (3) his prayer, (4) his longing, (5) his purpose, (6) his indebtedness, and, (7) his readiness.

These items are essential and should be normal characteristics of every true Christian life. Practically, it would not help us to study what Paul was like unless these characteristics somehow come into our lives and transform us too.

PAUL'S THANKSGIVING

"First, I thank my God, through Jesus Christ, for you all, that your faith is spoken of throughout the whole world" (1:8).

45

Thanksgiving for his fellow Christians seems always to have been first in the heart of the apostle Paul. Whatever epistle you may read in the New Testament from Paul to a church, soon after the salutation or greeting is over, he expresses his gratefulness to God for the church. There is just one exception to that rule, the epistle to the churches in Galatia. But there is a reason for that exception; those churches in Galatia had left the grace of God and had turned aside to what Paul called "another gospel."

Paul's thanksgiving is rendered to God "through Jesus Christ." That passage can be read in two ways. Either the apostle's thanksgiving was rendered to his God through Jesus Christ, or Paul was saying that his right to call God "my God" is through Jesus Christ. In other words, that God is *my* God through Jesus Christ. It does not matter which way you read it, because both interpretations are true. Every good thing we have—whether it is the glorious privilege of thanking God for the favors received, or the right to look up into the face of God and say, "My God," comes through Jesus Christ.

His thanksgiving is "for you all." The idea of thanking God for our fellow Christians is not new to us. We have often done it. We thanked God for those who have led us to Christ, for those who taught us the Word of God, for those who have helped us in time of need. But how many can say, "I thank God for *you all*"? Even for those who have spoken evil of you and misunderstood you, as they had Paul, who have caused you sorrow—can you thank God for all those who, nevertheless, trust the name of Jesus? We must be acquainted with the deep things of God in order to do it. Isaiah 53:11 points the way, speaking of the suffering of our Lord: "He shall see the travail of his soul and shall be satisfied." Out of Chirst's anguish on the cross, there are born into the kingdom of God individual souls, and when He sees that, He is satisfied! If every soul saved is the fruit of the travail of His soul and brings satisfaction to Him, shall I not thank God for every one of them, even though there may be among them some that mistreat me?

Paul thanks God that their faith is spoken of through the whole world. That phrase *the whole world* was very customary in the days of Paul. To say "the whole world" meant the whole

Roman empire. Luke's gospel says that Caesar Augustus issued a decree that the "whole world" should be taxed (See Lk 2:1). Of course, Caesar had no jurisdiction outside of his own empire, but the Romans were accustomed to speaking of their empire as "the whole world." The faith of the saints at Rome was so rich and remarkable that wherever Paul went throughout the whole Roman empire, he heard it spoken of. Today when our churches are spoken of throughout the world, it is too often notoriously. Frequently information comes through the newspaper that there is immortality in the church, or blasphemous pastors—and not faith. And this brings reproach on the faith for which our Lord died.

Paul's Service

"For God is my witness, whom I serve with my spirit in the gospel of his Son" (1:9). I want to call your attention first of all to that word *serve*. It means literally "to serve as a priest." It was the Greek word used in the Septuagint translation of the Old Testament to refer to the service of the priests in the temple, including also the idea of worship. The same word is translated "worship" in Philippians 3:3. This word is a commentary on what true Christian service ought to be: we serve God as priests, and therefore every act of our service should be rendered to God as an act of worship. In this light the distinction between sacred and secular disappears. The very ground you walk on is holy, and every trivial act acquires meaning. If you remember that, all your Christian service (no matter what it is) will become to you significant of that time when we shall be before the throne of God and "serve Him day and night in his temple" (Rev 7:15). Again the same Greek word is used that Paul uses here.

This exalted conception of service fits in perfectly with the next phrase that Paul uses: "with my spirit." Since all Christian service partakes of worship, it dare not be a mere fleshly service. It must find its origin in the spirit and be rendered with the spirit, which is why Paul says, "Whom I serve in my spirit." This echoes what our Lord said to the Samaritan woman: "God is a Spirit: and they that worship him must worship in spirit and truth."

Our Lord Jesus Christ Himself served God with His spirit
The greatest act of service that He ever performed was when
He humbled Himself and became obedient to the death of the
cross. "How much more shall the blood of Christ, who through
the eternal Spirit offered himself without spot to God, purge
your conscience from dead works to serve the living God?"
(Heb 9:14). "Christ . . . through the eternal spirit" does not
necessarily mean the Holy Spirit, although it does not exclude
the Holy Spirit, but rather describes the kind of service. It
came *of the spirit*—from His spirit, and the verse says that the
effect of His service on the cross was to purge our consciences
from dead works that we too might serve the living God as an
act of worship.

The place of Paul's priestly service was "in the gospel of His
Son." Paul was no priest ministering at a manmade altar,
ministering a sacrifice which could never take away sins. But
he had an altar nevertheless: "We have an altar, whereof they
have no right to eat who serve the tabernacle" (Heb 13:10).
Paul has an altar in the gospel of the Son of God. That is our
place of service, at the altar of the cross of Christ. We are to
stand and persuade sinners to come there and be cleansed. Our
priestly service today is not a wafer, not a cup of wine. Our
service today involves that for which those things stand: the
cross, His broken body.

PAUL'S PRAYER

"God is my witness . . . that without ceasing I make mention
of you always in my prayers; making request, if by any means
now at length I might have a prosperous journey by the will of
God to come unto you" (1:9-10).

This prayer is a most illuminating commentary on true
prayer. Let us note its important characteristics:

CONSTANT

Paul says he prays "without ceasing . . . always." Paul
probably reached more souls with his praying than with his
preaching, for the apostle could never say, "I preach without
ceasing, I preach always," because there were times when he
was laid on a bed of sickness or was in prison alone. There

his preaching must cease, but his praying could go on, a part of his priestly service. He is thinking not only of his preaching, but of his praying, when he says, "I serve God." Prayer is a service to God in which you can serve God day and night continually. Luke's gospel speaks of Anna, the widow who was in the temple serving God with prayers and fasting day and night (Lk 2:36-38). The modern world would say, "That is not service at all," but we who have come to know Him and to know that He answers prayer can realize that perhaps that is the greatest service we can render in the kingdom of God, in the church of God.

PERSONAL

"Making mention of you." Paul, in the last chapter of Romans, mentions no less than twenty-six of the members of this church which he has never visited. There is power in personal prayer, in mentioning names.

PARTICULAR

Paul's prayer included various details. He even asked for a prosperous journey to Rome. There is no detail in life that is so trivial that we cannot make it a matter of prayer.

SUBMISSIVE

Paul recognized that the request must be in the will of God, including this phrase: "By the will of God." He is repeating the divine formula, "If we ask anything according to his will, he heareth us" (1 Jn 5:14). This prayer of Paul breathes the very spirit of his life, following the pattern of Christ who said, "Father, if it be possible, let this cup pass from me: nevertheless, not as I will, but as thou wilt" (Mt 26:39).

UNDEMANDING

His prayer was not dictatorial. Paul desired that he might go to Rome, but he made no attempt to dictate to God by what means he should go. He was willing to accomplish this "by any means"—just as long as he got to Rome. Perhaps Paul looked forward to going there with friends in a ship. When he finally went, it was as a political prisoner, wearing a chain on his wrist, and yet, he got there!

GENUINE

He was not playing with words. Paul could say, "For God is my witness" that he prays for them unceasingly. It is a great thing to call upon God to witness that one's prayer life is genuine. This is a part of the Christian life where there can exist much sham, because God alone witnesses it, other men do not. In public, men may hear us pray and conclude we are remarkable in prayer. But their conclusion might be different, if they could only see us as God sees us.

PAUL'S LONGING

"For I long to see you, that I may impart unto you some spiritual gift, to the end that ye may be established; that is, that I may be comforted together with you by the mutual faith both of you and me" (1:11-12). Paul's statement does not lack dignity, and yet it breathes the very spirit of love and tact and delicacy. It begins with an expression of love—"I long for you," literally, "I am homesick for you"—and then he mentions his immediate purpose. He says, "I want to come that I might impart unto you some spiritual gift." He explains that the result will be to establish them. But he begins to think that some will misconstrue what he is saying and think that he is trying to assume a position of spiritual authority. So he anticipates this by further explanation, that it is not just that he may give them something, but that at the same time he may receive something back from them: that he may obtain comfort while they get the spiritual gift. In other words, the benefit will be mutual.

We cannot give without receiving. That is an impossibility. We cannot impart something without taking back something in return. It is a monumental mistake to suppose that the preacher always gives and never receives. Every true teacher and preacher of God's Word is acquainted with that mysterious reflex aid he is receiving while he is pouring out to others. There is a life that flows from one to another. There is a con-

tribution that every saint of God makes to that wonderful
fellowship, to that knowledge of the love of Christ.

PAUL'S PURPOSE

"Now I would not have you ignorant, brethren, that often-
times I purposed to come unto you, (but was let hitherto)."
The word *let* is old English; we don't use that word any more.
"Hinder" is the meaning. This is Paul's explanation for the
long delay in his visit to Rome. He had been a called apostle
for more than twenty years to the Gentile world, but he had
not yet found time to preach Christ in the capital of that world
to which he was called. It was no wonder that this church
could say, "Why is it that this visit is so long delayed?" There
are also other verses that speak of Paul's purpose and how he
was hindered: "Paul purposed in the spirit" (Ac 19:21). "I
have been much hindered from coming to you" (Ro 15:22).
Apparently Paul had held to his purpose throughout the years
in spite of those hindrances, and he clung to that purpose to go
up to Rome. But he was human after all, like the rest. Perhaps
he began to wonder if he would ever arrive at Rome. There is
just a hint of this in the book of Acts. In one of the darkest
hours of his life, when his own countrymen had tried to tear him
to pieces and the captain had to put him in a cell to save his
life, the angel of the Lord came to him and said, "As thou hast
testified of me in Jerusalem, so must thou bear witness also at
Rome" (Ac 23:11). The Lord seemed to think he needed a
little encouragement.

Hindrances are not always an evidence that our purposes are
wrong. Too often we purpose to do something that we think
is according to the divine will, and when we start to do it, a
hindrance comes up (or two or three). Immediately, with un-
seeming haste, we decide that this is not God's will for us, and
so we abandon it. But our purpose may be exactly according
to the divine will, only perhaps we are trying to carry it out
at the wrong time, and the very hindrance that appears as an
obstacle in our path may be a divine testing of our purpose, as
well as the assurance that it will be carried out at God's appointed time.

PAUL'S INDEBTEDNESS

"I am debtor both to the Greeks and to the Barbarians; both to the wise, and to the unwise." It is very possible that these words reveal Paul's reason for going to Rome—because he is a debtor. Paul wrote these words not at the beginning of his missionary labors, but after he had preached the gospel in a multitude of cities and lands and had endured untold sufferings and persecutions. He had rendered perhaps the most splendid missionary service that the world has even seen, yet after all that, he writes these words. This is Paul's conception of Christian service. Because God had saved him, Paul was made a debtor, but not to God. The Lord Jesus Christ had paid that debt to the last farthing, but Paul had been constituted a debtor *to the whole world.* He only regarded himself as an honest man ready to pay his debts. It cost Paul his life to pay the debt at Rome.

Every one intelligent in the Word of God feels that he can go to Romans 8:38-39 and say, "I am persuaded, that neither death, nor life, nor angels, nor principalities, nor powers, nor things present, nor things to come, nor height, nor depth, nor any other creature shall be able to separate us from the love of God, which is in Christ Jesus our Lord." Do we not feel that we have a right to apply that to ourselves? But we have no right to say, "I am persuaded," if we are not also ready to say, "I am a debtor." The two are in the same book, they were written by the same man, inspired by the same Holy Spirit, and they were written to us; and if the one is true, then the other is true. If nothing can separate us from the love of God, then we are debtors to the whole world of sinners! This debt to the heathen is just as important as our debt to the grocer, or to the tax collector. If it is wrong to repudiate the one, it is wrong to repudiate the other.

PAUL'S READINESS

"I am ready to preach the gospel to you that are at Rome also" (1:15). It is not enough to have a missionary purpose, to feel indebtedness to the heathen world. We must be able to say with Paul, "I am ready"! Here we can put our finger on that terrible thing that has hindered and dragged out the evangelization of the world for nineteen centuries, and has made it a failure even in this present day. God is ready. But we are not ready. God has prepared His feast, but we are not ready to go out and invite men to the feast. When our Lord was about ready to depart out of the world, He said, "Be ye also ready: for in such an hour as ye think not the Son of Man cometh" (Mt 24:44). There is not the slightest doubt in my heart that when He comes, He will take unto Himself every last one of His own. He will not take part of the church and leave the rest here; He will not take the strong ones and leave the weak ones. You will not be able to say, "I am ready for His coming" if you are not able to say, "I am ready to do all in my power to preach the gospel where it is needed." Paul says, "As much as in me is, I am ready." Whatever you can do, look up into the face of God and say, "I am ready!" It may be praying; it may be giving; it may be going.

Paul was a wonderful man, and he stands revealed in the light of these verses. No tribute, no praise is too great for such a man. It is a delight to honor such a man. And yet, we are not to forget what he himself wrote: "Let no many glory in man, but he that glorieth, let him glory in the Lord." If Paul could be here in person to speak to us, he would turn aside all our praise and repeat these words: "By the grace of God, I am what I am" (1 Co 15:10). The Holy Spirit would have us remember that this very man was once the Saul of Tarsus, a fierce hater and persecutor of all them that called on the name of Jesus. It is a testimony to the power of Paul's Christ to change the heart! All the credit for the mighty transformation of the life of Saul of Tarsus belongs to Him and not to Paul. Let us not glory in Paul, but let us glory in the Lord of Paul, the Christ of God that made him what he was.

5

The Theme of the Epistle to the Romans

IN THE INTRODUCTION following Paul's salutation and personal comments, comes a statement of the theme of the book. In those oft quoted and remarkable verses, the apostle Paul states the theme of his letter to the Roman church. The theme is the gospel, or literally, the "good news." And this good news is of Christ, as the third verse says, "concerning Christ."

But the gospel is more than only news concerning Him: Christ Himself *is* the good news.. Apart from Jesus Christ there is no good news. If somebody should ask, "What is the gospel?", we ought to answer, "The gospel is not *what,* it is *who!*" The gospel is the Lord Jesus Christ, in His blessed person and in His mighty work. To lose Jesus is to lose the gospel. One of the strangest things in the religious life of the world is that the world would like to have Christianity *without* Christ. It would like to get rid of Jesus and at the same time keep the gospel. The world would like to have good news from God without the Son of God. People are not offended by good news from God (they love that); but they hate the name of Jesus, and the two are inseparable. Christians must stand with the apostle Paul and proclaim that apart from Jesus Christ, God has no good news for any man. Eliminate Him, and there remains no good news for the world, but only a fearful expectation of judgment and of fiery indignation (see Heb 10:26).

In stating the gospel as he has here, Paul has used some great words. He talks about power, God, salvation, righteousness, faith, and the just. And then he talks about life. Seven powerful words. It is Jesus Christ, the Son of God, who gives meaning and value to those words; take Him out of those words and nothing is left but empty words and high sounding phrases.

For instance, take the first great word. He says, "I am not ashamed of the gospel, for it is the power." But what about power? "Christ [is] the power of God" (1 Co 1:2*a*); that is what makes the gospel the power of God! Let us take the word *God*. First Timothy 3:16 declares that Christ was God manifested in the flesh, for He is the image of the invisible God (Col 1:15). How much would you know about God if you did not have Christ?

The next one: "The power of God unto salvation." Simeon, the old man, took Mary's child in his arms and looked up into heaven and said, "Mine eyes have seen thy salvation" (Lk 2:30). Jesus is our salvation.

The next word (which comes right in the middle of that perfect number seven; it is the heart of it): "righteousness." "Jesus . . . is made unto us wisdom and righteousness" (1 Co 1:30). The next word is "faith": "Jesus [is] the author and finisher of our faith" (Heb 12:2). Without Him, we would not have any faith.

The next expression is "just," in which Paul quotes from the Old Testament. Acts 22:14 speaks of the Lord Jesus Christ as "that Just One." Romans 5:9 declares that in His blood we are justified (declared just); we become just in Him. There would not be any such thing as a just man except for Him.

The last word is "life." John 6:51 reads, "I am the *living* bread which came down from heaven: if any man eat of this bread, he shall *live* for ever: and the bread that I will give is my flesh, which I will give for the *life* of the world." So the word *life* occurs three times in one verse.

Thus it becomes evident that Christ is everything. When you take Him out, you have nothing left of the gospel: you have lost the power, you have lost the God that gave the gospel, the salvation that the gospel brings, the righteousness that it reveals, the faith by which we appropriate it, justification—yes, and we have lost life!

The first statement Paul makes about the gospel is, "The gospel is the power of God unto salvation." He does not say the gospel *contains* power, or that it *is* powerful, or that it *has* power, or that it *exerts* power. He doesn't say any of those things. But he does say that "the gospel *is the power!*"

Power is awe inspiring. No man can stand by Niagara Falls and see all that mighty torrent plunging over the rocks without feeling insignificant. Radium has the faculty of hurling out power 186,000 miles per second, a power that can pierce walls of stone and destroy every living tissue that is in its path; no man can handle a tube of radium without feeling awed. The stars also represent great power, as they are sustained in their orbits and maintained in their brightness.

The most condensed statement of the gospel is contained in I Corinthians 15:1-4. In that passage is all the gospel: Jesus Christ, His death for sins, His resurrection again from the dead. This is the gospel in less than two verses and about twenty-six words, just a scrap of paper and a few drops of ink! "Not very impressive," someone may say. "Nothing to get excited about"; and yet those few words contain the most amazing power that is known in the universe today: *the power of God* which can save men's souls!

This power can take a sinner who is depraved in mind, body, and soul, a man who is spiritually dead, with no thought of God, bound by the law of choice and nature to an eternal hell and can arrest his course, cleanse him from all sin, make him righteous in the sight of God, raise him up with Jesus, and guarantee him future glory and happiness forever! What a marvelous, awesome thing the gospel is!

The gospel, of course, is not bound up in paper. You can go outside, stop the first man you meet on the street, and say, "Jesus died for your sins and rose again from the dead," and if he believes it, instantly his sins are blotted out forever. He stands righteous before God, and the eternal life of God enters into his soul. The words which you have spoken have been the power of God. Someone will say, "Is it possible that mere words can save the soul of man?" In Acts 11:13-14, the angel came to Cornelius and said for Cornelius to send to Joppa for Simon, who would come and "tell thee words whereby thou and all thy house shall be saved." God said words would save him, and they did. Peter came to the home of Cornelius, and they were all gathered together waiting for him. He began to speak *words,* and the record says, "While Peter yet spake these words, the Holy Ghost fell on all them which heard the word"

(Ac 10:44) and they were saved! Peter had nothing we do not have today. We have the same words of the same gospel, and it has the same power—to save the souls of men.

The Greek word which is translated *power* in Romans 1:16 is the word *dunamis*. From that Greek word we derive our English words *dynamite, dynamo, dynamic*. It is possible therefore to translate the verse like this: "I am not ashamed of the gospel, for it is the dynamite of God unto salvation." Or, if you want to put it this way: "It is the dynamo of God." Those two English words are very appropriate words with which to describe the mighty power of the gospel, for the power of the gospel has two aspects. *Dynamite* is a destructive power, it blows things to pieces. A *dynamo* has a constructive power, it produces energy. The gospel too tears down; it blows to pieces the old life. But at the same time it has the constructive power to build up the new life. It is absolutely true that the gospel is not only the dynamite of God but the dynamo, too.

Power is a dangerous thing if it is not handled carefully. Electricity is very useful. It lights our cities, cooks our food, washes our clothes; but if a man handles it carelessly it will kill him. Dynamite, too, has been very useful; and yet if a man handles it carelessly, it will blow him to pieces! This is true also of the gospel. Let men beware how they handle it: it is a "savour of life unto life," and "death unto death" (2 Co 2:16). To the man who receives the gospel and has the right attitude toward it, it will bring the life of the eternal God into his soul; but to the man who turns his back on it, it spells eternal death to his soul!

We are told the church has no power today. The diagnosticians and experts are running around in circles trying to find what is the matter and discover a remedy so that the church may recover its lost power. They tell us that all the churches must unite; that they must hold the young people; that they must get into politics; that they must teach the Fatherhood of God and the brotherhood of man; that they must cease preaching the theological dogmas of the Bible. All these are mere quack remedies. If the church has lost its power, it is because it has lost the gospel, because the gospel *is* the power. God has vested His power in the truth we preach. The church is not the power nor the preacher nor the members in the pew nor methods, organization, and money. Some say we ought to pray more. "When we pray more, we will have more power." That is true. But the most astounding spectacle in all the universe is an apostate church which, having cast away the true gospel, is now on its knees praying to God for power! An astonishing contradiction, and yet, that is the tragic situation today: on the one hand, throwing away the power, and then on the other, praying for it. It is like going into a cave and praying for sunlight; or going on a hunger strike and praying for food; refusing to breathe and at the same time praying for air. It must make the angels weep and the devil laugh!

To add on to the first: "It is the power of God unto salvation to every one that believeth; to the Jew first, and also to the Greek." The gospel is for everyone. The word *Greek* in the text was a term very often used by the Jews to mean all the Gentiles. The gospel has no racial boundaries. It even ignores degrees of goodness or badness. The ignorant and the wise, the high and the low—the gospel is for all. It is like the air we breathe, the rain that falls from heaven—it is for everybody.

The Holy Spirit is gracious to tell this at the beginning. The human writer is about to begin the first section of the book, and in that section he will prove that as far as sin is concerned, every man is lost. "All have sinned." But before he takes that awful plunge into the condemnation of the world, he must first assure us (thank God!) that the gospel goes just as far as even sin has gone. In other words, before he shows that every man is a sinner, he tells that the gospel saves sinners.

That thought accompanies the reader through the gloomy section of the book which takes man, brings him down, and stands him naked before the judgment bar of God. The Holy Spirit must have anticipated that a good many people who started to read this section would need comfort before getting through. Logically, the discussion of the gospel belongs later, but the Holy Spirit mercifully reveals it first.

The sole condition attached is faith. The gospel is "to every one that believeth." There is no other condition. The gospel is not the power of God to everyone who is circumcised or baptized, or who keeps the law. "It is the power of God unto every

one that *believeth";* that is the only condition. If any other
condition were attached to the receiving of the gospel, then it
would not be for everybody. For if God required any work or
character before a man could receive the gospel and be blessed
by it, then certain individuals would be excluded. There is one
thing that everyone (man, woman, and child) can do, and that
is believe. No matter where you are, what you are, you can
believe, you can trust.

What does faith mean? The book of Romans speaks of faith
many times. Faith is nothing complex and mystifying, as some
theologians have implied. But faith is just the simple, trusting
acceptance of what God gives. God says, "I give," and the
heart responds, "I take." An illiterate, simple African was once
asked, "What is faith?"; and his answer deserves attention from
the wise as well as the ignorant. He answered, "Faith is the
hand of the heart." That agrees perfectly with what Paul said:
"With the heart man believeth unto righteousness" (Ro 10:10).

The last statement: "For therein is the righteousness of God
revealed from faith to faith." That is the secret of the power of
the gospel. The sixteenth verse never should be read apart
from the seventeenth. God has joined those two verses together, and "what therefore God hath joined together, let not
man put asunder" (Mt 19:6), whether it is a man and woman
or two verses in the Bible.

The explanation of the gospel's power is in the seventeenth
verse: The gospel is the power of God for salvation because in
the gospel is a revelation, and that revelation is a manifestation
of the righteousness of God; that is the reason the gospel has
the power to save a sinner. Man has no righteousness; but
God, in the gospel, has provided a righteousness, and He gives
that to man if he will only take it. This fact makes Christianity
different from every other religion the world has ever seen.
Every great scheme to save men has failed on just one point:
its success depended on man's righteousness, when in reality
there is *no* righteousness in man. Christianity attacks the problem at this point of righteousness. It recognizes that man has
no righteousness and then brings the righteousness of God and
clothes the man in that righteousness and saves him!

In the very next verse the wrath of God is to be revealed

against all ungodliness and unrighteousness of man. We are to stand and hear the thunderings and the crash of the judgment of God; we are to stand and be stripped of every rag of our own righteousness. But before He reveals His wrath, He reveals His righteousness. We are not to feel the wrath of God until we know there is a righteousness for all those who need it; we are not to know anything about that wrath of God which is *against* us until we know that there is a righteousness of God *for* us. In other words, righteousness is before wrath. He always anticipates our needs and He supplies them fully. It is the old story of the Lamb slain *before* the foundation of the world (1 Pe 1:19-20) —before human sin ever started. Isn't that right? Righteousness comes first.

Paul was preaching not a plan, not a philosophy, but a *person*—The Lord Jesus Christ—in preaching the gospel. When he says, "I am not ashamed of the gospel," in reality he is saying, "I am not ashamed of Jesus," for He *is* the gospel. There is an echo there of those words of our Lord, "Whosoever . . . shall be ashamed of me and of my words in this adulterous and sinful generation; of him also shall the Son of Man be ashamed when he cometh in the glory of his Father with the holy angels" (Mk 8:38). Paul says, "I am not ashamed of Him," and he never was ashamed of His Lord nor of the gospel that told of His Lord. Paul was called to stand before the dignitaries of the world, before the high priest of Israel, before the philosophers at Athens, before the governor, the emperors of Rome, even before Caesar himself, and not once in the record can be found the blush of shame upon his face for His Lord. Almost the last word we have from him was written to Timothy, from his dungeon in Rome, with the chain upon his hand; and he wrote this: "For the which cause I also suffer these things: nevertheless I am not ashamed: for I know whom I have believed, and am persuaded that he is able to keep that which I have committed unto him against that day" (2 Ti 1:12).

May we go out as Paul did, with a gospel that is the power of God for salvation, and not be ashamed of it—or rather, I would say, not be ashamed of Him, for that is who it is!

6

The Pagan World Under Sentence of Condemnation

As POWERFUL as this gospel is, there is one thing that this gospel cannot do: it cannot save any man until that man sees himself as a guilty, lost, condemned sinner. Therefore, before Paul even begins to talk about God saving sinners, he takes a whole section of his letter to demonstrate that men need the gospel. It is a universal gospel for a universal need. If no one is sick, why send for the doctor? If no one is lost, why preach the gospel? If the world of men is not lost, absolutely condemned, then preaching the gospel is foolish.

This next section of the book of Romans deals with condemnation and answers the question, "Is the world really lost?" That section extends from verse 18 of the first chapter to verse 20 of the third chapter. It unfolds logically from the very start through to the end.

This section on condemnation has four distinct movements of thought: (1) the condemnation of the heathen world, (2) the condemnation of the moral man (the better class, so to speak), (3) the condemnation of the religious man (represented by the Jew), and (4) the condemnation of the whole world.

THE CONDEMNATION OF THE HEATHEN WORLD

This condemnation is covered in verses 18 to 32, thus completing chapter one. There are three distinct divisions in this passage: (1) the wrath of God revealed (v. 18), (2) the wrath of God deserved (vv. 19-23), and (3) the wrath of God inflicted (vv. 24-32).

THE WRATH OF GOD REVEALED

"The wrath of God is revealed," Paul says. What is the wrath of God? The word *wrath* makes most of us think of an arbitrary outburst of temper. But when we speak of "the wrath of God," we do not mean that. The wrath of God is His holy aversion to all that is evil, and His purpose is to destroy it. The wrath of God might be compared to the wrath of the judge or the wrath of the law, for it is proper to speak of "the wrath of the law." If a man murders another man, the wrath of the law will be revealed—he will be punished for his crime. The wrath of God is like that.

The question that arises is, *"How* is the wrath of God revealed? Where can I see its revelation?" The wrath of God is revealed plainly in three ways:

The wrath of God is revealed in the Bible. "He that believeth on the Son hath everlasting life; but he that believeth not the Son shall not see life; but the wrath of God abideth on him" (Jn 3:36). Throughout the Bible the wrath of God is revealed right alongside the love of God. There are many who would like to omit the wrath of God yet keep the love of God; but the two attributes are inseparable.

The wrath of God is revealed in the cross of Christ. There is no greater revelation of God's wrath than is revealed in the cross of Christ at Calvary. When Christ hangs on the cross and cries, "My God, my God, why hast thou forsaken me?" (Mt 27:46), God's wrath against human sin is revealed. Paul says about his gospel, "For therein is revealed the righteousness of God." The place where righteousness is revealed is the cross. The same place where God reveals His righteousness, He also reveals His wrath, and through His revelation of wrath He brings forth a revelation of an obtainable righteousness.

The wrath of God is revealed in the natural world, and that is the greatest revelation, perhaps, of the wrath of God to a man who rejects the authority of the Bible and the historicity of the cross. An example can be found in a hospital ward where a man, because of some social sin, is being eaten up by disease. There is no need to wait until the day of judgment to see the wrath of God.

According to the text this revelation is from heaven. The Bible is from heaven; the cross of Christ originated from heaven; and the laws of nature also came from heaven.

Something in this verse not apparent to the English reader is that this revelation of God's wrath is a standing revelation. The tense of the verb *is revealed* is the present in the original Greek and might well be translated like this: "The wrath of God is being revealed continuously." Consider how true this is. The Word of God continues to stand in the world. The cross of Christ, although it occurred nineteen hundred years ago, continues to stand as the great witness of the wrath of God and has stood for the last nineteen hundred years. Similarly, the wrath of God is being revealed continuously upon those who break the laws of God in nature. It is a standing revelation!

Notice the object of God's wrath. Paul, in two words, has summed up all of human sin, placing it in two great divisions: ungodliness and unrighteousness. "Ungodliness" is sin against the *being* of God. "Unrighteousness" is sin against the *will* of God. Man is not only a moral sinner (he is unrighteous), but man is a religious sinner (he is ungodly). The unrighteous man lives as if there were no will of God revealed; the ungodly man lives as if there were no God. That is the relationship between those two things. While unrighteousness has to do with morality—our relation with our fellow man, ungodliness has to do with religion—our relation to a sovereign God.

Some say, "I am righteous; I live a moral life; I do not sin against my fellow men." Such a man—even if he were perfect in that respect, never breaking the laws of man's relationship to man—would still be guilty of ungodliness. It is not enough to keep the laws between man and man for the sake of morality, but he must live righteously for the glory of God, and that is what godliness means. This was the godliness of our Lord Jesus Christ. Every righteous act that He performed, every righteous thought He thought, every righteous word He spoke—was all to the glory of God. He was both godly and also righteous!

Paul mentions "ungodliness" first. Here is an evidence of inspiration in the order of these two words, because ungodliness precedes unrighteousness. The first thing the heathen do not do: "They glorified Him not as God" (v. 21). That is ungodliness. In a later verse they are presented as "being filled with all unrighteousness." Their moral decline started with *ungodliness!* Men have reversed the order, however, in religious teaching. Men are emphasizing primarily righteousness, when in reality everything flows from a godly life. We must first of all worship God, and then our lives will line up in the realm of righteousness.

The eighteenth verse in the King James Version says, "Who hold the truth in unrighteousness." The American Standard Version translates it, "Who hold *down* the truth in unrighteousness," which is a different thing. The King James Version may be wrong, for this reason: the apostle Paul is talking about why they did not hold the truth. "They exchanged the truth of God for a lie" (v. 25). Obviously, they did not hold it. This translation is more clear: "Who hold down the truth in unrighteousness," or "Who hindereth it in unrighteousness." Sin has a tendency to suppress the truth, and no matter how much truth a man has, it will not manifest itself in his life as long as he continues to disobey God. So at this point the American Standard Version correctly uses the word *hinder* instead of the word *hold*.

There is one great thing that can hinder or hold back the operation of the truth of God: unrighteousness in the church. It must be purged out in order that the truth of God may have full freedom to work. There must be righteousness in order that the truth may prevail.

THE WRATH OF GOD DESERVED

Those ancient civilizations had some truth. Therefore, it is correct to state that the wrath of God was deserved.

Paul, in this passage (19-23), anticipates an objection. Concerning the wrath of God being revealed, someone may say, "What about the ancient heathen world? They had no revelation of God. How can people like that be expected to honor and worship God? Do such people deserve the wrath of God?" That is an old question. Are the heathen really lost? Were they responsible, those people living back there in the darkness? The apostle answers this question. He says they *do* deserve the wrath of God!

The key word is *because:* "Because that which is known of God is manifest in them, for God manifested it unto them" (v. 19); "because that, when they knew God, they glorified Him not as God" (v. 21).

First, "that which is known of God is manifest in them." God did what? "He showed it unto them." There are two tenses there. First is the present tense: "That which *is* made known of God." The verse closes with the past tense: "for God *showed* it to them." Verse 20 says, "The invisible things of Him since the creation of the world are clearly seen, being perceived through the things that are made, even His everlasting power and divinity, that they may be without excuse." God revealed Himself through the created universe, and every man has that revelation. His eternal power and Godhead, the fact that He is God, and has power to punish ought to be revealed to every man by looking up at the starry heavens. "They are without excuse."

That settles the question of the responsibility of those people; they had a revelation of God. Every man has the same revelation. It is the evidence of creation. When a man can look out at the created universe and fail to see the power, the Godhead, and the divinity of God, he is a man who is holding down the truth—not because he cannot see it, but because he is unrighteous. That is what Paul is talking about in relation to the ancient people. They had the truth, and if they had not held down the truth, it would have prevailed.

The second reason they deserved the wrath of God was "because that, knowing God, they glorified Him not as God." Then comes the downward trend involving seven steps. Undoubtedly in this twenty-first verse the apostle Paul was talking about a different revelation than in those other two verses. There is the revelation of creation spoken of in Psalm 19: "the heavens declare the glory of God." The heavens tell us there is a God, a God who has power, yet the heavens can never make us *know* God. We can never know God in the actual sense of the word without a special revelation. Paul says in this twenty-first verse that these people not only knew *about*

God, but they *knew* Him. They could not know God without a revelation. God apparently revealed Himself to man back there in a special way, before the Word of God was given. Archeology has discovered in the records that there are traces of an original, primeval revelation. We know that God revealed Himself to Adam and to Noah and his sons. There may have been others.

These ancient people took a path of seven steps downward:

1. They knew God, but refused to honor Him. "Knowing God, they glorified him not as God."
2. They were not thankful for God's goodness to them. "Neither gave thanks."
3. They began speculating foolishly. "Became vain in their reasonings."
4. Their minds became senseless and darkened. "Their senseless heart was darkened."
5. They thought they were wise. "Professing themselves to be wise."
6. In reality, they had become very foolish. "They became fools."
7. Instead of worshiping the eternal God, they preferred idols patterned after mortal man. "They changed the glory of the incorruptible God for the likeness of an image of corruptible man."

That is total descent. They knew God, but when they arrived at the bottom, they were worshiping sticks and stones, carved out in the shape of animals and "creeping things." Compare the theory of evolution with this picture. As a pattern of development, evolutionary theory permeates everything today, so of course it has been applied in the realm of religion. Evolutionists say religion developed in a process like this: When man was primitive (when he had graduated from the ape tribe, lost his tail, quit climbing trees), he felt an impulse to worship something, so he took a stick, carved out an image, and began to worship that. That was the first step. As his intellectual powers grew, he began to make moral distinctions, saying, "This is right, and that is wrong." The next step in his reasoning process was to realize that the rain and the seasons must come from one or more superhuman beings and so he gave thanks to the gods for their gifts. From that point he rose to the conception of the true God and became a monotheist.

Paul's description of man's religious development does not follow the evolutionary order. His arrangement is the reverse, going from monotheism to idolatry. Man did not begin with the worship of sticks. Archeology confirms that man began with monotheism and later degenerated. This is, therefore, an accurate, scientific statement of Paul's.

In Isaiah, God exposes the foolishness of idolatry. He says, "The smith maketh an axe, and worketh in the coals, and fashioneth it with hammers, and worketh it with his strong arm; yea, he is hungry, and his strength faileth; he drinketh no water and is faint. The carpenter . . . shapeth it after the figure of a man, according to the beauty of a man . . . he planteth a fir tree, and the rain doth nourish it" (Is 44:12-14). Who gives the rain? Who gives him his strength? Who gave him the water he needed to drink while he was making his idol? Isn't that wonderful irony? "Then shall it be for a man to burn; and he taketh thereof, and warmeth himself; yea, he kindleth it and baketh bread" (Is 44:15). He couldn't bake his bread if God didn't give him wood. "Then he maketh a . . . graven image; he falleth down in front of it" (Is 44:17).

THE WRATH OF GOD INFLICTED

How did God inflict His wrath on the ancient heathen world? "Wherefore God gave them up." God stayed with them all the way as they descended into the pit, until they come to the point where they carved out wood and stones and made idols and worshiped them. Then God surrendered them! That is the key phrase of this passage: verse 24—"God gave them up"; verse 26—"God gave them up"; verse 28—"God gave them up." All three verses are alike: "God gave them up!" The number three signified completeness. When these folks had turned to idols, God completely abandoned them to their own ways!

First of all, "God gave them up to the lusts of their hearts unto uncleanness." They became depraved in heart when God gave them up. First it is the heart, then it is the body. Next,

"God gave them up to a reprobate mind." A depraved heart, a depraved body, a depraved mind. The word *reprobate* means "tested and found to be no good"—like a piece of tested steel in a machine shop. God tested man and gave him up. Men vied with one another to invent new forms of vice in the days of Paul.

There you have the list. You may ask this question: "Is every man in the world guilty of those things?" No, not in outward act. The best man on earth may never do outwardly one thing in this catalog of sins, but let him turn his back on God! Someday every one of these things would develop in that man's life, for it is there in germ and needs only the proper environment to come out. A drunkard went reeling along the street, and an onlooker said, "There, but for the grace of God, goes John Bradford." Our hearts are all the same. It is only because God has not given us up that we are here today.

Some people have asked, "What is the wrath of God like?" The wrath of God inflicted, whatever else it includes, includes one thing: abandonment. If you can look at the world when God removes all His restraining forces and His love, and lets sinners wander in their sins—that is hell; that is the wrath of God! No man can say this response of God is not righteous. Even as they refused to know God, God gave them up.

Notice the final charge: "Who knowing the ordinance of God, that they that practice such things are worthy of death, not only do the same, but also consent with them that practice them." The word *consent* may be translated "applaud." People not only do these things, but they applaud others who do them. There is one great lesson here: evil (sin) is progressive and you cannot stop it, once it is started.

Some people ask, "Why should I go to church Sunday morning to worship God?" Why should we come here to thank God for the things we have received during the week? "Neither give thanks" is one of the first steps in declension. If we keep close to Him, if we worship Him as God, if we have a thankful heart, He keeps us from taking the plunge such as these men took.

7

The Moral World Under Sentence of Condemnation

IN THE LATTER PART of the previous chapter, the apostle drew a terrible picture of the sin of the heathen world and its awful condemnation and punishment. All the time Paul was talking about that heathen world and telling about their descent into idolatry, he was conscious that there was a class of men in the world who could say amen to everything he was saying. They would say, "Yes, Paul, that is right. We know the heathen world has fallen into those sins, and in our judgment they deserve all they got." They were standing right beside him and approving his condemnation of the heathen world.

Now Paul turns to those very fellows and says to them, "Wherefore thou art without excuse, O man, whosoever thou art that judgest: for wherein thou judgest another, thou condemnest thyself; for thou that judgest dost practise the same things" (2:1, ASV).

Precisely to whom is the apostle referring, and who falls beneath the ban of this judgment? Some commentators and expositors declare that the apostle is talking to the Jew here, but they say that Paul was approaching the subject very carefully and therefore does not name the Jew until the seventeenth verse. Let the Word settle the identity of those to whom God is speaking here through Paul: "O man, whosoever thou art that judgest." Then to whom is he talking? Any man (it does not matter who he is) who judges. To finish it, look at the latter part of the ninth and tenth verses. What two classes are mentioned both times? Jew and Gentile. Then this passage is addressed to any man, whoever he may be (Jew or Gentile) in the whole world that judges. It is sufficient to say that this is a man who knows right from wrong, who has moral discernment. Paul is talking to *him* right here.

The key word of this section is the word "judgest" (or "judgment"). Nine times that particular word occurs, and it sums up everything in this passage. The first and the last verses of this section provide a contrast: "O man, whosoever thou art that judgest"; and later, "In the day when God shall judge." This section starts out with *man* on the throne of judgment, and it ends with *God* on the throne of judgment, which is proper and right. *Judgment* is the keynote of the section.

There are two great divisions of thought in the whole section: (1) in the first verse, the moral man (for that is the man under consideration) is condemned by his own judgment; (2) the rest of the section (2-16) shows the moral man condemned by God's judgment. Condemned by his own judgment, condemned by God's judgment: those are the two main divisions and everything in the passage falls under those two heads.

The Moral Man Condemned According to His Own Judgment

At the very beginning in the first verse is the key word that will analyze the verse. It is the word *thou;* it occurs five times in the first verse. Four of these fit into an analysis of the passage:

1. "Thou . . . that judgest"—the identification of the man
2. "Thou condemnest thyself"—the indorsement of the man
3. "Thou . . . dost . . . the same things"—the inclination of the man
4. "Thou art without excuse"—the indictment of the man

"thou that judgest"

What does it mean? On the negative side it does not mean what we have often thought—that is, a mere condemnation of somebody else; but on the positive side it means the faculty of moral discrimination that every man has to a more or less degree. Let me illustrate: I see a man steal something, and I say in evaluating that deed, "That is wrong." This means I have judged. I have exercised the faculty of judging right from wrong. That is precisely the significance of the words, *"Thou . . . that judgest."* I can conceive of the fact that some men might fall so low that they could almost lose that faculty—for instance, those men in the first chapter. But even *these* men had that faculty to a degree. They could look and say, "This is right; or that is wrong."

"THOU CONDEMNEST THYSELF"

I have heard sermons which say, "It is wrong to judge somebody else. If a person does that, God will judge him." The thing that this man is condemned for here is his act of judging. But nothing could be more wrong than this conclusion. The faculty of moral judgment is right. God approves it. Every man ought to have it. Everyone ought to be able to look at another man and say, "That is wrong" or "That is right." This man was not condemned because he condemned others. He was condemned because while he was condemning others, *he was doing the same thing and therefore condemned himself for his own sins.*

A wonderful illustration comes from the Old Testament. David committed murder because he wanted a man's wife. David had many wives. This man had only one, but the king desired her. He then had one of his officers take her husband and place him in front of the army to be killed. Then David took his wife! Nathan came to him. (David had the faculty of moral discrimination.) Nathan told him the story of a man who had many herds and flocks. He had a neighbor who had one little ewe lamb. Instead of taking one of his own flock to entertain a stranger, the man with many flocks took the neighbor's lamb. David became very angry. He said, "Show me that man!" Then Nathan said: *"Thou art the man!"* In other words, "You who judge are condemning yourself because you do the same thing."

Never let anybody tell you that it is wrong to judge things in the lives of others. It is right. If we did not have the faculty of moral discrimination, think where we would be. However, God wants us first to judge things in our own lives.

"THOU . . . DOST . . . THE SAME THINGS"

That may seem a little difficult to believe. It may seem impossible to you that these men who were moral men should be doing the same things that we found in the first chapter. You may even say, "It is impossible. If they were doing that, then it is wrong to call them moral men."

However, several explanations may be made, for there are perhaps three or four ways in which they did the same things.

First, they may not have done all the things, but only some of them. You will notice that they were covetous, envious, boastful. You can find things in that catalog of which every moral man is guilty; though he may not fall down before a graven image, he does some of those things.

Then perhaps he may not do them outwardly but inwardly. There is an intimation in verse 16 that this is what the apostle is thinking about, as he says, "God shall judge the secrets of men." Have you ever seen someone who outwardly was good, but inwardly wicked, and that very man condemning other people who were outwardly bad? That is what Paul has in mind. "Thou . . . dost . . . the same things."

Then again (and this is probably the greatest sin of all), what was the outstanding sin of the people in the first chapter? They sinned against light. "Knowing God, they glorified Him not as God" (1:21). These men were doing in their lives the very things they disapproved. In that sense, they were doing the same things.

"THOU ART WITHOUT EXCUSE"

This indictment is doubly true. If these men did the same things, they are without excuse. But their guilt was heightened by their own morality, by their own ability to judge.

Look at verse 32 of the first chapter. Pagan men not only do evil things, but they have pleasure in others that do them. The word *consent,* you will recall, means "applaud" or "approve." These people in the first chapter knew that these sins brought death, yet they approved of them. The difference between the two classes now becomes clear. Both kinds of men were sinners, both did the same things; but the pagans did something of which they approved, and the moralists did something of which they disapproved. The second is worse.

So the conclusion to be drawn from verse one is this: man is condemned by his own judgment.

THE MORAL MAN CONDEMNED BY GOD'S JUDGMENT

Paul has shown that this moral man is self-condemned, and now he is going to show that he is God-condemned. He first turned his own judgment against him, and now he is going to turn the judgment of God against him (2-16). In these verses, Paul explains four great principles of judgment which constitute the four features in this section:

A. "According to truth" (verse 2). Truth is the first principle by which God is going to judge men.
B. "According to his works" (verse 6). Practice is second.
C. "There is no respect of persons" (verse 11). When God judges men, there will be no partiality.
D. "According to my gospel" (verse 16). There will be a searching judgment of the secrets of men.

We are going to find some "things hard to be understood" (2 Pe 3:16). Some say, for instance, that Paul teaches salvation by works, and at first glance it looks that way too. But remember that Paul is not trying to show men how to be saved; he is trying to show men why they are lost. So you will find no gospel in this section. He is dealing with a crowd of men who stand off and say, "We are righteous in ourselves." He is trying to sweep away their refuge, to cut the foundation from beneath them. God is talking about judgment!

"ACCORDING TO TRUTH"

It is *the* truth, not "truth." Perhaps you have been in court at some time and have seen a witness called to the stand. He swears "to tell the truth, the whole truth, and nothing but the truth," but he does not do it, and so justice is miscarried. Paul is saying that when God sets Himself up to judge man, there is going to be the truth—"the whole truth, and nothing but the truth." In other words, the moral man will have to face the naked and awful truth when he comes before God. That is

what the apostle wants him to face here; there will be no eva-
sions. Paul intimates here that these people knew that very
principle. He says, "We are sure" that this is so. In this way
he reaches out and includes all these men, whether Jews or
Gentiles. The Jews knew that God is true and righteous; the
Gentile believers also knew that God would judge according to
truth.

Now, in view of that knowledge, here is the way Paul sets
forth man's attitude toward God:

In verses 3-5, there are three words which are key words—
one in each verse. The first key word (v. 3) is "thinkest."
(My version is "reckon"; it means "reason.") Second (v. 4) is
"despisest." Third (v. 5) is "treasurest." Each word indicates
the contents of its verse.

These men knew that God's judgment was according to the
truth. How are you going to explain their attitude in going on
in sin? Paul says it is their false reasoning: "Did you *think* you
are going to escape the judgment of God?" Any man who
thinks so is the victim of false reasoning.

Suppose a man denies that. "I did *not* think that way." Paul
says there is just one alternative—you *despise!* It's either one
thing or the other— either you are the victim of false reasoning
or you "despisest . . . the riches of His goodness and forbearance
and longsuffering, not knowing that the goodness of God leadeth
thee to repentance." That expression *not knowing* is one word
in the Greek. It does not mean that the man is absolutely
ignorant of it, but he *ignores* it.

That God has not punished sinners for nineteen hundred
years, that He has not broken through the heavens and struck
men down, because God has not brought a judgment on the
whole world since the flood has led men to draw a false conclusion from this delay. They are concluding that God will
never punish sin because He is now silent. They ought to learn
from this that God is longsuffering, that He is "not willing that
any should perish" (2 Pe 3:9). That is what they ignore: "Not
knowing that the goodness of God leadeth thee to repentance."
From the silence of God, men draw wrong conclusions.

In either event (it does not matter which), a man who
reasons this way is treasuring up wrath for himself. He is like

the man who goes to the bank every week and puts away twenty dollars. He is treasuring up his wealth. To think that every thought, word, and deed of a man out of Christ is laying up wrath. Contrary to this, Jesus said, "Lay up . . . treasures in heaven" (Mt 6:20). That is a different kind of treasure. In reality, the righteous do lay up treasure in heaven, but the wicked are laying up a different kind of treasure that is going to be poured out on them in the day of wrath and revelation of God! According to 1:18, the wrath of God is being revealed, but a time is coming when it is going to be fully revealed.

"ACCORDING TO HIS DEEDS"

In this passage Paul is accused of teaching salvation by works. Notice in the seventh verse, when he starts to explain: "To them that by patience in well-doing seek for glory and honor and incorruption, eternal life." Some say Paul there teaches that if a man does a certain kind of work, he will have eternal life. But in answer, note the following points.

In the first place, even before looking at the passage before us, this could not be possible, for Paul says, "By the works of the law shall no flesh be justified in his sight" (3:20, ASV). And again, "But to him that worketh not, but believeth on him that justifieth the ungodly, his faith is reckoned for righteousness" (4:5, ASV). Paul never taught salvation, or justification by works.

Nevertheless, from the phrase in the seventh verse, "Patience in well-doing," comes the question, "what is welldoing?" In every age of man God has revealed certain truth, and obedience to that truth in that age constituted welldoing. Paul here is not dealing with simply one age—the age of grace, the age of law, or any other age. He is laying down an eternal principle by which God is going to judge men in all ages, and he says: "To them that by patience in well-doing seek for glory and honor and incorruption, eternal life." Let us go back to the age of conscience, and see what is welldoing. Genesis 4:3-7: "If thou doest well"—the same expression. "If thou doest not well, sin coucheth at the door." Abel brought the sacrifice of an animal; Cain did not. God said one man did well; the other man did not. Welldoing in that age was bringing the appointed sacrifice. In the words of 1 John 3:12, Cain is condemned "because his works were evil." So, welldoing back there was bringing the sacrifice that God appointed. The age of law required that they keep God's law, and if they broke it, bring a sacrifice.

What is welldoing in this age? Welldoing in this age is believing on the name of the Son of God. "What must we do, that we may work the works of God? Jesus answered and said unto them, This is the work of God, that ye believe on him whom he hath sent" (Jn 6:28-29, ASV). Now if you want to do well in God's sight in this age, believe on the Son of God. That is welldoing.

When the end comes and God judges men, He is going to judge them by their life attitude, their heart attitude toward the truth in the age in which they lived. This is a general principle which is not confined to one dispensation at all, but is applicable down through the ages.

When God reveals a certain truth in a certain age, there are two classes that emerge. One class is obedient to the truth, and the other is rebellious. For them that rebel there shall be "wrath and indignation" from God's side (v. 8); "tribulation and anguish" on man's side (v. 9). This will be true for "The Jew first, and also the Greek." That is an awful priority, isn't it? Did you ever think of it? What was the Jew morally? He said, "I am first." And he was first, too. But in a larger sense than he ever dreamed of! For if God would render to him first from the standpoint of righteousness, He would also render to him first from the standpoint of responsibility. Revelation of truth determines priority in the mind of God. On the positive side the principle of judgment follows the same order (v. 10).

"NO RESPECT OF PERSONS"

God is absolutely and always impartial, and this is specifically true in judgment.

Verses 12-15 have been found very difficult. But there is a method of explaining these verses that simplifies their meaning. Look at the first word in the twelfth, thirteenth, and fourteenth verses. It is the word *for*, which is the key word explaining the principle that is stated in verse 11. First, read the principle: "For there is no respect of persons with God." Why? "For as many as have sinned without the law shall also perish without the law; and as many as have sinned under the law shall be judged by the law." Paul is saying that ignorance of the law will not save the Gentile. He will not be judged by the law, but he will perish! When a man sins, it does not matter if he knows nothing about the law, he is going to perish. But when one is inside the law, he will be judged by the law. Possession of the law will not save the Jew. Therefore, both are condemned alike.

There are two parts to the twelfth verse. The first deals with the Gentiles; the last with the Jew. Verses 14 and 15 explain those two halves. Let us take the latter part of verse 12: "As many as have sinned under the law shall be judged by the law." That explains why the Jew will be judged—because a man must *do* the things, not simply hear them (see Lev 18:5). He thought the mere possession of the law would save him, whereas the possession of the law constitutes the context within which he will be judged.

Verse 14 should be read with the first part of verse 12: "For as many as have sinned without the law shall also perish without the law . . . for when Gentiles that have not the law do by nature the things of the law, these, not having the law, are the law unto themselves."

Paul states the principle in verse 11; in verse 12 he speaks of the two classes and applies the principle; in verses 14 and 15, he deals with the first half of verse 12—all connected by the word *for,* and in verse 13 he deals with the last half of verse 12, also connected by the word *for.*

The first thing affirmed in verse 14 is this: *The Gentiles do not have the law.* That means the *written law.* But they sometimes "do by nature the things that are contained in the law." For example, consider the commandment "Thou shalt not kill." You may go into any primitive culture and find men there who never heard of that law, but who keep it. Their conduct proves that they have a standard of righteousness. Therefore, they "are *the* law unto themselves." (The article *the* ought to be there.) God has only one standard of righteousness—not two. The Jew does not have one while the Gentile figures out another by himself. Paul is saying that these Gentile nations sometimes did these very things that are in the law, and because of that, they "are the law unto themselves."

In verse 15 he gives a most searching analysis. The standard of righteousness is written in the very inner conscience of every moralist, no matter how far from the law of God he is. He shows this by his conduct. "They show the work of the law written in the hearts." The word *hearts* is the first word for you to notice. The passage continues, "Their conscience bearing witness therewith." That is not all: "Their thoughts one with another accusing or else excusing them." *Hearts, conscience, thoughts:* they all bore witness to the existence of this standard which shows itself in the man's conduct. In other words, just as the Jew had a court where he was tried (there was the law, a judge, and witnesses—a regular court), this was also true for the Gentile. This man had a court within himself comprised of the same three things: the law was written on his heart; his conscience sat as a judge; and the thoughts of the man accused or excused him.

Every man has gone through the same experience. His desires lead him to do something. Then his conscience sits in judgment on him, weighing the testimony of the witnesses as to whether it is right or wrong. His thoughts act as the witnesses, either accusing him or excusing him. Every Gentile moralist had been through that experience, and therefore he knew the basis for moral judgment, the very seat of his morality.

Here is the conclusion: God will judge every man by the standard that man actually has, not by the standard he does not have. He will judge the Jew by the written law, the Gentile by the law in his heart. If God does that, what will happen to man? He will perish! Any moralist can be judged by his own standards, and he will be a lost man! What a searching thing Paul has done; he has gone right into the heart of a man and shown him his sin and his own condemnation!

Ignorance of the law then, will not save the Gentile, because he has a standard that agrees with God's standard, even though only partially. Possession of the law by the Jew will not save the Jew, because he does not keep his own law.

This answers the question: "Will the heathen be saved if he follows the light he has?" No one has ever lived up to the light he has.

Consider the fourth principle of judgment: "God will judge the secrets of men." Notice how strange that last phrase in verse 16 is: "According to my gospel, by Jesus Christ." Some of the commentators have tried to tie in that phrase with nearly every verse in this passage. Grammatically, it is difficult to know where it belongs. It is the conclusion of the whole passage. Read it with verse 2, with 6, with 11, with 12.

Some commentators have said that God is going to judge the secrets of men according to the gospel; but that is impossible, because there are millions of men who have never heard of the gospel. What is said here is that God is going to judge men *according to Jesus Christ*. Paul preached that Jesus Christ is to be the Judge. At Athens Paul said that God has appointed a day when He shall judge the world *by Jesus Christ* (Ac 17:31).

The principle stated here is that God is going to judge the secrets of men. This means not only the secrets that are hidden from others but those also hidden from each man himself (Ps 19:12). These secrets will be measured by the pattern of that pure gospel which is centered in Christ and was exhibited at the cross for sinners (1 Co 15:3-4).

Now a final summary of the ground just covered: (1) Man is condemned by his own self-judgment, as a moralist; (2) he will be condemned by the judgment of God because of four principles: (*a*) God will judge according to the truth; (*b*) God will judge according to works; (*c*) God will judge with impartiality; (*d*) God will judge the secrets of men.

The best man in the world cannot stand before such principles of judgment.

At this point Paul does not tell us what the gospel is, but how I thank God for the gospel! There is refuge in the gospel. Today that gospel is a message of deliverance; at the great white throne it will be a message of destruction. Let me bring to your mind one verse: "He that heareth my word and believeth him that sent me, hath eternal life, and *cometh not into judgment,* but hath passed out of death into life" (Jn 5:24, ASV).

The one who is in Christ cannot come into judgment! I praise God, for if God applied those principles to my life, I could not stand before Him.

However, Paul is not talking about the gospel here but is trying to bring these men to their knees in order that when he does bring the gospel to them in the next chapter, they will be ready for it.

8

The Jew Under the Sentence of Condemnation

WHAT CLASS OF PEOPLE is the Holy Spirit dealing with in this section? Look at verse 17: "Behold, thou art called *a Jew*" (2:17). In the ASV: "But if thou bearest the name of *a Jew*." Look at verse 28: "For he is not *a Jew*." Or verse 29—"But he is *a Jew*." "What advantage then hath *the Jew*" (3:1). Four times the word *Jew* appears. Certainly that should identify the group to whom he is addressing this argument.

When Paul started to condemn the world, the Jew claimed to be exempt from condemnation on three grounds. Paul knew this, for he himself was a Jew. These were the three grounds:

1. Because he was a son of Abraham. When Christ was condemning those Jews, they replied, "We are Abraham's seed" (Jn 8:33, ASV).
2. Because he had the law. The Jew rested his hope on possession of the law.
3. Because he was circumcised. The old rabbinical writings of the Jews contain such statements as this: "No circumcised man will be lost." In the days of Paul there was a saying that Abraham stood at the gates of Hades or Hell, seeing that no circumcised man was ever cast into Hell.

Since these three claims had a basis of truth, the apostle Paul needed to deal with each one in showing that the Jew is condemned with the rest of the world.

Three words are the key words. In the first section the emphasis is on the law: "resteth in the *law*" (v. 17); "instructed out of the *law*" (v. 18); "the form of knowledge and of the truth in the *law*" (v. 20); and "Thou that makest thy boast of

the *law*, through breaking the *law* dishonorest thou God?"
(v. 23).

In the second section the emphasis is on circumcision: "circumcision verily profiteth . . . thy circumcision is made uncircumcision" (v. 25). Paul uses this word in 26 and 27, too.

The third section emphasizes lineage: "He is not a Jew . . ."
(v. 28), "but he is a Jew . . ." (v. 29).

Now then, take those three ideas, and with them let us make
our outline for the section. It would be something like this:

1. The *law* cannot save the Jew (vv. 17-24).
2. *Circumcision* cannot save the Jew (vv. 25-27).
3. *Birth* cannot save the Jew (vv. 28-29).

Paul deals with exactly the three things that the Jew would
rest his hopes upon.

His Law Cannot Save the Jew

The apostle Paul first states the position of the Jew (2:17-
24). There were five advantages upon which the Jew based
his hope.

HIS NAME

The name *Jew* is from "Judah" and means "one who is
praised." The Jew was proud of that name, believing anyone
who bore that name was praised of God. "Whose praise is not
of men, but of God" (2:29). Paul was thinking of the meaning of that name when dealing with the Jew.

HIS TRUST

He trusted in the law. He trusted that the law would save
him.

HIS BOAST

The Jew boasted that the God of the Jew was the true God.
Certainly He was. That is an Old Testament doctrine. From
the forty-fifth chapter of Isaiah, last verse, can be seen that
the Jew was commanded to glory in God, and that is the word
here. But there is a boasting in God which is good, and there is
a boasting in God which is nothing less than blasphemy! And

the latter is what the Jew and the Pharisee had done. But Paul is not discussing that here.

HIS KNOWLEDGE

"And knowest His will, and approvest the things that are excellent, being instructed out of the law" (2:18). The word *His* is in italics. We can drop it out then. The real word that is in the Greek is the article *the*. It reads, "And knowest the will." There is only one will—the divine will.

HIS CONFIDENCE

His confidence involves four roles he believed were his: "a guide for the blind," "A light of them which are in darkness," "An instructor of the foolish," and "A teacher of babes" (2:19-20).

Paul's words carry just a touch of sarcasm. "Thou art confident," he says to this Jew. Paul knew the religious Jew and that is exactly what that Jew thought in those days. He thought that the Gentile was blind in darkness, and that he was a fool and did not know anything. The Gentile was considered immature, only a babe. The Pharisee believed he had to get the blind Gentile, and guide him, enlighten him, and instruct him.

Every one of these five aspects of the Jew's role revolves about the law. The Jew's name came from the law. His trust was in the law. He boasted in the true God, who was revealed in the law. He knew the will of God; it was shown in the law. The Jew was confident that he was a teacher of the law.

When Paul reaches verse 21, he begins to ask some searching questions. First of all, Paul affirms the Jewish role: "Thou therefore which teachest . . . thou that preachest . . . thou that sayest . . . thou that abhorest . . . thou that makest thy boast." On the basis of these attitudes and actions, Paul is going to ask questions. He says, "Do you teach yourself? Do you steal? Do you commit adultery? Do you desecrate temples?" (For that is what "commit sacrilege" means.) "Do you break the law?" Paul does not accuse him of these things; he merely inquires about them. Paul did not say, "You are a thief"; Paul says, "Are you a thief?" He arouses the conscience by searching questions.

Paul put his finger on a terrible inconsistency of the Jew (2:22). The Jew would shudder righteously if he saw an idol in a temple, or in speaking of idolatry; and yet he was willing to deal, as a merchant, in the very plunder that men stole out of those temples!

Not every Jew was guilty of all that Paul names here. Not every Jew was an adulterer nor a thief, but there was one respect in which every Jew failed. The first thing Paul asks is "Teachest thou thyself?" Every Jew failed to teach himself, and the Jews are not peculiar in that respect. We might put that question to the church and a good many Bible teachers today. "Thou therefore that teachest another, teachest thou not thyself? Thou that preachest a man should not steal, dost thou steal?" What a man says is worth nothing unless it has come into his own life and been worked out there in righteousness and service for God.

Paul stops asking questions and makes a direct charge: "For the name of God is blasphemed among the Gentiles because of you." And then he adds, "as it is written." The Jew trusted in the law (or what we would call the Old Testament), and Paul says in effect, "This charge is not mine. The very law in which you trust condemns you and proves that you have blasphemed the name of God through your life among the Gentiles" (see Is 52:5). Jesus made a similar statement: "Think not that I will accuse you to the Father; there is one that accuseth you, even Moses, on whom ye have set your hope" (Jn 5:45, ASV). The prophet Ezekiel was told by God: "They profaned my holy name; in that men said of them, these are the people of Jehovah" (Eze 36:20, ASV). When the Jews lived among the Gentiles, the Gentiles looked at them, saw how they lived, and said, "If this is the people of Jehovah, what kind of God must Jehovah be!" That is the charge.

In Paul's own words, they were "Instructed out of the law" (v. 18), "having in the law the form of knowledge and of the truth" (v. 20), he made his boast in the law (see v. 23), and yet he broke it. Paul's conclusion: the Jew dare not take refuge in the law, because he had broken that law, and that same law now condemns him.

What will be the Jew's answer? He will say, "Perhaps that

is true, therefore I cannot take refuge in it, but I am circumcised, and circumcision is the mark of God upon His own. No circumcised can be lost."

HIS CIRCUMCISION CANNOT SAVE THE JEW

"Circumcision indeed profiteth, if thou be a doer of the law: but if thou be a transgressor of the law, thy circumcision is become uncircumcision" (2:25). It can be summed up in a sentence: Circumcision could not save the Jew because he had not kept the law.

"If therefore the uncircumcision [the Gentile] keep the ordinances of the law, shall not his uncircumcision be reckoned for circumcision?" (2:26, ASV). Lack of circumcision would not condemn a Gentile just as the possession of circumcision would not save the Jew. The whole question rests upon the law. The Jew cannot be saved by his circumcision, because he has not kept the law; but if the Gentile did keep the law, lack of circumcision would not condemn him. And furthermore, the morality of the uncircumcised Gentile will judge and condemn the Jew who is circumcised. The very fact that the Jew was a circumcised man would only heighten his guilt in the eyes of God, because it showed he had the law.

This situation has a parallel among religious people today, too. The man who trusts in the rite of baptism, in membership in the Christian church will face a heightened guilt and condemnation in the eyes of God. His contact with the doctrines of Christianity increases his responsibility.

The conclusion here is that circumcision could profit a man if he kept the law. But the Jew had broken the law; therefore it was worthless to him as a means of salvation. The Jew's answer would be: "Perhaps I have broken the law, and perhaps that divinely appointed rite, the seal of God, is worthless to me, but I am still a Jew. I am a son of Abraham, and God has made certain promises to the sons of Abraham and the Jews, that He dare not break. That will save me."

HIS BIRTH CANNOT SAVE THE JEW

Paul turns to that in the third section and deals with that very question: "For he is not a Jew who is one outwardly;

neither is that circumcision which is outward in the flesh: but he is a Jew who is one inwardly, and circumcision is that of the heart, in the spirit, not in the letter" (2:28-29, ASV). Paul shows that there is such a thing as being a Jew merely in outward form. But God demands an inward reality and would not recognize any man as a Jew unless he has that. Some people think this statement teaches that every Christian is a Jew, but what it really teaches is that every Jew is not a Jew. No man can be a Jew unless he is born outwardly as a son of Abraham, and also inwardly in spirit; therefore, a man born only outwardly of Abraham is not a true Jew.

Notice these contrasting word pairs: outwardly—inwardly; flesh—heart; spirit—the letter; man—God. Those two verses are similar to the words of the Lord Jesus Christ to Nicodemus. He was a Jew outwardly. He had everything outwardly. The Lord Jesus Christ said to him, "Except a man be born again, he cannot see the kingdom of God" (Jn 3:3). That matter of heart circumcision was not anything new; the Old Testament is full of it. No Jew could deny that Paul was on safe ground when he talked about circumcision of heart (see Jer 4:4).

By the way, these two verses solve a difficult question raised later (see 11:26), where Paul says that all Israel shall be saved. People ask, "Is it possible that every Jew from the beginning of time is going to be saved?" Yes, every one of them, but "he is not a Jew who is one outwardly, but he is a Jew who is one inwardly." The Jew, in order to be a real Jew had to be born of God. The new birth is not a distinctively Christian doctrine. It belonged to the Jew as an Old Testament revelation. Nicodemus should have known it. Christ said, "Art thou a teacher of Israel, and understandest not these things?" (Jn 3:10, ASV). God demanded the inward reality, not merely the outward shell of profession that the Jew had.

Paul is dealing with this inward and outward profession. Look back at the seventeenth verse and you will see why he uses a peculiar expression there. He says: "Behold, thou that are *called* a Jew." They are just *called* Jews. There is a wholesome lesson here for us. Perhaps we may paraphrase the twenty-eighth and twenty-ninth verses in this manner: "For he is not a Christian who is one outwardly, neither is that baptism which is outward in the flesh, but he is a Christian which is one inwardly, and baptism is that of the heart, in the spirit, not in the letter; whose praise is not of men but of God." That does not mean that we are not emphasizing the importance of the outward rite, but we are saying that the outward rite is a worthless thing apart from the inward reality in our own lives.

The Jew does like sinners do today—he takes refuge in argument. If a man is uncovered, he will flee to another refuge and hide; finally he is entirely uncovered and convinced that he has no place to flee from the indictment that he is a sinner. It is then that he will resort to argument. That is what the Jew does. First he had taken refuge in the law; then in circumcision; then in Jewish birth. Now he takes refuge in argument! This is frequently the refuge of the sinner. Show him that he is a sinner, and he will begin to raise objections. Answer his objections and he will leave them and object to your answers. Often he will just keep on doing this.

Some have said that this is the hardest portion of the book of Romans to understand, and it may be. But I hope I can help you to understand it. I am going to call this the fourth division:

ARGUMENT CANNOT SAVE THE JEW

There are in these 8 verses four objections and four answers:

Verse 1. An objection	Verse 2. Paul's answer
Verse 3. Another objection	Verse 4. Paul's answer
Verse 5. Another objection	Verse 6. Paul's answer
Verse 7. Another objection	Verse 8. Paul's answer

Paul had been a Pharisee once and knew the pattern of their thinking. So he states their arguments here and answers them. These four objections in verses 1, 3, 5, and 7 are not independent of one other. There is only one real objection, and that is in the first verse; and when Paul answers that, the Jew squirms and varies his objection slightly, though to something that Paul says has already been answered.

"What advantage then hath the Jew? or what is the profit of circumcision?" (3:1, ASV). The Jew did not like to ask that, did he? "What advantage is there in being a Jew if all you say is true, Paul? If we are condemned with the rest of the world, what good is it to be a Jew?" The Jew had a right to ask that. So Paul answers, "Much every way: first of all, that they were entrusted with the oracles of God" (v. 2).

The Jew somehow thought that by being a Jew, he could escape the judgment of God. But nevertheless there is an advantage in being a Jew (see 9:4-5). A great deal, but Paul is not going to discuss all the various reasons; he is just going to take one, "the oracles of God—Scripture." That word *oracles* singled out a certain element in Scripture—the prophetic element—the promises concerning Jesus Christ. Was not that a tremendous advantage for the Jew to have: that in his hands God committed the oracles that told of the coming of the Messiah? The Jew ought to have known Christ when He came. The very advantage that the Jew had was the very thing that condemned him, because he did not believe in the Messiah when He came. He did not make the most out of his advantage.

The Jew knew that this was a good answer. But he sidesteps the answer by objecting to something in it (3:3). The Jew knew that he had not believed those oracles, and so he says, "Well, what if some of us did not believe? We had the oracles —we will admit that. But we did not all believe them. Shall the unbelief of some cancel out the faithfulness of God?" Do you see what he is saying? He is saying, "Supposing that God back in the Old Testament did promise the Jews a Messiah; supposing that He came and some of us did not believe? Won't God have to keep His promise to the Jewish nation anyway?" He is arguing that God must keep His promises whether the Jew is a sinner or a righteous man.

Paul answers: "God forbid!" God's faithfulness cannot fail —it cannot be made "of none effect." Paul expands: "Yea, let God be found true, but every man a liar" (3:4). If every man in the world becomes a liar, *God will still remain true*—it does not matter what happens. "That thou mayest be justified when thou speakest, and be clear when Thou judgest" (Ps 51:4). The very song of David showed God to be righteous when He condemned him.

The response of the Jew is clever but wicked. The Jew took this Scripture, twisted it out of shape, and made a terrible thing. He said, "But if our unrighteousness commendeth the righteousness of God, what shall we say? Is God unrighteous who visiteth with wrath?" (3:5). If God's righteousness appears in a clearer light because of our sin, can God blame us for our sin? The word *commend* means render conspicuous or bring out in a clearer light. To put it in other words, the Jew says, "If our unrighteousness makes clearer the righteousness of God, He would be unrighteous to take vengeance on us."

What is Paul's answer to that? Again his answer takes on tremendous force. "God forbid: for then how shall God judge the world?" Every Jew believed that God would judge the world. Paul is saying that if God cannot judge a sinner because his sin makes the righteousness of God more conspicuous, then He cannot deal with any sinner. That sort of reasoning would clear the slate for the Gentiles as well as for the Jews, and it would get rid of all judgment.

The Jew loved that argument, so Paul pursues the movement of this objection a step further. "If the truth of God through my lie abounded unto his glory, why am I also still judged as a sinner?" (3:7, ASV). He is still arguing that somehow, if the sin of man would make conspicuous God's righteousness—if man's lie made God's truth appear the greater—how then can God justly judge the sinner? The Jew is trying to argue that he ought to escape somehow. That is clever but fallacious reasoning. It is an attempt to escape the real issue and serves as a present refuge of sinners, and the Jew was one such.

Paul takes him on his own ground: "If you fellows are going to say that, then let us press that argument to its logical conclusion and see just exactly where it leads, as some people say." And what is the logical conclusion of that doctrine? Here it is, "Let us do evil that good may come." That is the logical outcome of that doctrine, and that is exactly what the Jesuits of the Catholic Church hold, namely this, that the end justifies the means. It does not matter what you do, just so the end is good. "Let us do evil that good may come." Paul says, "That is exactly what they say about *us,* and it is slander." Do you know why they said that about Paul? Paul taught salvation by grace apart from works. So the Jews used this doctrine against him. In effect they said, "This man Paul says that the more you sin, the more good comes out of it." So now Paul turns what

they said about him right back on them! What is his answer
to the whole thing? "Whose condemnation is just!"

There are two very solemn lessons from this. First, the
strictest legalism leads to the worst license. Many well-meaning
people want to keep the law today. They want to impose it
on us Christians. They say, "If you do not teach the Ten Commandments, soon your folks will be sinning, and they won't
care what they do." That is wrong. Those very Jews who would
not accept the fact that they were condemned and would not
accept Christ as Saviour, while depending on their law, finally
said, "Let us do evil that good may come." This is the logical
outcome of that frame of mind.

Second, by the same token, there are many professing Christians who are trusting in similar things today. Just as the Jew
trusted in his law, his circumcision, and his birth, so those who
are born of Christian parents and christened when they were
babies keep the Ten Commandments (they do not really keep
them) and think God will let them by! They need to read this
passage and realize that there is no refuge for a sinner in keeping the law, in church ordinances, in mere human birth, no
matter how good the family may be from which they come.

"What then? Are *we* better than *they?*" (3:9). Who are the
we? The Jews. Who are *they?* The Gentiles. Read it that
way: "Are the Jews better than the Gentiles? No, in no wise;
for we before laid to the charge both of Jews and Gentiles that
they are *all under sin.*" *All under sin*—that is his conclusion.

From the argument of this passage, is there not reason to
praise God that He has made a way of escape from the condemnation He has brought upon the world?

9

The Whole World Under the Sentence of Condemnation

THE CONCLUSION of the first section of Romans, called condemnation, answers the question, "Is the world lost?" This division comes almost in the center of the chapter. I have always been sorry that when they divided the Bible into chapters, they did not begin one there. There is no more definite division in the whole Bible. Note verse 21 begins "But now." He is introducing a new thing into the text.

Three sections of this first division deal with the Gentile, the moral man, and the Jew. Paul now comes to the conclusion of this section. Notice what particular class of men he is dealing with: "both of Jews and Gentiles" (v. 9). He has dealt with them separately, and now he is going to bring them together in the final section of the first division. In the world there are only two classes of people in the eyes of God: Jews and Gentiles.

Paul answers the question, "How many Jews and Gentiles are there who are righteous": verse 10, "there is none"; verse 11, "there is none," and again, "there is none"; verse 12, "there is none."

Four times the expression *none* is used. But that is only the negative side. "None" is the answer to the question, "How many righteous are there?" Now for the positive side. How many sinners are there? How many of all these people are sinners? The answer is to be found in the latter part of verse 9. It is the word *all,* appearing also in verses 12 and 19.

The word *none* appears four times, and *all* appears three times; three and four equal seven. If the number seven marks completeness, then the indictment that God brings against the world is a complete one—sevenfold—a complete indictment of evil. This section sums up all that has gone before, in order that Paul may bring the whole world to the judgment bar of God and leave them standing there—trembling and silent!

In this section is a picture of a courtroom with a criminal on trial. The very terms that the apostle uses are legal. There are several elements involved in a human trial. First, a charge. Then, very often there is an indictment, written and carefully prepared, and it has perhaps one, two, three, four, or a dozen counts. Then there is an opportunity given for the prisoner to make his defense. Finally, there is a verdict brought in specifying the guilt or innocence of the party. These four elements appear in this passage: (1) The Charge, verse 9; (2) The Indictment, verses 10-18; (3) The Defense, verse 19; and (4) The Verdict, verses 19-20.

THE CHARGE

"What then?" Paul is summing up all that has gone before. He has talked to the Gentile, both the heathen and the moral man; he has talked to the Jew. And he has condemned all of them. Now he is going to conclude, and so he says, "What then? What shall we say in conclusion? Are we better than they?" ("We," the Jews.) "Are we Jews better than the Gentiles?"

His answer is, *"No, in no wise."* Then he explains why. He says, "For we before laid to the charge both of Jews and Gentiles, that they are all under sin." The word *prove* is a very bad translation, for it means "to lay a charge against somebody in a court." It does, however, include the idea of proving that charge, because Paul not only laid a charge against the world, but he proved the charge. So we might speak of it as a proven charge. Just like a charge might be laid before a criminal in a courtroom.

What was the charge? "All under sin." He does not say that all have sinned. He will say that later on. He does not say, "I charge Jews and Gentiles that they are all sinners," but "They are *all under sin.*" This is a very striking phrase, especially in the original. It means that these people are not only under sin, but they are under all that goes with sin. Sin has its guilt, sin has its power, sin has its condemnation, and sin has its doom! Paul is saying that every one of these people (both Jews and Gentiles) is under the guilt of sin, under the power of sin, under the condemnation of sin, under the doom of sin! All these ideas are gathered up in this statement.

This is really no new charge. He says in essence, "We made that charge before." But when did Paul make that charge? In the three sections we have been studying. He is only gathering the whole thing up in one great sweeping statement, making the charge that every man in all this world is under sin! Now then, that is the charge.

The Indictment

Next in the order of judicial procedure is the indictment, which must be written. "As it is written," Paul says. These passages that he quotes in verses 10-18 are all taken from the Psalms (14 and 53) and from Isaiah. He paints the picture of the world just as an artist might, picking out a passage here and there and drawing a picture with a sweep of the pen.

There are fourteen counts in this indictment:

1. "There is none righteous, no, not one" (v. 10).
2. "There is none that understandeth" (v. 11).
3. "There is none that seeketh after God" (v. 11).
4. "They are all gone out of the way" (v. 12).
5. "They are together become unprofitable" (v. 12).
6. "There is none that doeth good, no not one" (v. 12).
7. "Their throat is an open sepulchre" (v. 13).
8. "With their tongues they have used deceit" (v. 13).
9. "The poison of asps is under their lips" (v. 13).
10. "Whose mouth is full of cursing and bitterness" (v. 14).
11. "Their feet are swift to shed blood" (v. 15).
12. "Destruction and misery are in their ways" (v. 16).
13. "The way of peace have they not known" (v. 17).
14. "There is no fear of God before their eyes" (v. 18).

These are God's fourteen points; God has drawn here a com-

prehensive picture of the human race. These fourteen counts
settle some questions.

RIGHTEOUSNESS

The world has talked a great deal about righteousness; it has
talked about righteous men and righteous nations. How many
righteous men and nations are there? "None," says God. The
whole trouble with us is that we do not know what righteousness is. What is righteousness? Being right—*perfectly right.*
Sometime ago some scientists wanted to make a ruler that was
perfectly accurate and straight. It cost $10,000 to make, and
then it was still not right. Where is the man, where is the nation
that is perfectly right in the light of God's standards? There is
none.

UNDERSTANDING

We are proud of the fact that we know a great many things
today, and yet after all, how many are there that understand?
"None." We might apply that in the physical world. We know
something about electricity, about radium, but where is the
man that *understands* them? But God is not talking about
physical things here. He is talking about spiritual things, the
things of God. He says, "There is nobody that understands."
It is derangement in mentality, spiritual incomprehension.

SEEKING AFTER GOD

All the new theologians and the preachers are telling us that
the world is *seeking after God.* Have you ever heard that before, that men are reaching and stretching up, trying to find
God? What does God say about it? How many are seeking
after God? "None." Not one, really.

TURNED ASIDE

"They have all turned aside" (ASV). The picture intended
is that of a caravan crossing the desert, which has gotten off the
route. So men have deviated from the right way of God.

UNPROFITABLE

"They have become unprofitable." The Greek word is used

to translate a Hebrew word, and the Hebrew word is one used to speak of milk that has turned sour. It does not say that God made man originally the way he is now. It says he *became* that way—became unprofitable.

NONE DOETH GOOD

Look at the course of life in the phrase *doeth good*. We talk about men doing good, and yet God says that "There is none that doeth good," meaning as a course of life (not speaking of single acts). There is not one man of whom it can be said, as a course of life, that "he doeth good."

GRAVEYARD THROATS

"Their throat is an open sepulchre." What is an "open sepulchre?" In the East, the grave of a buried person is sometimes left open. This is a dangerous situation; people coming along at night might fall in. Paul says that is what the throat is like. What did James say about the tongue? We can defile ourselves and other people with what we say. In reality, is it not true that the throat of some folks is like an "open sepulchre?" It is like the stench emanating from a decaying body. It gives expression to the vilest and most loathsome thoughts.

DECEITFUL TONGUES

"Their tongues are filled with deceit." They may speak nicely to you while at the same time they are intending to insinuate deadly poison.

POISONOUS LIPS

"The poison of asps is under their lips." The poison of the asp was stored in a bag under the lips. Like this deadly poison, so is human speech.

CURSING MOUTHS

"Mouth is full of cursing and bitterness." There are men in the world who have never opened their mouths except to utter an oath. There are others who have never yet spoken an oath; yet this remains true—their mouth is full. God is not telling so much what man does as what he *is*. Man is *full* of cursing and bitterness. A man may have lived all his life who never used indecent language, but when he is about to die and unconscious, he pours forth a stream of profanity! God knew it was there all the time. He knows that you or I may have never lived in an environment to bring it forth, but potentially it is there, in embryo; our mouths are full of it!

SWIFT FEET

"Whose feet are swift to shed blood." What a picture this draws of the condition of our time. It is true of the world—nations: quick, not in peace, but quick in war. Our feet are swift to do violence right now, and sad to say, the same sort of spirit exists in the churches themselves.

DESTRUCTION

"Destruction and misery" are at issue. Wherever man walks, there are destruction and misery! You only have to read history to find that out, or follow the telecasts of the day.

PEACE UNKNOWN

"The way of peace they have not known." Capitalize "Way" and "Peace," for *He* is our Peace and *He* is our Way, but He is unknown to the vast majority in the world.

NO FEAR OF GOD

"There is no fear of God before their eyes." Solomon says in the book of Proverbs that the fear of God is the beginning of wisdom. Perhaps the source of all other sins is found in this last indictment: "There is no fear of God before their eyes!" Without reverential fear of God, there is the absence of wisdom, increasing mental confusion, and moral and spiritual darkness.

That is an awful picture of the human race! There are three general divisions in this list of indictments: (1) Man is depraved in *character* (vv. 10-12); Man is depraved in *his speech* (vv. 13-14); (3) Man is depraved in *conduct,* "his feet," his ways (vv. 15-18).

That is remarkable, isn't it—that God should make a diagnosis like that? Character is what a man *is*. Speech is what a man *says*. Conduct is what he *does*. In all that man is, in all that he says, in all that he does, there is the taint of depravity and sin. That is the meaning of *total depravity*. God's Word teaches that each area of human life has been corrupted. Paul is not saying that there are not differences in degree among men concerning moral failures, but as far as the man's character, and his speech, and his conduct are concerned, everyone without exception has been touched by sin.

Perhaps some of you may say, "Is that *my* picture? Have *I* been guilty of all these things?" Yes, it is. It is your picture and mine—apart from Jesus Christ. We are herein described apart from Jesus Christ. God is not describing what we *do* as much as what we *are*. "The poison of asps is under their lips." You may never have poisoned anybody, but the poison is there. "Mouth full of cursing." You may say, "I have never taken an oath upon my lips," but it *is there,* and if you had been born in some families and trained like some people, it probably would have come forth. If you have never taken an oath upon your lips, it is by the grace of God. You have nothing to boast of.

There are only two things that God says we have without exception done: "They have all turned aside"; "They have used deceit." He does not say we have actually sinned in all these points. He is saying we are not righteous and thus the others are potential sins.

It would seem as though all these Scriptures piled one upon another would be sufficient to prove that every man is a sinner, but Paul knew his countrymen well. Paul had been a Pharisee once, and he knew the Pharisaical mind would listen to all these quotations from the Jewish Scriptures, say, "Amen" to every one of them, and then calmly pass them over to the Gentiles. That is human. We listen and say, "That means Jones—not me." Paul knew his countrymen would do this very thing, so he says in verse 19, "They that are under the law." He is not going to let the Jew escape. Does the law just speak to the Jew, not to the Gentile? There are some people that say that is true, but look back at the ninth and tenth verses. Just Jews? No, *everybody!*

Paul knows that when he gets through, the Jew will need an

extra reminder that all this applies to him too. So Paul says, "Now listen. All these things may apply to the Gentiles, but this law that I am talking about (the Old Testament: the five books of Moses, the Psalms, the Prophets) speaks first to them that are under the law— *to Jews!* You can't escape!"

That ends the indictment. Now then, let us look at the defense.

THE DEFENSE

In a human court, when the charge has been made and the prisoner is given a chance to speak for himself, sometimes (when he feels greatly the tremendous burden of his guilt and his sin) he will only bow his head and say, "I have nothing to say."

When the apostle Paul brings the whole world before the judgment bar of God (Jew and Gentile), it is not a blustering, noisy world. *It is a silent world!* Mark the words: "That every mouth may be stopped!" The mouth of the heathen idolater, the mouth of the man of exemplary morals, the mouth of the proud Pharisee, even the mouth that was full of cursing and bitterness: *every* mouth is stopped!

There is a foregleam here of the day of judgment. There is no defense! Men have wondered what that day will be like. Some men have been so presumptuous as to declare when that day comes they will stand before the throne of God and make their own defense. The great French infidel Rousseau, a man who shunned wedlock and sent his children to an orphanage, said, "I will stand before God and defend my conduct!" Many men say, "I will stand before God and defend myself." When I hear a man say that, I think, "Poor fool!" When men stand before that dread bar of God, there will be no defense, no alibi, no excuse. *Their mouths will be stopped!*

There is only one reason why human courts permit a defense. That is to protect against a mistake. Therefore, in order to protect everyone, we say, "You have an opportunity to make your defense. But when God brings a charge against a man, *He makes no mistakes!* There will be no defense in that day; the day of judgment will be a day of silence! Only one voice will speak, the voice of the Judge. Every mouth stopped!

That is guilt! God will not stop the mouth. Every man will be free to talk but will know in his heart that he is guilty!

THE VERDICT

The charge has been made, the indictment has been read, no defense given. The verdict: *guilty!* What a terrible word that is, even when it drops from the lips of a human judge. How much more terrible when it comes from the lips of God! It is God who is speaking here. "Guilty!"

What does the word mean? In our speech it means merely that the man did it, but Paul's statement means more than that. It means not only that he committed the crime, but that he is *obligated* to suffer the penalty for doing it. "All the world . . . brought under the judgment of God" (3:19, ASV). Man not only did it, but he must suffer for it.

In verse 20 Paul tells why God has rendered this verdict. The *therefore* of the King James Version should read *because* as in the American Standard Version. That gives it a clearer meaning. Just let me read it that way: "All the world may become guilty before God, because by the works of the law shall no flesh be justified in His sight." That is why. Man is guilty for two reasons: first of all, because he is a sinner; and second, *"because* by the deeds of the law shall no flesh be justified in His sight." The sinner has taken the impossible way for him—the wrong way. The law could justify a righteous man but never a sinner.

Notice something more: the apostle is leaving the specific law of Moses. He is no longer talking about *the* law. The definite article *the* is not present in the Greek. It ought to read, "by works of law." I have talked with Seventh Day Adventists and quoted this verse. They have said, "By works of *the* law. You cannot be justified by *the law of Moses,* but you can by *the law of Christ."* Paul includes *all* law, whether it is moral law, the law of Moses, ceremonial law, law of conscience, or whether it is the law that Christ laid down in the Sermon on the Mount, no matter what law, Paul says, "By works of law no flesh shall be justified in His sight" (3:20, ASV).

There is only one thing the law can do: "Through the law cometh the knowledge of sin." It is a remarkable end to the passage. *"Knowledge of sin."* If you have learned what God intended during this study, you will take that verse on your own lips something like this: "I know that I am a sinner." If you have learned that, you have learned the lesson that God would have you learn.

In the whole section on condemnation, the apostle has brought three witnesses against the world:

1. Against the Gentile world he brought the witness of *creation*. He says, "They ought to have known better, because they could see the created universe."
2. Against the moral man the witness of *conscience*. The conscience excuses or accuses. A man ought to know what is right or wrong by the conscience he has.
3. Against the Jew the witness of *the Scriptures*.

All three of these witnesses speak with one voice: "man is guilty!" and the conclusion can be summed up in three statements in this last section: *"All under sin"* (3:9); *"Every mouth stopped"* (3:19); *"All the world guilty before God"* (3:19).

There you have it. Paul has done his work; he has brought the whole world before the judgment bar of God and left everyone standing there, trembling and silent—not a mouth open!

Now we are ready for salvation. The argument is conclusive. If the whole world is under sin; if the whole world has its mouth stopped; if the whole world is guilty before God— thank God that He "so loved the world, that he gave his only begotten Son, that whosoever believeth in him should not perish, but have everlasting life!" (Jn 3:16).

10

Salvation: The Divine Method of Justification

"BUT NOW" marks a great transition. Those two words, *but now* make a great difference. They form a favorite expression with Paul. In his epistles he may at times paint the blackest picture possible and then say, "But now." (See Eph 2:11-13 and 1 Co 15:16-20.) "But now" is his particular phrase for making the transition from a dark, gloomy picture to something wonderful God does for us. Paul has the whole world standing with nothing to say before the judgment bar of God. "But now."

This section is the very heart of the book of Romans. For this reason, all Christians ought to memorize verses 21-26. If someone should ask me, "Brother McClain, if you could have just six verses out of the Bible, and all the rest be taken away, which would you take?", I would select these six verses. All of God's gospel is there, and in a way found nowhere else in the Word of God.

In order to get an outline, look at verse 21, "the righteousness"; verse 22, "even the righteousness"; verse 25 (about the middle), "to declare His righteousness"; the beginning of verse 26, "to declare . . . His righteousness." Four times the word *righteousness* is mentioned in this passage.

Another concept in this passage also appears: verse 24, "being justified"; verse 26, "and the justifier"; verse 28, "a man is justified"; verse 30, "which shall justify." This term also appears four times.

So we have *righteousness* occurring four times and forms of the verb *justify* used four times. While in the English these two words do not look alike, in the Greek they are practically the same word (*dikaiosune*—righteousness; *dikaioo*—justify). The first two syllables are exactly the same; they come from the same root and both emphasize the idea of righteousness.

Righteousness is the key, as it were, to this whole section, and using that idea, this outline emerges: (1) righteousness provided (vv. 21-22); (2) righteousness needed (v. 23, also a phrase in v. 22); (3) righteousness bestowed (v. 24, when God gives it to us); and (4) righteousness declared (vv. 25-26).

There is the main section of the passage. The concluding verses (27-31) constitute the conclusion and contain three questions: (1) "Where is boasting then?" (v. 27); (2) "Is He the God of the Jews only?" (v. 29); (3) "Do we then make void the law through faith?" (v. 31).

RIGHTEOUSNESS PROVIDED

About this righteousness that God provides, seven observations may be made:

THIS RIGHTEOUSNESS IS OF GOD

Back in the first chapter Paul mentioned righteousness in verses 16 and 17. In the eighteenth verse, he started on condemnation and said no more about God's righteousness again until the third chapter. Now he takes it up again. He had mentioned righteousness in the first chapter for our encouragement, before plunging into that dark section on condemnation.

So this righteousness is from God. This righteousness is not the righteousness that designates God's character. That particular kind of righteousness appears in the latter part of the passage, where Paul says, "To declare God's righteousness." But this righteousness is God's gift. It is the righteousness that He gives through the gospel and works out through the cross. At the end of this passage, Paul then turns to God's character. God *is* righteous at the same time He *gives* righteousness to man.

RIGHTEOUSNESS WITHOUT THE LAW

The word *without* is a very, very strong word in the Greek. It means "absolutely apart from." It is the same word used in

Hebrews 4:15, speaking of Jesus Christ, "in all points tempted like as we are, yet without sin," absolutely apart from sin. Law has nothing to do with this righteousness; it is not a legal righteousness in any sense of the word. Above all things, remember that!

THIS RIGHTEOUSNESS IS WITNESSED TO BY THE LAW

It is a righteousness that is without the law but the law witnesses to it, and also the prophets. The whole sacrificial system bore witness to the righteousness of God in Christ. When a man took his sacrifice as a sin offering to the temple, laid his hand upon the animal, confessed his sin, then killed the animal, he witnessed by that very act to the fact that he had faith in a righteousness that was not his own; and by faith he looked forward to the cross of Christ where the righteousness of God was manifested.

How do the prophets witness? The prophet Isaiah says, "All we like sheep have gone astray: we have turned every one to his own way; and the LORD hath laid on him the iniquity of us all" (Is 53:6). So the prophets as well as the law bear witness to this righteousness, though they have nothing to do with bringing it. It is *without* the law.

In Romans 4:3 Paul proves that this righteousness is without law. "For what saith the scriptures? Abraham believed God, and it was counted unto him for righteousness." We read about Abraham in the law.

The sixth verse of the same chapter refers to David, one of the prophets: "God imputed righteousness without works, saying, Blessed are they whose iniquities are forgiven, and whose sins are covered. Blessed is the man to whom the Lord will not impute sin." As one of the prophets, David knew something about this righteousness, just like Abraham did in the law. Paul proves what he is talking about.

THIS RIGHTEOUSNESS OF GOD IS MANIFESTED

The ASV reads, "hath been manifested"; the KJV says, "is manifested." It is that peculiar Greek tense, the perfect tense, which refers to something that was done in the past, the effects of which abide right up to the present. So both renderings can be considered right. God manifested His righteousness at the cross nineteen hundred years ago. He *hath* manifested; but the righteousness of God is still manifested today, because the cross is eternal in the sense that its effects last forever. The righteousness of God has been and is yet being manifested.

There is quite a remarkable contrast between this statement and the one in 1:17: "For therein is the righteousness of God revealed." The verb *revealed* in this passage is present tense; that is to say, in the gospel the righteousness of God is being revealed all the time. Every time the gospel is preached, God's righteousness is revealed. But here (3:21) he is not talking about the preaching of the gospel, but the fact that God manifested His righteousness in the cross.

RIGHTEOUSNESS WHICH IS BY FAITH IN JESUS CHRIST

It is remarkable that the righteousness of God will not come to the one who has faith in God. If you want to have the righteousness of God, you must have faith in Him: *Jesus Christ.* Of course, Jesus *is* God. But remember that faith in God is not enough! You must have faith in the Son of God, Jesus Christ, the appointed way, or you do not have the faith which brings righteousness.

THIS RIGHTEOUSNESS IS UNTO ALL

A lot of folks wonder why Paul said "unto all and upon all," seeming to repeat himself. "Even the righteousness of God which is by faith of Jesus Christ unto all and upon all them that believe" (3:22). They ask, "Doesn't the righteousness of God in Christ come to every last man that lives? Isn't it universal? Isn't it for everybody?" Certainly. "Does it *save* everybody?" No! Whom then does it save?

A RIGHTEOUSNESS UPON ALL THAT BELIEVE

It is "upon all," with a condition: "Them that believe." The precision of language at this point is significant. God's righteousness is for all men, if they want it, but it only comes to *rest upon* those who believe in Jesus Christ.

RIGHTEOUSNESS NEEDED

Verse 23 and the last phrase of verse 22 constitute a parenthetical interjection. It is therefore possible to move from the word *believe* in verse 22 right down to verse 24. But Paul introduces the statement here because he cannot let the people forget that they *need* God's righteousness. Man needs righteousness for three reasons: (1) because "there is no difference"; (2) because "all have sinned"; (3) because "all . . . come short of the glory of God."

THERE IS NO DIFFERENCE

Is there no difference between a drunkard down in the gutter and the man of morality (but out of Christ)? Yes, there is a difference. The one fellow is worse than the other, as far as sensual sin is concerned, but as far as being a lost man, there is no difference! Neither one has righteousness with God. A state penitentiary may contain several hundred men. Some of them are in for life, some are murderers, others are thieves. Some may be more deeply criminal than others. But there is no difference as far as one thing is concerned: they are all there in prison because they are all lawbreakers.

This phrase *no difference* occurs in one other place in Romans: "For there is no difference between the Jew and the Greek: for the same Lord over all is rich unto all that call upon Him" (10:12). That is the other side. If there is no difference when it comes to man's need, thank God there is no difference in God's meeting that need.

ALL HAVE SINNED

In the clause, "For all have sinned," the tense indicates something done in the past. It does not matter how many times a man does it—a man may sin a hundred times, but as God looks back, He simply says, "All *have* sinned."

ALL COME SHORT

Then Paul uses the present tense: "all . . . come short." Let us read it this way: "And are continuously coming short of the glory of God." That is the result of "all have sinned." What if someone denies that and says, "I have not sinned"? To such a one there comes the answer from the first epistle of John, "If we say we have not sinned, we make him a liar, and his word is not in us" (1 Jn 1:10).

That verb has another significant meaning, indicated by its grammatical voice. The middle voice points to the fact that the cause of man's condition is not from outside himself, but *in* him.

What is this glory of God that men are constantly coming short of? John 1:14 gives us the explanation: "And the Word was made flesh, and dwelt among us (and we beheld his glory, the glory as of the only begotten of the Father,) full of grace and truth." What is that glory there? Was that the glory that made John fall down when he saw Him, as stated in the book of Revelation (1:17), or as in Isaiah when he saw Him in the temple (6:1)? No, because He did not have that glory then. This is simply His moral and spiritual glory. "He was in the world, and the world was made by him, and the world knew him not" (Jn 1:10). *He was sinless,* and that was His glory. Every man, woman, and child is conscious of coming short of that glory, day by day, hour by hour, and every moment. We praise God for Paul's statement: "But we all, with open face beholding as in a glass the glory of the Lord, are changed into the same image from glory to glory, even as by the Spirit of the Lord" (2 Co 3:18). We are going to be "like Him," for we are going to "see him as he is" (1 Jn 3:2). We fall short of the glory now, but some day we shall attain it by His blessed power. That is what he is talking about here. Every man knows that he is coming short of the glory of God as it is in Christ Jesus.

RIGHTEOUSNESS BESTOWED

BEING JUSTIFIED

What does it mean to be justified? Some people say it means to make a man righteous. Catholic theologians say that when God justifies a man, He makes him righteous. Therefore it is progressive. This means that when God justifies a man, He makes him better and better. However, let us settle the meaning of this word by noting in the Scriptures the use of the word.

"The doers of the law shall be justified" (Ro 2:13). Think about that. Suppose it means to make the man righteous. Isn't the man that does the law already righteous? How could you make the doer of the law righteous, if he is already righteous? But actually, the word *justify* means to pronounce a man righteous. He is not *made* righteous, but pronounced righteous. In speaking of God, Paul says, "that Thou mightest be justified" (3:4). Suppose we insert the phrase "to make righteous" in place of the phrase "mightest be justified." Can God be *made* righteous? No, because God *is* righteous. All that a person can do is to say, "Oh, God, You are righteous." That means that God is pronounced righteous, which is exactly what *justify* means: to pronounce a man righteous and to treat him as such. Remember that definition: *justify means to pronounce and treat as righteous.* It is vastly more than being pardoned; it is a thousand times more than forgiveness. You may wrong me and then come to me; and I may say, "I forgive you." But I have not justified you. I cannot justify you. But when God justifies a man, He says, "I pronounce you a righteous man. Henceforth I am going to treat you as if you have never committed any sin." Justification means sin is all past and gone—wiped out—not merely forgiven, not merely pardoned; it means clearing the slate and setting the sinner before God as a righteous man, as if he had never sinned, as if he were as righteous as the Lord Jesus Christ Himself.

FREELY

How does God do this? "Freely!" The Greek word is *dorean.* A whole sermon is contained in that word. When the Lord Jesus Christ said, "They hated me *without a cause,*" that Greek word was used in the text. "They hated me *dorean.*" Let us read this text that way: "Being justified without a cause." There is no cause in the sinner that God should justify him; the cause is all in Christ. The same word is used by Paul in saying, "Neither did we eat any man's bread *for nought*" (2 Th 3:8), that is, "for nothing." Paul is saying, "We did not eat any man's bread for nothing." Insert these two words into the text: "Being justified for nothing." How much does it cost to be justified? Not a thing! "Being justified without a cause;

being justified for nothing." You did not pay a cent for it. But that doesn't mean that it was cheap.

BY HIS GRACE

Now the next phrase. How was it done? "By his grace!" He first of all says that we had nothing to do with it, then he turns around and shows God did it. It was the unmerited, undeserved favor of God!

REDEMPTION

He did it through something, namely, "the redemption that is in Christ Jesus." *Redemption* means to set free, to liberate by the paying of a price. That is what God did in Christ. He set you free from your sins because He paid the price. They say, "Salvation is free," and so it is. Salvation does not cost *you* a thing, but salvation cost *God* sacrifice of His only Son.

Verse 24 is part of the flow of thought from verse 22. "They that believe are justified freely by His grace through the redemption that is in Christ Jesus." Remember, verse 23 is a parenthesis.

RIGHTEOUSNESS DECLARED

We have here in these two verses (25-26) some things that ought to make men tremble as they behold the majesty of that God who sits in the heavens and establishes His justice through the cross of Christ. Cowper, the poet, was a lost man. He began to realize that he was a sinner and came to the point where he was almost ready to take his life. He was in despair because he knew he had no righteousness of his own. He said, "One day when I was walking the floor, I decided to pick up the Bible and see if there was anything to help me. My eye fell on Romans 3:25. I saw the light in that verse and it saved me!"

First of all, Paul says that God has "set forth Christ to be a propitiation." A *propitiation* is a reason for not executing punishment which is deserved. The Greek word is the same word that is applied to the mercy seat in the Old Testament, where the blood was sprinkled. The only reason that God set aside judgment was that a broken law was covered by the blood on the mercy seat. The mercy seat was the only thing that saved them. "God hath set forth Christ to be a propitiation."

But there are two other things there: "Through faith" and "in His blood." There ought to be commas after "propitiation" and after "faith," because His propitiation is *in His blood* and not through faith in His blood. Propitiation cannot be had without blood, yet propitiation is not operative without faith. Propitiation may be made, but it avails me nothing until I believe, and so the two elements must be present to have propitiation and to have it operative. First, the propitiation, Jesus Christ; He must be slain, His blood be shed. Then there must be faith in Him.

Why did God make Christ a propitiation? Why was it necessary for there to be the cross? Why did Christ die on the cross? A quick answer might be that He died to show God's love. Thank God, He *did* die to show God's love, but that is not the primary purpose. "To declare His righteousness for the remission of sins that are past, through the forbearance of God" (v. 25). *To declare His righteousness,* not His love. But why did God's righteousness need to be declared? Doesn't everybody know that God is righteous? "For the remission of sins that are past." That is a poor translation for the Greek word rendered *remission.* The sins of the Old Testament were never taken away until the cross of Christ. This word *remission* means that His judgment was suspended. God "winked" at sin, as the word is translated in Acts 17:30. In the Old Testament, God's character was under a shadow. Psalm 50:16-23 explains the situation: "These things hast thou done," and God says, "I kept silence." God did not do anything about it. Then what happened? "Thou thoughtest that I [God] was altogether such an one as thyself!" Man went on and sinned, and because God did not do anything, man said, in his estimate of God, "God is just like I am. He does not punish sin; He is indifferent." And God says, "I will reprove thee and set them in order before thine eyes."

Down through the ages of the Old Testament, God overlooked sin; He passed over it. God's character thus came under a cloud, and men were saying, "God doesn't care if men sin." In order therefore to show that He is righteous, He set forth the cross of Christ, and there, in Christ, He punished every last sin that man has committed. God's righteousness in this way is cleared and vindicated.

That is the first reason for the cross. It was a moral reason. God cannot forgive sin apart from the cross. If Christ had not died on the cross, the Old Testament saints would be compelled to come back from heaven. As someone has said, "Elijah and Moses were only there on credit." They could not have stayed there. God sets forth Christ as a propitiation to show that He is righteous. "To declare . . . at this time His righteousness" (v. 26). It is important when He says it twice. "That He might be just."

There was another way that God could have been just. He could have punished sin on the spot. When a man sinned, He could have destroyed Him. That would have proved that He was just. But think for a moment of the alternative. Not a soul in the world could have been saved that way. Never! But God did not show Himself to be righteous in that way. He wanted to do something else, namely, "That He might be just, and the justifier of him which believeth in Jesus."

Praise God for those two phrases. God could be just, holy, and righteous on His throne, punishing sin, upholding His law; and yet at the same time He can take a sinner like me, pronounce me righteous, and treat me like a righteous man! There is not a man in all the universe that can find fault with God for doing it. God, in Christ, came down and suffered for our sins, and He is righteous because of that. "Mercy and truth are met together; righteousness and peace have kissed each other" (Ps 85:10). Mercy has all that is coming to her, and the law has all that is coming to it.

Now he closes on this point by asking, "Where is boasting?" His answer requires three words: "It is excluded." In modern English: "It is shut out." There is no room for boasting when God faces man that way. No boaster will ever get into heaven.

Revelation 5:9-14 depicts a scene in heaven where praises are sung to the Lamb, and all say, "Worthy is the Lamb that was slain," "for thou wast slain," and "hast made us . . . kings and priests." In this statement, there is no boasting of personal attainments and character. The boasting of heaven is in the Lamb of God!

His second question: "Is He the God of the Jews only?" The answer is no, but in this way he shows that this method of salvation is the only method that is in accordance with the universality of God. Paul said that God is God of all nations, therefore when He shuts man's mouth and says, "I will save any man by faith," that is the way it ought to be.

He asks in the thirty-first verse: "Do we then make void the law through faith?" Paul answers again: "God forbid!" We do not make it void but we *establish* the law. It is done by God in satisfying holy demands of the law in the infinite penalty inflicted on His son, therefore making possible for any man, Jew or Gentile, to appropriate the benefits of the cross by faith.

There is only one religion in all the world that can save men and still establish, exalt, and honor the law: Christianity. All other systems that are based on legality, on salvation by works, dishonor the law, because nobody ever kept it. The inevitable result is that they pull the law down a little bit so that man can win his salvation by keeping it. But God punished Christ, His Son, for our transgression, and in so doing, He not only saves us, but at the same time He also establishes His throne in the heavens as a throne of justice and mercy.

11

Salvation: The Old Testament Illustration of Justification

WHEN THE APOSTLE PAUL, in the latter part of the third chapter, discusses how God justifies a man, he shows that God does it by faith, apart from works. This is in accord with what *justification* means, namely, "to declare and treat as righteous." This is one of the things the devil would like to confuse in our thinking. Justification does not mean to *make* a man righteous. That belongs to sanctification. In order to make this clear we shall see in this chapter how God justifies the ungodly. A concrete instance of this remarkable procedure on the part of God is now presented.

When the apostle Paul shows that divine justification comes by faith and not by works, the first response of the Jew would be, "What about our father Abraham?" And until Paul has dealt with Abraham, he can get no place with the Jew, because Abraham was the father of all the Jews and the great prototype of all the saved. Israel looked back to him as the father of the faithful; and so Paul must explain the question of how he was justified, which he does in chapter 4:

Verse 1 begins, "What shall we say then [about] Abraham?" At the outset let me clarify that it does not mean "Abraham is our father as pertaining to the flesh." More particularly it means "what has Abraham found as pertaining to the flesh?" Paul is using the word *flesh* to stand for human activity, fleshly activity, works. The Jew, of course, held that justification and salvation must come by the works of the law, and so Paul is going to discuss that point. "What has he found? What did he get?" Every Jew would hold that Abraham received at least

112

three things: (1) *righteousness,* the very essence of justification; (2) *an inheritance,* "I am the LORD that brought thee out of Ur of the Chaldees, to give thee this land to inherit it" (Gen 15:7); (3) *a posterity,* "And thou shalt be a father of many nations" (Gen 17:4).

These three items stood out in the mind of the Jews. The question: How did Abraham get those three things? The answer will settle the whole matter, and the apostle Paul is going to show how Abraham acquired his righteousness, his inheritance, and his posterity. Paul's discussion will form the outlines of the chapter. The movement of thought is very logical.

The chapter starts out with an introduction of two verses. In the order of discussion he takes up righteousness first. This is the subject of verses 3-12. Then he turns to Abraham's inheritance, which is the theme of the second division (vv. 13-16). Finally, he comes to Abraham's posterity (vv. 17-21). "As it is written, a father of many nations have I made thee" (v. 17, ASV). The chapter closes with an application in which he confronts believers with the personal implications (vv. 23-25).

You many wonder why we should be discussing Abraham, a man of ancient times. The answer is clear. Even though this was written back there it contains lessons for us today, and so Paul closes with an application.

ABRAHAM'S RIGHTEOUSNESS

How did he get it? By faith: "For what saith the scripture? Abraham *believed* God." And then what did God do? "It was counted unto him for righteousness." *Count, impute,* and *reckon:* all three of these words are one word in the Greek, not different words. The men who translated the King James Version were seeking to produce a good English version, and they thought the translation would become too monotonous if the same word were used too often. So they varied the translation and confused the English reader by using different words for the translation of the same Greek word. The same Greek word is used eleven times. The rendering is either *count, impute,* or *reckon* all the way through, which means "to put to one's account." It is like taking five dollars to the bank and putting it on deposit. The bookkeeper puts that to your account.

So Abraham believed God, and God in effect got out His book and put it down to Abraham's account as righteousness. Paul quotes Scripture which takes on particular force for the Jew, because it takes him right back to Genesis 15 where it is recorded that God promised to Abraham certain things. Abraham ". . . believed in the LORD, and he counted it to him for righteousness" (Gen 15:6).

In essence the Jew asks, "Didn't works have something to do with it?" So Paul addresses himself to this question in verses 4 and 5. "To him that worketh *not,* but believeth on him that justifieth the ungodly, his faith is reckoned for righteousness (v. 5). You might have something put to your account that you earned. There are two ways you may get your righteousness: someone might give it to you or you might earn it. Paul is going to discuss those two ways. He says, "If it is a reward for works, it is not from grace at all, but out of debt" (v. 4).

That verse, and especially one phrase in that verse, is without doubt the greatest presentation of free grace and righteousness by faith in all the Word of God. God justifies whom? "The ungodly." That is a strong word. He does not mean merely a sinner, but a man whose sin is ungodly. God justifies that kind of man. He declares him righteous and treats him as righteous, and He does it on the ground of faith.

So Paul rules out all works. Righteousness is not "to him that worketh," but it is "to him that worketh *not."* He is the man whom God justifies, even though he is an ungodly man. That was a new thought to the Jews about their father Abraham.

In verse 6 Paul is not introducing a new case but is only bringing testimony from David to support his argument. David was another great man in the mind of the Jew, second only to Abraham.

Verses 7 and 8 declare that sins are covered. Sins were not taken away in the Old Testament, only covered. But they were taken away at the cross of Christ!

So Paul finishes with the "works" part of it. He shows first of all that Abraham received his righteousness by faith; he shows second that works had nothing, absolutely nothing, to do with it.

Verse 9 introduces a new aspect of the case, of which the Jew would say, "There *was* a righteousness that Abraham had. Abraham was circumcised, and that helps towards his righteousness." So Paul now confronts that problem. Abraham was righteous; he had it by faith, not by works. But did circumcision have any place in it? Paul meets the issue: "How then was it reckoned? When he [Abraham] was in circumcision, or in uncircumcision? (v. 10). Could you prove it? In Genesis 15:6 is the record of when Abraham received his righteousness. The seventeenth chapter records when Abraham was circumcised. The last verse of the sixteenth chapter says that Abraham was "fourscore and six years old" when Hagar bare Ishmael. According to Genesis 17:25-26, he was ninety-nine years old (thirteen years later) when he was circumcised. Abraham already had his righteousness thirteen years (according to the Jews' own Scripture), probably fourteen years before God required the rite of circumcision. Certainly this was sufficient evidence that circumcision did not enter into the acquisition of righteousness.

"Well, then," the Jew might say, "what was the rite of circumcision for?" Some folks ask the same question today about baptism, thinking that one must be baptized to be saved. "Well," they say, "what is baptism for, then?" It has a place, and circumcision had a place. Because the rite was not what secured righteousness for the man did not mean that it was excluded from any place in the plan of God. "And he received the sign of circumcision, a seal of the righteousness of the faith which he had yet being uncircumcised" (Ro 4:11). Though circumcision does not secure righteousness, it is a seal of righteousness already received. That is exactly what baptism is. Baptism does not secure righteousness for any man. But it is a seal of the righteousness received by faith and by grace, and when put in its proper place, it is a benediction and a blessing, as is circumcision according to this fourth chapter of Romans.

Since the Jew thought that the Gentile had to come in by the door that the Jew had entered, Paul reverses the order to show that the Jew must come in by the way the Gentile entered. Abraham was a Gentile before called to be a Jew, the father of the nation. This was also before he was circumcised, which was a sign of Judaism. So Paul puts the Gentile first here. The Jew comes last instead of first.

Verse 12 makes it clear that circumcision alone will not suffice for the Jew. He must also walk in the steps of his Father Abraham. Paul takes the Jew away from external rites and sends him back to that faith which Abraham exercised.

Abraham had righteousness; he got it by faith, apart from works and apart from human ordinances.

ABRAHAM'S INHERITANCE

Abraham and his seed are heirs of the world, and we are heirs because we are his seed by faith. In that light, consider 1 Corinthians 3:21: "Therefore let no man glory in men. For all things are yours." And the reason everything is yours is because you are the seed of Abraham—spiritually, of course.

The promise was made to Abraham that he should be heir to the world. How did he get the promise—by works? "It was not through the law, but through the righteousness of faith" (Ro 4:13). He puts the two things together in this expression, "through the righteousness of faith."

The inheritance that the Jew looked forward to was the world. He wanted his Messiah to come in order that they as heirs might take over the world. Abraham received that promise by faith.

Now the question arises, "Why could not this inheritance come through the law?" The Jew could not understand that. But Paul is going to give the reason.

Verse 14 raises the question about the promise. Is it not good? If God would offer this inheritance through the law, then this promise would fail. Why? Nobody ever kept the law. He proved that back in the first part of the book.

Isn't it strange that the very people who admit that they have never kept God's law are the ones who are insisting that they will some day be saved by keeping the law? For those who reason this way, Paul settles the question. He says in effect,

"If God had made this promise through the law, it would have amounted to nothing."

Verse 15 expresses the fact that nobody ever kept it, and because they had broken the law, God's wrath must fall upon anybody who tried to keep it and failed.

Aren't you glad you are not under the law? "Where there is no law, neither is there transgression" in God's sight (15). Oh yes, you are a sinner, but not in God's sight! This is a legal proposition *before God,* in a courtroom, where you are not under God's law and there is therefore no transgression and He counts you righteous!

In verse 16 he tells why it positively came by faith: "to the end that the promise might be sure!" That is why. "That the promise might be made sure to all the seed."

Praise God that there is just one way that anything that God can give to the world is made available, and all must receive it on the principle of grace through faith. That can't fail because it all depends upon God. God is the giver. If you are going to depend upon law, it will have to depend upon you; and if you are the person upon whose works and whose faithfulness the promises of God depend, then "the promise is of none effect." On the other hand, if it is the grace of God, apprehended by faith (which is "simply the hand of the heart"), then "the promise is made sure to all the seed" down through the ages. It cannot fail, because God cannot fail, even though you may fail. That is the reason Peter said, "Our inheritance is undefiled; it is reserved in heaven for us." It is sure because it depends upon God absolutely!

Abraham's Posterity

He was to be "the father of many nations." How did he get that promise?

Verse 17 declares that "He believed God." That is to say, he got his posterity through believing. In the unfolding of this section, I want to point out five things about his faith. I think you will agree that it is one of the most thrilling climaxes about a man's faith!

HE BELIEVED GOD

In the first place, it is affirmed that "He believed God." Notice the kind of God he believed in—the God who "quickens the dead and calleth the things that are not, as though they were." Did he say, "I *will* make thee the father of many nations?" No! He said, "I have made thee!" As God states it, it is already an accomplished fact, and yet Abraham did not even have a son when God said it, and he was 100 years old. That is certainly "calling the things that are not as though they were." God does that very thing for us today. He says that we are predestinated; He says that we are called; He says that we are justified; He says that we are glorified! He says it! (Ro 8:29-30). Are we glorified yet? No, of course not. But that is certainly following the same pattern of dealing as with Abraham. "He calls the things that are not as though they were!" He is able to do it because He can bring it to pass. He says we are "seated with Christ in the heavenly places," and we are down here in the church. He can say it because He can do it!

HE BELIEVED AGAINST HOPE

In the second place, verse 18 records something that is no less wonderful! He "believed against hope." That looks like a contradiction. But it means simply that there was no human ground for any hope, but he believed God anyway, and his faith gave him a hope. That is the way we do today. Sometimes when things are going wrong, if we can just believe God, then we have hope. Out of our faith comes hope.

HE BELIEVED IN SPITE OF CIRCUMSTANCES

In the third place, verse 19 asserts that he believed in spite of "his own body now dead, when he was about an hundred years old, neither yet the deadness of Sarah's womb." I have mentioned this circumstance to pinpoint an amazing achievement. Here is a man a hundred years old, with his wife almost as old, and yet God comes to him and says, "Abraham, your seed shall be as the stars of heaven"! Now this man believed God in spite of circumstances, and that is the kind of faith God wants us to exercise. The devil can always raise up circumstances and say, "Now, look here and look there. God can't fulfill His promise." But never mind the circumstances. Believe God, "who quickeneth the dead and calls the things that are not as though they were."

HE BELIEVED WITHOUT STAGGERING

In the fourth place, verse 20 declares that he believed without staggering. The Greek word *stagger* means "to divide." The idea seems to be that a man is divided—he is two men; one part of him wants to go this way, the other that way. That is the way folks are when they come to believing. One part says, "I believe God," the other part says, "I don't know," so that person is parted in two. Abraham was not that way. "He staggered not." He believed God with all his heart. "He staggered not at the promise of God, but was strong in faith."

HE BELIEVED GOD COULD PERFORM

In the fifth place, Abraham believed that God could perform whatever He promised (Ro 4:21). That is, Abraham was fully persuaded in his own mind that God was able to carry His promise to fulfillment. That brings the reader to the point of personal salvation. One must believe that God will do what He promises. Do you believe that God can make you like Christ? He has promised to do it. All human and natural circumstances were against Abraham, but he said, "I know that God can do this thing." So Paul repeats once more: "Therefore it was *imputed* unto him for righteousness." This is the key to the whole passage. It occurs four times in the chapter: "It was *counted* unto him for righteousness" (v. 3); "His faith is *counted* for righteousness" (v. 5); "That faith was *reckoned* to Abraham for righteousness" (v. 9); "Therefore it was *imputed* to him for righteousness" (v. 22).

Now then, what is the conclusion of this matter? Did Abraham get anything by works? Not a thing! He got his righteousness by faith; his inheritance by faith; his posterity by faith. Abraham did not get a single thing by human works, and yet the Jews looked back to Abraham and said, "We are walking in his steps," while trying to keep the law.

At this point Paul not only answers the argument, but he

also turns it against them. This is the great faith chapter of the Bible. The word *faith* or the word *believe* occurs no less than sixteen times in the chapter. Everything that Abraham had was by faith.

With inescapable logic, Paul introduces the application. "Now it was not written for his sake alone, that it was imputed unto him; but for us also, to whom it shall be imputed, if we believe on him that raised Jesus our Lord from the dead" (vv. 23-24).

God has but one way of saving men in all ages. It is by faith, apart from works. Revelation may change, but down through the ages, salvation is through faith in God! Back with Abraham, He came and said, "You are going to have a son" and Abraham believed Him. Now that was looking forward. The Messiah was to come through that son, and so Abraham's faith, in a way, was in the Lord Jesus Christ, because without that son we could not have had Christ. That was really the beginning. It was faith in the ability or omnipotence of God—looking forward, however, to a promise.

Today we do not look forward to a promise; we look back to an accomplished fact and believe that. But it is faith, just the same. In both these instances it was not simply faith in a fact, but faith in God that He would bring it to pass. Mere faith in something that happened nineteen hundred years ago will not save. We believe God, and a God incarnate in human flesh who died on the cross and was raised from the dead and lives today, our personal Saviour and Lord!

This chapter of Romans contains the whole history of redemption. It began with life from the dead, because Abraham, the father of Israel, was an old man. It began with Israel, with the son of Abraham; it ended with Jesus Christ, raised from the dead. The beginning and the end: life from the dead (Ro 4:24-25). The only way we can apprehend and secure the benefits of redemption is by simple faith in God, for "without faith it is-impossible to please him" (Heb 11:6). That is the argument of the chapter.

12

Salvation: The Blessings That Accompany Justification

THE LAST WORD in the fourth chapter is the word *justification* which means to declare and treat as righteous. With the close of the fourth chapter, Paul is finished with the discussion of how God justified a certain man, who is representative of all men. He turns to another aspect of justification in the next chapter.

A good many people think of justification as the first or initial blessing of the Christian life, its value ending at that point. But while justification is the initial blessing, it is more than that in the Christian life. Justification is not only the first or initial blessing, but justification carries with it every other blessing of the Christian life, and when a man is justified, he has everything that God has to give.

So, let us never think of justification as being a small thing. It is the greatest thing in the Christian life, because it carries with it everything else. There are a great many Christians who are not enjoying every blessing. There may be some Christians who do not know what they received when God justified them and of course can't enjoy what they are ignorant of. But that does not change the fact that when God gives justification by faith, He gives with that justification everything that He has to give. In these first eleven verses of chapter five, Paul will give a summary of the blessings that go with justification.

There are two key phrases which occur twice in this section. Following the first comma in the first verse, "Therefore being justified by faith," come two words. *"We have."* This means we have some possessions that come with justification. Then look at the ninth verse: "Much more then, being now justified by his blood, *we shall be*."

First, being justified by faith we *have* something; and then, being now justified we *shall be* something. One phrase has to do with the present, the other with the future.

I have spent a good many hours on these eleven verses, and I admit failure to make any outline of them that satisfies me, because the thought and the argument are so close and continuous that it is almost impossible to analyze it without breaking the thought. So I have not tried to do that but am going to point out to you twelve blessings that go with justification using *being justified* as the key phrase:

1. Being justified by faith, we have *"peace with God."*

2. Being justified by faith, "we have *access*, by faith, into this grace."

3. Being justified by faith, we have *a standing* in grace.

4. Being justified by faith, we have *joy* ("we rejoice") "in hope of the glory of God."

5. Being justified by faith, "we *glory* in tribulations." *Glory* is the same word in the Greek as *rejoice*. Being justified by faith, we "rejoice . . . in tribulations." We have *joy* in our tribulations. The unsaved man cannot rejoice in his tribulations.

6. Being justified by faith, we have a *hope* that "maketh not ashamed."

7. Being justified by faith, we have *"the love of God* . . . shed abroad in our hearts." We have an experience of the love of God.

8. Being justified by faith, we have *the Holy Spirit*. A justified man need not anxiously look for a future time when he will receive the Holy Spirit. He has the Holy Spirit as a justified man. This fifth verse is a remarkable verse, for it is the first occurrence in the Book of Romans of the Holy Spirit, and here too the love of God is first mentioned.

9. Being justified by faith, we have *the proof of God's love* because "Christ died for us."

10. Being justified by faith, we are going to be *"saved from wrath."* We have immunity from wrath to come.
11. Being justified by faith, we are going to "be *saved by his life."* This is no denial of the fact that we have already been saved, but this is looking forward to something else.
12. Being justified by faith, we *"rejoice in God."* We are not afraid of Him any longer, but we actually rejoice in God. We look at Him, see Him in all His holiness, and we rejoice in Him!

First of all, notice the preface: "Being justified by faith." The word *justified* is in a Greek tense that points to an accomplished fact. It occurred at the time of faith. This is a great testimony to the fact that justification is a thing that takes place instantaneously. In this statement the apostle Paul is looking back to the time when these people believed, hence the expression, "being justified by faith." Here is a most practical point. You cannot grow into justification. You cannot be more and more justified. It is not a continuous process at all. It is something that happens suddenly, instantly, in the twinkling of an eye, in the moment you look up into the face of God and say, "I receive Your Son." At that moment you are justified!

"Now then," he says, "being justified by faith, we have some benefits!"

PEACE WITH GOD

Peace with God does not mean that we have a *feeling* of peace. An unbeliever may *feel* in his heart perfectly at peace, and yet not *have* peace with God. A Christian who is untaught and does not know the truth may *have* peace with God, and yet *not feel* at peace in himself.

Between the sinner and God there exists a state of enmity. It could not be otherwise. "O that thou hadst hearkened to my commandments! then had thy peace been as a river" (Is 48:18). If Israel had only kept the commandments of God, then there would have been peace. Look at the twenty-second verse: "There is no peace, saith the LORD, to the wicked." Does he mean a feeling of peace? Not at all. Some wicked men are perfectly at peace in their hearts, not disturbed at all by the thought of facing God in judgment. Even where this is true, there is still a state of enmity between God and wicked men, set forth in Romans 5:10 by the clause, "when we were enemies." In other words, the sinner is an enemy of God. It could not be otherwise. Unsaved men have rebellious hearts. "Because the carnal mind is enmity against God . . . [it] is not subject to the law of God" (Ro 8:7). If a man rebels against the American government and flees to another country, even though he is a refugee in that country, there exists a state of enmity between him and the American government. It does not matter how tranquil this man may feel in this foreign refuge, he is *not* at peace with the American government. If he comes back to the United States, the government will immediately initiate action against him.

Here is the point about being justified: when a man is justified, that enmity is taken away and there is peace between the sinner and God. When the justified man realizes that peace has been declared between God and him, the result is peace in the soul; he then *feels* at peace. However, do not confuse the feeling of internal peace with the external relationship of peace with God, which is the subject about which the apostle is now talking.

A prophecy in Isaiah refers to this peace: "He was wounded for our transgressions, . . . the chastisement of *our peace* was upon him" (Is 53:5). He suffered for our sins. He was punished for our sins, and that brought *peace* between us and God.

The apostle speaks of this in his letter to the Ephesians: "He is our peace" (Eph 2:14). Not making you *feel* peaceful, but *making peace* in your relationship with God. "Having slain the enmity," Paul continues in that thought, "He came and preached peace to you that were near and to them that were afar off" (Eph 2:17). He took away the enmity and then He preached *peace* to us.

Whereas in time past we looked forward to someday standing before God in judgment, and if we knew the truth, we trembled. But now we have no dread of Him, because the state of enmity centered in sin has been removed.

As Paul concludes this section, you will remember he says we even *rejoice* in God! We can look at Him and realize that

He is a Holy God, and we can rejoice in Him because we have peace in Him.

ACCESS TO GOD

"By whom also we have *access.*" In ancient times a king might have a man who had rebelled against him, but the king would forgive him and peace would be restored. But that pardon did not necessarily carry with it the right to come into the presence of the king. It was perilous to go into the presence of the king without permission. Thus, the man did not have the right of *"access."*

Paul says that God, in Christ, has not only taken away the enmity, but He has made it possible for the sinner to have access into the very presence of God. The tense of the verb in the original language does not appear in the English version, unfortunately. The perfect tense indicates that Christ has achieved a completed and continuous access for us. He led us into the presence of God and we still have that access today. "We both have access by one Spirit unto the Father" (Eph 2:18). Peace and access in the Bible always go together.

OUR STANDING WITH GOD

Let us face a real problem, one that has been the problem of the ages: how can a sinner stand in the presence of a holy God? "If thou, LORD, shouldest mark iniquities, O LORD, who shall stand?" (Ps 130:3). Let somebody answer that question. If God would begin to pick out iniquities in your life, would you stand under that scrutiny? The same thing the apostle is talking about in this passage is referred to in Revelation when the wicked cry out in the presence of the wrath of God: "Who shall be able to stand?" (Rev 6:17). The Psalmist declares the same thing in the first Psalm: "Therefore the ungodly shall not stand in the judgment." He will go down to wreck and to ruin when he comes to the day of judgment!

But "being justified by faith, we have" a standing. *We stand,* and our standing is in Christ Jesus. In Christ Jesus is the only place any man will ever be able to stand.

How is that standing maintained? *By grace.* Any man who tries to stand in his own works, his own character, his own righteousness, will fall. Grace is the only thing that can maintain his standing. I praise God for His grace this day, and you ought to, too.

OUR REJOICING IN HOPE OF GLORY

"Being justified by faith, we rejoice in hope of the glory of God." The apostle introduces a subject he later discusses in full (see Ro 8:18). In this introductory statement he is saying, "We rejoice in hope of the glory of God." We have a hope that some day we are going to have the glory of God and because of the hope, *we rejoice!*

What is the glory of God? To put it simply: the glory of God is the likeness of God. God's glory is what God *is* in character, in essential power, and in external appearance. That is the glory of God. Hebrews 1:3 says that Jesus Christ is the brightness of His glory, and that word *brightness* means "outshining." Jesus Christ is the outshining of God's glory; He is the image of God's glory.

Paul means our hope is to be like Jesus Christ in every respect. As he says, "Whom He did foreknow, he also did predestinate to be *conformed to the image of his Son*" (Ro 8:29).

When we have the image of Christ, then we shall have the glory of God. Glorification for the Christian is putting on to the full the likeness of God Himself as it is revealed in Jesus Christ. That is "the hope of the glory of God," a wonderful hope! The apostle says we *rejoice* in it! You know the hopes of men—oh, how they fail! But here is something that cannot fail. Paul says we rejoice in it!

OUR REJOICING IN TRIBULATION

"We also rejoice in tribulation." Let me emphasize the verb, we *rejoice* in them! The unbeliever is unable to do that. To the unbeliever this life is all he has. He has no prospect of joy or happiness hereafter. He doesn't even know whether there is another life. If, in this life, his joy and happiness is marred by tribulation and affliction, he is miserable, because he has lost all he had.

But it is not thus with the Christian. No matter how dark it may be, he knows the morning still comes. There is not an experience nor a tribulation, no matter how hard it is, that will take away his hope. He can actually take a tribulation, look it in the face and say, "I thank God for this! I rejoice in it!"

The King James Version reads, "We glory in tribulations," and it is commonly interpreted, "We rejoice in the midst of tribulation," that is, we rejoice in spite of tribulation. But it does not mean that "I thank God in spite of my tribulations." Paul says in effect, "I thank God *for* my tribulations!"

Look at the eleventh verse: "We . . . rejoice in God." Does that mean we rejoice in spite of God? It means that we look at God and we take pleasure in Him. Now it is the same Greek construction here: "We . . . rejoice in tribulation." It means that we praise God for the things that come into our lives. You may say, "How can I do that?" There are a good many reasons why you should. "If children, then heirs; heirs of God and joint-heirs with Christ; if so be that we suffer with him, that we may be also glorified together" (8:17). Then suffering leads to glory. If you can rejoice in the glory of God, and suffering leads to glory, can't you glory in suffering? "For I reckon that the sufferings of this present time are not worthy to be compared with the glory which shall be revealed in us" (8:18). "For our light affliction, which is but for a moment, worketh for us a far more exceeding and eternal weight of glory" (2 Co 4:17).

The text here in this fifth chapter tells us why we should rejoice in tribulation. It is because we *know* something: "Tribulation worketh patience" (5:3). Let us leave the *patience* for a moment, and dwell on the word *worketh*. Tribulation works patience for us, and not merely patience but steadfastness.

Here is a principle by which you can discover the difference between a true child of God and one who is just a professed child of God. It is by the effect that tribulation has on him. In the life of a true child of God, tribulation brings him close to God, makes him steadfast, makes him patient. There is another sort of person. Troubles come into the life and instead of bringing him close to God, tribulation makes him hard. If tribulation comes into your life and does not make you more tender, if it does not make you love Him more, then it would be wise to examine your life in order to discover what the trouble is. In justified people, tribulation works steadfastness and patience.

PATIENCE WORKS EXPERIENCE

It is further affirmed that "patience worketh" something else, namely, *experience*. The word *experience* means proof or testing, for that is what experience is. Here is the explanation: You enter into tribulation and that tribulation makes you steadfast, and your steadfastness becomes an experience, or a proof that you are a child of God.

EXPERIENCE WORKS HOPE

Paul does not stop there. He says that "experience" works something else, namely, hope! Here is a beautiful circle! It started with hope, "Hope of the glory of God." Then tribulation worked steadfastness, and steadfastness proved to us that we are children of God, and when we were proven children of God, we were encouraged in our spirits and we completed the circle with "hope of the glory of God."

HOPE MAKETH NOT ASHAMED

Paul is not talking about hope in any abstract sense. Some of our hopes have made us ashamed. Some of our hopes have disappointed us. How many there have been in my life and in your life! A father may stand by his son, a dissipated wretch, and say, "I had hoped." A mother may stand by the casket of a loved one that has gone and say, "I had hoped." Or a man may look upon the fragments of his fortune, when it has been distributed to the winds and is gone, and say, "I had hoped," but his hopes did not issue in fruition. They failed, and that failure made him ashamed.

He is not talking about *all* hope here, because many a hope there is that has failed utterly. He is talking about a certain, specific hope—a definite hope. This is the way it reads in the original—the little article *the* is before the word *hope*. "And *the* hope maketh not ashamed!" Not any kind of hope—not hope in the abstract, but *"the* hope"—a certain hope, a Christian hope. That hope will never make you ashamed. It will never fail you. It will never disappoint you. That little article *the* points back to the second verse. What is "the hope"? Hope of the glory of God!

The rest of the section is devoted to showing us why this hope can never fail. "[The] hope maketh not ashamed; *because* the love of God is shed abroad in our hearts by the Holy Ghost which is given unto us" (Ro 5:5). How does Christ dwell in our hearts? By the Holy Spirit, and Christ in you is "the hope of glory" (Col 1:27). So this hope of ours cannot fail or make us ashamed, because He has come into our hearts and shed His love abroad by the Holy Spirit.

If God loved us so much as to come into us and live in us, and if our body is the temple of the Holy Spirit, can that hope ever be disappointed? Certainly not! "There is a hope that maketh not ashamed!"

Verse 6 opens with the word *for*. Now read the next three verses. Paul compares God's love with human love. "For scarcely for a righteous man will one die: yet peradventure [perhaps] for a good man some would even dare to die." That is what men would do. "But God commendeth His love toward us, in that, while we were yet sinners [or enemies] Christ died for us"! Now, what does that mean? It simply means that in the death of Christ for us we have such a proof of God's love that we know He will not forsake us. He rescued us when we were enemies by a supreme act of love. Now that we are His, He will take us all the way through to the end.

That is what Paul argues for in the ninth verse. He says, "How much more then." If while we were sinners and enemies He *died* for us, will He allow us to come into wrath? Not at all! "Much more then, being now justified by his blood, we shall be saved from wrath through him." Wrath would be the thing that would destroy our "hope of glory." If, while I was a sinner, God loved me enough to give His Son for me, now when I am justified, *how much more* will He continue in His love for me. "Much more, being reconciled, we shall be saved by His life" (5:10). Read it this way: "We shall be kept safe by His life."

A Christian Scientist one time quoted this passage to me, saying that we were saved by Christ's life, and not by His death, but I said, "You are not reading the whole passage. He recon-

ciled us by *His death."* "He is able also to save them to the
uttermost that cometh unto God through Him. Seeing he ever
liveth to make intercession for them" (Heb 7:25). Jesus
Himself said, "Because I live, ye shall live also" (Jn 14:19).
So, we are kept safe by His life. Romans 8:32 reads: "He that
spared not his own Son, but delivered him up for us all, how
shall He not with Him also freely give us all things?" Romans
8:34 goes on with the same theme: "It is Christ that died,"
but Paul doesn't stop there, "Yea rather, that is risen again, who
is even at the right hand of God, who also maketh intercession
for us." So, if it is the death of Christ that wipes out all our
sins and gives us justification and righteousness in the sight of
God, it is His life that keeps us safe forever!

A real Christian cannot talk about being afraid of losing his
salvation. When Jesus Christ went to the cross, He took upon
Himself the debt for our sin, and He paid it. If Christ had not
paid the debt of sin in full, He would still be dead. The only
reason God raised Him from the dead was because He paid it!
When Jesus Christ went to the cross and paid our debt in full,
He was raised from the dead. "Death hath no more dominion
over Him," because sin's penalty is paid forever. The fact that
He is alive today is the pledge that His payment is eternal. He
would have to be dragged down from heaven in order for us to
fall. If He lives, we live. If He dwells in heavenly places, we
will sit there.

Now Paul closes this section by saying, "And not only so,
but we rejoice in God" (5:11, ASV). The passage closes as it
began: "Through our Lord Jesus Christ." It had begun: "Being
justified by faith, we have peace with God, *through our Lord
Jesus Christ,"* and it closes: "We rejoice in God, *through our
Lord Jesus Christ!"* No man has any hope apart from the Son
of God. There is no approach to God the Father, save through
the Son of God.

These are the blessings which accompany justification. Perhaps they are not all new to you, but if any one of them is
new, may this be the day you begin to enjoy it. It is yours, so
enjoy it, and especially your tribulations.

13

Salvation: Condemnation in Adam But Justification in Christ

THE PASSAGE now before us looks difficult. Perhaps the apostle Peter was thinking about this passage when he wrote that the apostle Paul had written some things that were hard to be understood (2 Pe 3:16). Even though this is a very difficult passage, the outstanding ideas are plain. A constant reading of this passage under the leadership of the Spirit of God never fails to bear fruit.

This particular paragraph closes the section called "Justification." In reality it is the conclusion of the first two sections, one on condemnation and the other on justification. This section is a wonderful comparison, but also a contrast between condemnation and justification.

KEY IDEA

To find the key idea, first look at verse 16: "For the judgment was by one to *condemnation,* but the free gift is of many offences unto *justification.*" That is one contrast between condemnation and justification. In verse 18 the same idea is repeated. Condemnation and justification are laid side by side.

But then again, this section is more than that. It is not only a contrast and a comparison between condemnation and justification, but it is also inevitably a comparison and a contrast between Adam and Christ, for our condemnation flows from Adam. And our justification flows from Jesus Christ. So any comparison between condemnation and justification will involve necessarily a comparison between the two men from whom these two states come.

You will find this indicated in verse 14, the last phrase: "Who [Adam] is the figure of him that was to come." What does *figure* mean? It means type. "Who is the type of Him who was to come," that is, Christ.

So we have the key. This passage will set forth not only a contrast and a comparison between condemnation and justification, but also a comparison and a contrast between Adam and Christ.

SEED THOUGHT

In reality this whole section is a development and an expansion of a text which is found in 1 Corinthians 15:45: "The first man Adam became a living soul; the last Adam became a lifegiving spirit" (ASV). The first letter to the Corinthians was written before the letter to the Romans. Therefore, Paul in chapter 15 of 1 Corinthians expresses the seed thought of this whole section of Romans. In this section Paul concentrates on the first Adam and the last Adam—compares the two, compares their work and the consequences and results that flow from their work.

If in Adam we are all condemned, then in Christ everyone (who knows Christ) receives justification. Naturally, as he has now dealt with condemnation and justification fully, nothing remains except to demonstrate that justification in Christ is many times greater than the condemnation in Adam.

CHARACTERISTICS OF THE PASSAGE

A few outstanding characteristics of the passage can be noted before a more complete and detailed study of the passage.

BEGINS WITH ADAM, ENDS WITH CHRIST

First of all, the section begins with Adam and ends with Jesus Christ: "That grace might reign through righteousness unto eternal life through Jesus Christ our Lord." We have the "bad news" first, while the best news is held for the end.

SIX CONTRASTS

This passage contains at least six pairs of contrasting terms: (1) Adam and Christ (vv. 14, 15); (2) disobedience and obedience (v. 19); (3) sin and righteousness (v. 21); (4) law and grace (v. 20); (5) condemnation and justification (v. 16); and (6) death and life (v. 21).

FOUR KINGS

There are four "kings" mentioned in this section: (1) "Death reigned" (v. 14); (2) "Sin . . . reigned" (v. 21); (3) "Grace reign[s]" (v. 21); (4) "They [believers] shall reign" (v. 17).

These are the four kings. *Death* reigned; *sin* reigned; *grace* reigns; and *we* shall reign!

WORK OF CHRIST AS DEEP

This whole passage demonstrates that the work of Jesus Christ goes as deep as the work of Adam and is as far-reaching in its effects. One significant phrase has three occurrences. "So then as through one trespass the judgment came unto all men to condemnation, even so . . ." (v. 18, ASV). "For as through the one man's disobedience the many were made sinners, even so . . ." (v. 19, ASV). "That, as sin reigned in death, even so . . ." (v. 21). The effect of *even so* is to equate Christ's work with Adam's work.

WORK OF CHRIST GREATER

But that is not all. The apostle shows that Christ's work not only goes just as deep, but that the work of Christ goes deeper and is vastly greater than the work of Adam. He indicates this three times: "Much more the grace of God . . ." (v. 15); "Much more . . . abundance of grace . . ." (v. 17); "And grace did much more abound" (v. 20). In the Greek, Paul's phrase *much more* implies "much more *exceedingly*," and is translated that way in the ASV.

Many commentators have covered this passage in hundreds of pages. After much investigation, it becomes difficult to be original. But both with the help of others and through independent study, the following outline has become clear:

1. Adam, sin, and death (vv. 12-14)
2. Adam and Christ contrasted (vv. 15-17)

3. Adam and Christ compared (vv. 18-21)
4. Christ, righteousness, and life contrasted with Adam, sin, and death (v. 21)

ADAM, SIN, AND DEATH

The first word of this passage is "wherefore," or in the ASV version, "therefore." Whenever a man says "wherefore," in his mind is something that has gone before. He is about to sum up an argument, and in this case, Paul is about to sum up all that he has said about condemnation and justification.

"Therefore, as by one man sin entered into the world, and death through sin; and so death passed unto all men; for that all sinned." That is not a complete sentence, which has made commentators frantic in their effort to find out how to complete the sentence. It starts out, "Therefore," but has no concluding phrase.

A passage with a parallel construction is Matthew 25:14. Present in it are a number of italicized words. While it is possible to read the passage and leave out those italicized words, it is then an unfinished sentence. The Greek does that very often. The reason the translators put in the italicized words *the kingdom of heaven is* was because Christ had been talking about the kingdom of heaven. The ASV has put in three other words: "It is . . . when." We ask the question, "What is?" The answer must be the thing he was talking about, namely, the kingdom of heaven. With this guide, turn to Romans: "Therefore, it is." What is? The thing Paul had been talking about, namely, justification in Christ. "Therefore, justification in Christ" is like something else. It is like condemnation in Adam. This makes a complete sentence, and the translators are right in supplying the two words *it is.* They are understood in the Greek, but must be supplied in the English translation.

Sin has entered into the world, and there is something else that came in too. Sin has not come in alone. "Sin entered . . . and death through sin." The two always go together, like that other pair in the Bible, grace and peace. When grace comes in, peace comes in. When sin comes in, then death comes in at the same time. So the movement is "death through sin."

Is death natural? Certainly not! Death is the most unnatural thing in the world, and it is possible to put your finger on the spot where it entered into the race. God did not start out this world with death, as far as the human race is concerned.

You may say, "What if Adam had not sinned?" Perhaps if Adam had not sinned there would have come a time in his life when he would have been changed, as we are going to be changed when the Lord comes—raised to a higher life and to reign. But Adam did sin, so there came "death through sin."

But that is not all. "And so death passed unto all men." The two Greek words used here are descriptive, *sin entered.* The figure is that of a house; somebody opens a door and enters. When sin came in, death entered through the same door. After death entered, death moved into all the rooms of the house—"unto *every* man." Sin entered, but that was not all. Death did not remain isolated—he began to penetrate to everyone. Eventually death will come to every one of us, unless the Lord comes. Death penetrated to all men.

Some protest that it is not fair of God to bring death upon all because of what Adam did back there. They insist it is wrong to argue that sin entered into the world through Adam, and therefore death passed to all men. To answer that objection, Paul gives that last clause: "For that all have sinned."

The man who objects to condemnation in Adam needs to be reminded of the fact that he himself has sinned. Paul has dealt with it—this is just a reminder. Paul says, "If you cannot accept the fact of condemnation in Adam, then reflect upon the fact that *you yourself* are a sinner and deserve condemnation on the basis of what you have done."

A great many commentators have taken this phrase to mean that all have sinned through Adam. And that is true. But it is laying direct responsibility on each individual man. Paul is dealing with facts. There is a great mystery in connection with sin: how can sin start with one man and spread until it permeates the whole world? Why should the whole human race be condemned by the sin of one man? Paul answers these questions, and in doing so he deals with the facts. It is a fact that sin entered into the world and that death entered as a result. It is a fact that men sin. Paul does not attempt to expand his explanation.

Can sin exist without law? Yes, it can. "Until the law, sin was in the world." Read Genesis 6:5-8. Paul has the Jew in mind, and he reminds the Jew that sin was real before the law came into existence. How could man then expect to be justified by law? Even if it had existed, all it could do was to condemn him. But the Jew would say, "Sin is not imputed where there is no law. Sin is not put to his account. God can't put sin down to a man's account where there is no law." Paul admits it, but he does not argue. He merely says, "Yes, but nevertheless, sin was there, even though it was not put down to man's account."

Sin is a vastly greater thing than mere transgression of the law. Sin is lawlessness. It exists where there is no law. In the second chapter of this book, the apostle said, "As many as sinned without the law shall perish without the law." And if men have sinned under the law, then they shall be judged by the law. God puts it down to their personal account.

At this point the statement of verse 14 confronts men with a fact. "Nevertheless death reigned." That is proof of it. If you do not believe that sin is in the world, and you do not believe that it is a real thing, go out to the cemetery. There is the evidence of the reign of death! That is the final proof whether sin is a real thing or not.

The apostle says death reigned from Adam to Moses. That depressing fifth chapter of Genesis gives the book of the generations of Adam. It is the record of an endless funeral train interspersed with a hopeless refrain, "And he died . . . and he died . . . and he died." Then a little light breaks through: "Enoch walked with God and he was not." But the funeral train moves on again and Methuselah was nine hundred and sixty-nine years old, "and he died." "Death reigned from Adam until Moses." It *reigned!* And it still reigns.

"It reigned even over them that had not sinned after the likeness of Adam's transgression." Who were they? How did Adam sin? Adam knew God's commandment. He had a positive commandment and he broke it. There were children then just as there are today. Over children who had never known the commandment, over mentally deficient ones who never understood the commandment of God—death reigned even over them. Where is the man who dares to deny that the human race is somehow tied up with Adam and his sin? Let him explain why babies die before they come to the age of accountability. There is only one explanation. Adam was the head of the race, and what he did had its effects in his race.

When Christ comes into the scheme of things, his reign goes just as far as that of Adam. You may say you do not think it right that we should die for Adam's sin. But by the same token, is it right for God to give you righteousness when you do not have any? The two things are equal. The ways of God are equal!

ADAM AND CHRIST CONTRASTED

THE CONTRAST OF QUALITY

It is not a contrast of quantity, but a contrast of quality. Here is what Paul says: "If the one trespass caused the death of many, *much more* will the grace of God abound unto many." In Adam we got what we deserved. Adam received death, and he deserved it: you receive death, and you deserve it. But on the other hand, God gives the saved (those in Christ) something they do not deserve.

THE CONTRAST OF QUANTITY

"The judgment came of one." He is referring, not to one man but to one offence—one trespass. "For the judgment came of one offence unto condemnation, but the free gift came of many offences unto justification." The contrast there is between one offence and many offences. Let me illustrate: Here is a man who goes out into a forest; he takes a match and sets fire to a tree. A small action that anyone could do. (That is what Adam did—he committed a small action anyone could do.) Then you know what would happen in that forest. The fire would travel up the tree and soon the whole forest would be blazing. Now, then suppose somebody came along and put the whole thing out. Would not the second operation be vastly greater, "much more" than the first?

That is what Paul is saying: that condemnation came from one offence, but justification blots out forever millions and millions of offences. Therefore, it is greater.

THE CONTRAST OF CERTAINTY

The reign of death is certain. Just as certain as death reigns through Adam, *much more certain,* we are going to reign through Jesus Christ! "Much more they which receive abundance of grace and of the gift of righteousness shall reign in life by one, Jesus Christ." Remember that if death is a certain thing in this world, just as certain and much more certain is our reign in eternal life through Jesus Christ!

ADAM AND CHRIST COMPARED

ONE ACT

"Even so by one act of righteousness." The comparison here is between the judgment that came upon all men and the free gift which came unto all men. The one goes just as far as the other—the one came to all men and the second goes to all men.

ONE MAN

"One man's disobedience" as over against "the obedience of one." The comparison there is as to effects. If Adam's sin constituted all sinners, Christ's obedience is going to constitute righteous all those who believe on Him.

THE REIGN OF GRACE

"As sin reigned in death, even so might grace reign through righteousness." The comparison there is very obvious. The Jew would say at this point in the chapter, "Well, what is the law for?" So Paul takes just a little phrase there, "The law came in besides," and it means to steal in. "That the offence might abound." It means that "the law came in that the offence might abound." Sin existed back there. Moreover, God brought the law in, but not to save men. Paul is not approving that old heresy that the law would save men! It was given that the "offence," or sin, might abound. The law came in to show man how great a sinner he is. Commandments stir up the "old man," and he will break the law. The law does not make a man a sinner, but it provokes sin and proves him to be a sinner. All you have to do is to tell folks what they can do and what they cannot do, and then you will have trouble. The way to get rid of sin is not through the law, but through grace! The Jew was glorying and boasting and rejoicing in the very thing that showed him how great a sinner he was. But he was no bigger a fool than some folks are today.

But, "where sin abounded, grace did abound much more exceedingly." Grace superabounded! That is what it means. Grace was greater.

Christ, Righteousness, and Life

In verse 12 Adam, sin, and death are featured. But at the end of verse 21, a direct contrast is made. "Jesus Christ our Lord" corresponds to Adam. "Righteousness" corresponds to sin. "Life" corresponds to death.

There is one more term that has no corresponding one. That is *grace!* It is that little word that makes all the difference between Adam, sin, death; and Christ, righteousness, life! It is the added term. And that is why the apostle Paul dares to lay the two things side by side and say, "Look at them! The one is *much more* than the other!" It is because the one contains the grace of God.

Some people say this passage teaches universalism—that every man is going to be saved, as all were condemned. But look carefully at verse 17. There is a qualifying expression, "they that receive." That is Paul's answer. Receive! Receive! That is what man must do in order to be saved.

14

Sanctification: The Right Way of Union with Christ

WHILE THE ACTUAL WORD *sanctification* does not occur in the KJV, it is in the ASV at verse 19. The Greek word means sanctification and has been rendered by the word *holiness*. It appears again in verse 22: "you have your fruit unto *holiness*." Perhaps it may properly be said that the word in the Greek is more correctly translated by the word *sanctification*. At any rate, this word occurs for the first time in the book of Romans, appearing twice in the sixth chapter.

What shall be done with the sinner in relation to the penalty for sin is the first problem God faced in saving men. The next problem concerned the power and pollution of sin that dominates his life. First of all, how does God deal with the sinner and his sin? Justification is the answer. God declares him to be righteous, and treats him as such. Second, after a man is justified, he discovers that he has a sin nature which gives rise to sinful acts. What will God do about that? The answer is sanctification, that aspect of the work of God which deals with the power and pollution of sin.

Justification deals with the guilt of sin. When a man sins, he is guilty and therefore he deserves to be punished. In justification, God declares that man righteous, by virtue of the death of Christ in his behalf. By that act He removed the guilt forever. Because Christ died in his stead, the sinner goes free. Thus justification is the declarative act of God. Justification does not *make* man righteous. It never means that. It means that God *declares* him to be righteous. God weighs the guilt, gets rid of it, and the sinner gets immunity from punishment.

140

What does *sanctification* do? In sanctification, God takes that same man (still a sinner, but also a justified man) and *makes him holy*. In sanctification, God deals with something that is actual, the power of sin. Whereas justification deals with the *guilt* of sin, sanctification deals with the *power* of sin.

Justification cannot be separated from sanctification, except for the purpose of study. No man can experience sanctification unless he has first been justified in the sight of God. Our human minds can only deal with one aspect at a time, but God never works that way. Justification and sanctification are two aspects of the one work of God in saving men.

"Moreover, the law entered, that the offence might abound. But where sin abounded, grace did much more abound" (5:20). No matter how great the sin was, grace was greater than the sin. The worst sinner in the world can find grace sufficient.

That is Paul's conclusion to the section on justification, that wherever sin appeared, grace came to the rescue in an even greater measure and covered it. "Grace did much more abound." It superabounded! Someone will say, "then if that is the case, it does not matter how much we sin. If our sin, no matter how great it is, only causes us to see that the grace of God is greater than our sin, let us go on and sin in order that we may see more of the grace of God." On the other hand, there are those who say, 'The doctrine of justification is a dangerous doctrine. If you teach that, you will have a sinning people. People will say, 'Then sin does not matter,' and they will go on in their sin."

Paul met this first charge that was brought against the doctrine of gratuitous justification. "They will rejoice in sin because it only magnifies the grace of God." Paul does not hedge the slightest bit. He does not say, "Well, I know that I said a man is justified apart from works and character, and after all, that is not quite it. He has to be good, or he will go to hell." Paul will not retreat one inch from what he said in chapters 4 and 5. He has insisted that believers are "justified freely," that "by grace ye are saved." But now he shows that once justification has been received, sanctification follows logically and naturally.

"What shall we say then? Shall we continue in sin, that

grace may abound?" (6:1). Paul anticipates the very thing
that men will protest. If, no matter how great sin is, grace is
greater, if that is the case, what shall be our response? Shall
we say that we shall continue in sin? That is the first question.

In verse 15 there is another question which must be faced:
"What then? Shall we sin because we are not under the law,
but under grace?" There is the other question.

Those two questions indicate the contents of this chapter
and give the divisions. We might paraphrase them like this,
"Shall we *continue in sin* in order that grace may abound, or
shall we *sin* because grace does abound?"

Everything between the first verse and the fifteenth verse is
in answer to the first question; everything from the fifteenth
verse to the end answers the second question. There are two
distinct phases—two aspects of sin: (1) one is *continuance in
sin*—"Shall we continue in sin?"; (2) the other is *committing
single acts of sin*—"Shall we commit sin?"

Here is a comprehensive view of the chapter before the
actual exposition of it.

In considering verses 1-14, the first question is "Shall we
continue in sin, that grace may abound?" What, in two words,
is Paul's answer to that? "God forbid!" The very thought of it
is abhorrent to him.

Then he asks a question to show how impossible it is to do
it. It is impossible for a Christian to continue in sin, which
is implied in this question: "God forbid. We who died to sin,
how shall we any longer live therein?" (6:2, ASV). And, of
course, if we died, we are dead. How shall we continue in sin
if we died to sin? There is no answer to that. Paul does not
attempt to answer it. It is an impossibility.

There are two views that fall short of the truth in dealing
with sanctification. One view is that there is nothing at all in
the cross of Christ that sanctifies, so when dealing with the
question of the Christian sinning, an attempt is made to place
the Christian back under the law. But this is contrary to the
Word of God.

The other view admits that believers come short and do not
live the high type of Christian life they should. So mysticism
is advocated. The proponents of this view are earnest and sin-

cere, and they talk about "dying to self." But the Bible does not teach this either. They say, "We must die to sin." But the Bible does not teach this. What does the Bible teach? *The Bible teaches that we have died to sin.*

This is not a quibble over words. The death of the believer is a thing that is in the past. It is a transaction that is complete, and what God wants us to do is to believe it and not try to do again something that has already been done. Of course, there is a sense in which we must appropriate what has been done and make it practical in our lives. But if we did not learn anything else in this study, let us remember that the Christian has died to sin.

Confirming the teaching of this verse is 1 John 3:9: "Whosoever is born of God doth not commit sin." The verb *sin* means to continue in a course of sin. It does not mean committing an act of sin. He that is born of God cannot continue in sin; It is an utter impossibility. God will break it off sometime.

How can a dead man sin? There is not a Christian who does not face this problem. You know you do things that are wrong. You know you do not have victory over the sin in your life. This is a serious problem: as we have been released from the guilt of sin, how can we be released from the power of sin? There is a way. Here are three key words: (1) *know,* or *knowing* (vv. 3, 6, 9); (2) *reckon* (v. 11); (3) *yield* (v. 13).

Let us now turn to the meaning of these three words in relation to the problem of the power of sin in the believer's life.

KNOW

First, we must know. "Know ye not, that so many of us as were baptized into Jesus Christ were baptized into his death? Therefore we are buried with him by baptism into death" (6:3-4). The article *the* is before the word *death* in the original Greek. It is *"the* death," not a death of our own. It is the death of the Son of God. "That like as Christ was raised up from the dead by the glory of the Father, even so we also should walk in newness of life. For if we have been planted [bodily united] together in the likeness of his death, we shall be also in the likeness of His resurrection" (6:4-5).

If we are to know victory over sin in our lives, we must first of all *know* that we died with Christ on the cross. When He died, we died; when He was buried, we were buried (in the mind of God). This passage does not discuss water baptism, only insofar as water baptism stands behind as a symbol of the thing he is talking about here. Paul is talking about the spiritual reality: when Christ died, we died; and when we believe, He baptizes us by the operation of the Spirit of God immersing us into the body of Christ.

"Knowing this, that our old man was crucified with him" (v. 6). And yet we talk about "crucifying the old man." Don't we? "The old man" *has been* crucified, if you are a Christian. It stirs up our pride for us to try *to do something* by "crucifying the flesh of the old man." *But Christ has already gotten the victory!* The "old man" means the old self; what we were in Adam. That "old man" was crucified with Christ at the cross, and the task is finished in the mind of God. (See also Gal 2:20).

When we exercised faith in Christ, we entered into that crucifixion. "That the body of sin be destroyed." Does the word *destroy* mean annihilation? No. Every one of us knows that although that "old man is crucified with Christ," there is still sin with us. "If we say that we have no sin, we deceive ourselves, and the truth is not in us" (1 Jn 1:8). Sin is still there. Therefore the word *destroy* does not mean annihilation, but what it does mean is this: "That the body of sin might be made of none effect, rendered powerless." The Greek word here gives the idea of sin being annulled, or rendered inoperative.

"The body of sin"—what is that? It is the body we have, in which sin finds an instrument: the tongue, the hands, the mind. Sin does not find its source in the body. Sin finds its source in the will, but uses the body as an instrument. Because we were crucified with Christ the body of sin is actually powerless in our lives. "That henceforth we shall not serve sin, for he that is dead is freed from sin" (v. 6). A corpse is in view. It does not matter how great a sinner that corpse was, it is now free forever. We are not to doubt the transaction back there when we died with Him. "He that is dead is freed from sin." You cannot take a man that is dead and punish him anymore.

When we died back at the cross with Christ, the question was settled. The penalty was paid. Sin has nothing more to do with us, because we are dead to it. "If we be. dead with Christ, we believe that we shall also live with Him." Death is past and believers are now alive in Christ and should conduct themselves as dead to the past.

"Knowing that Christ being raised from the dead, dieth no more" (v. 9). If He does not die anymore, do we? Certainly not. Some people say we can, but we died with Him, were buried with Him, raised with Him. "He dieth no more!" So we die no more. That is security! "Death hath no more dominion over Him." When He went to the cross, He paid the debt of sin in full. And when the debt is paid in full, the creditor has no more power over the debtor. We are in Him, therefore death hath no more dominion over us.

Verse 10 sums up the matter in just a few words. First of all, when Christ died, we died. When we died back there with Him, our old self was crucified. Second, being identified with Him, we are risen from the dead, to die no more!

RECKON

"Likewise reckon ye also yourselves to be dead indeed unto sin, but alive unto God through Jesus Christ our Lord" (6:11). We are to *know* this truth and then continually, second by second, moment by moment, hour after hour, day after day, we are to reckon it to be so! Don't ever lose sight of it. Don't doubt it! Don't let the devil say, "You did not die back there." You did die—you were buried with Him, raised with Him. That is the secret of a holy life. God declares it so, now reckon it to be so.

Whenever a young man who may be a member of an Orthodox Jewish family becomes a Christian, the father says, "This son is to me dead." He turns him out of his house. He never speaks to him again. If friends come in and ask about his son, he says, "My son is dead." He is not actually dead, but the father considers that boy as dead. In the same sense, even though the old self is still alive, God says, "Reckon ye yourselves to be dead unto sin."

It is like an old associate who exercised terrible influence

over you. There is only one way to get liberty. Break it off
once for all. Call him in and say, "You have exercised a powerful influence over me. From now on, it is to be as if I had
died."

"Neither yield ye your members as instruments of unrighteousness unto sin," but, on the other hand, "Yield yourselves
unto God, as those that are alive from the dead, and your
members as instruments of righteousness unto God."

That word *instruments* is a military term. It would be better
translated by the word *weapons*. Your hands, your feet, your
tongue—the members of your body—they are weapons in
"the good fight." "Now," Paul says, "don't take your weapons
and give them to the enemy." It would be foolish if a man
should hand over his arms to his enemy. But that is exactly
what happens, for instance, when a person takes the tongue,
which ought to be used as a weapon of righteousness, and uses
it to wound somebody.

From the original Greek a thought unfolds out of this passage. It starts out with the words, "Neither yield," and the
idea is a *continuous* yielding. "Do not yield all the time your
members—day after day, hour after hour—giving up your
weapons to sin, your enemy."

The thought goes on to imply *once for all* yield; here it is a
different tense. At one great crisis point in your life, once for
all yield to God. The Christian ought to come to this place
where he says, "Lord, I yield once for all."

And then he closes with a promise (Ro 6:14). If we know
these things—if we reckon these things to be so—if we yield
our members unto God—then remember this: "Sin shall not
have dominion over you." Why? Because you are not under
the law, but under grace. Some people falsely say that sin will
have dominion over you if you come out from under the law.
Paul says the opposite: "Sin shall not have dominion over you."
Paul says about sin and law (1 Co 15:56): "The sting of
death is sin; and the strength of sin is the law." It is the grace
of God that breaks the power of sin. The law cannot do it.

The reason that sin shall not have dominion is because you are under grace and not under law.

Up to this point we have dealt with the fact of continuance in sin. Somebody is bound to say, "Well, all right, I won't continue in sin. I can see that now. But surely it won't hurt if I drop into sin once in a while." So Paul deals with that. Shall we commit even an act of sin? Is it not permissible to drop into sin once in a while because we are not under law? Paul's answer: "God forbid."

He is going to show in this whole section from now on that no man can serve two masters. He will either serve sin or he will serve righteousness. He will either serve Satan or he will serve God.

There is one word that occurs eight times in this section. It is the word *servant*. That is the key word of the passage.

Paul starts with verse 16. "Know ye not, that to whom ye yield yourselves servants to obey, his servants ye are to whom ye obey?" In other words, if you start to obey sin, you are thereby admitting the mastership of sin, and your very confession of Christ said, "You are my Lord and master." You cannot, therefore, if you are a Christian, start to obey sin without saying, "Christ is not my master. Sin is my master."

It is simply a development of Christ's own words: "No man can serve two masters" (Mt 6:24). Notice what Paul says (17-18), "Being then made free from sin." How were we made free from sin? We died to it. Therefore, sin is no longer our master.

We have not only died, but we have risen from the dead and now have a new life and a new master. That master is Christ and righteousness. So he says, "You have become the servants of righteousness." Somebody might say, "Is Christianity slavery?" Paul says, "I speak after the manner of men because of the infirmity of your flesh." That is, "Christianity is not really slavery, but I have used that term in order that you might understand."

Verse 20 declares, "When ye were the servants of sin, ye were free from righteousness." There was a time in your life when you were a servant of sin, and righteousness had nothing to do with you. Now turn it around. Once you are free from sin, just the opposite is true. When you are the servant of righteousness, you have nothing to do with sin. You are free from it!

Verse 22 goes further and insists, "You have your fruit." You have something else also, namely, "the end." It is wonderful that you can have *the end* before you get there. The old way was explained this way: "if you are good, holy, and do not fall, someday, when you come to the end, God will give you eternal life." But Paul says if you die with Christ, if you reckon it to be so, you not only have the "fruit unto holiness," but *you have the end* right now.

Paul has shown us how to deal with sin in our lives. We are first to *know* that we died with Christ. Second, we are to *reckon* that thing to be so, never surrendering for a moment. Third, we are to *yield* our members. Then we are to remember that no man can serve two masters.

These great facts will grip the heart of a true believer and lead him in the paths of righteousness. But there may be among the professed people of God some that are not born of God. There are always some people who have never really bowed the knee to Jesus Christ; people who profess to be His but who have never obeyed Him and thus have never been born of God.

While all these truths may work in the lives of those who are truly saved, there may be some who are merely professed Christians who say, "Oh, we are saved, and it does not matter what we do." So Paul closes with a very solemn warning: "For the wages of sin is death" (6:23). Let no man take the grace of God and turn it into license. Let no man go on in sin (and, by the way, the true Christian cannot continue in sin). Therefore, should some man who is professing to be a Christian continue in sin, let him remember that "the wages of sin is death" and there has been no reduction in those wages!

But for such a man there is hope. "But the gift of God is eternal life through Jesus Christ our Lord" (6:23). There are two servitudes. If you serve sin, you will be paid wages. You will get just exactly what is coming to you. If you serve God, He cannot pay you any wages. You do not deserve any. But He does have a gift, that of everlasting life.

15

Sanctification: The Wrong Way by Works of the Law

HOWEVER DIFFICULT this seventh chapter of Romans may be, no trouble will be encountered whatever if we have actually mastered what the sixth chapter has taught. In the sixth chapter, God gives us the right way to be sanctified, and in the seventh chapter He gives us the wrong way. Of course, God has a purpose in this chapter. But why should we not learn the right way first? And the question is, have we learned it? Those three key words in Romans are crucial: know, reckon, yield.

One would think that these key words would be sufficient on this whole subject, that after He has given us the right way, what further need for anything else to be taught on this subject? Human nature is a perverse thing. The old nature loves to *do* things. It loves to depend upon its own works. It loves to merit what it receives. Human nature loves to trust God. Human nature, after it knows the right way, will very often take the wrong way; and so it is not surprising that sometimes the very man who has been brought face to face with Jesus Christ and has discovered that there is no righteousness or justification in the law, and has settled in the heart that he had to come to Christ and receive righteousness by faith alone—that even then, that very same person will then sometimes try to go back to law for holiness!

God has given this chapter of Romans to warn against acting in such a way. If we are not satisfied to get our holiness and sanctification just as we got our justification, trusting in Jesus, knowing that we died with Christ, reckoning it to be so, yielding ourselves to Him—if we are not satisfied with that, then this chapter is for us.

There has been a terrific controversy raging in Christendom over this chapter and over this question: was the apostle Paul converted or unconverted when he wrote the experiences recorded in the seventh chapter of Romans, when he said, "I am carnal"? Was he converted or not? I am inclined to believe he was converted, and that we have here a picture of a saved man trying to be holy by keeping the law. But the whole question as to whether he was converted or unconverted is immaterial and unimportant. It does not make any difference which view we take, for God did not introduce this chapter to give us a psychological analysis of either the sinner or the believer, to satisfy our curiosity. God wrote this chapter to warn men and women, whether believers or unbelievers. He wrote this chapter to teach all men that there is no holiness by works of the law. Paul was writing from the standpoint of a converted man, who has tried sincerely and earnestly to attain holiness in life and break the power of sin by keeping the law.

There is one view of this chapter that is terribly mistaken, and that view is the one that says what we find in here is the Christian's normal experience. That is the devil's own method. Some people in churches every Lord's Day stand up and recite, "O, Lord, we have done those things we ought not to have done, and have left undone those things which we should have done," and sit down very well satisfied with themselves, as if they had done something very virtuous.

If you ever must say that (and, of course, a great many of us do sometimes); if you are meeting defeat in your life (for that is what it is in this chapter), then at least be concerned enough about your defeat and your lack of victory to cry with Paul, "O, wretched man that I am! Who shall deliver me from the body of this death?" No one ought to repeat that as a litany without the cry of despair that the apostle Paul uttered when he said it. He certainly did not say it unconcernedly.

No Christian need ever enter into the experience that is recorded here in the seventh chapter of Romans, if he only receives with the heart what the sixth chapter has to teach him. But if we cannot know what God has done for us in Christ; if we fail to reckon it to be true; if we fail to yield ourselves to God—then there is nothing left for us but the dreary, depressing, desperate experience which we find in the seventh chapter. And it is for such that God has caused it to be recorded.

Notice several outstanding characteristics in this chapter. The sixth and seventh chapters will be considered together in contrast and comparison.

"Sin shall not have dominion over you: for ye are not under the law, but under grace" (6:14). In that verse is the key to these two chapters, for the sixth chapter deals with the first half: "Sin shall not have dominion over you." The last half, "You are not under law," is dealt with in the seventh chapter. The sixth chapter is about the believer and sin, and the seventh is about the believer and law.

Following those two thoughts, you will discover that the key word of the sixth chapter is *sin.* The word *sin* occurs seventeen times in the sixth chapter. In the seventh chapter the key word becomes *law,* occurring eighteen times. The two are very closely related—sin and law. Paul says, "The strength of sin is the law" (1 Co 15:56).

To contrast or compare these two chapters, read the first six verses in each. The first six verses of the sixth chapter teach that we died with Christ and are dead to sin; the seventh chapter, that we died with Christ and therefore are dead to the law.

Perhaps the most outstanding characteristic of chapter seven is the occurrence of those personal pronouns, which occur over and over again in the chapter. From verse seven to the end of the chapter, the personal pronoun *I* occurs thirty times! The personal pronoun *me* occurs twelve times; the personal pronoun *my* occurs four times; and *myself,* once. Forty-seven times the personal pronoun occurs in nineteen verses. That is the picture of the defeated Christian, the Christian who has failed to reckon the "I" to be dead and has not yet experienced Galatians 2:20. As long as a person is contented to talk about "I," "my," "me," and "myself," utter defeat is all that he will meet in the course of his life. It is most significant that this chapter which displays the most utter human defeat combines it with a persistent use of the personal pronoun.

The first verse of chaper 7 strikes the keynote of the chapter: "Know ye not, brethren, how that the law hath dominion over a man as long as he liveth?" Here are the divisions of the chapter: (1) law and the Christian (7:1-6); (2) law and sin (7:7-13); (3) law and the carnal man (7:14-25). There is a very close, logical connection between these three divisions. The first three verses set forth an established fact: the believer is dead to the law; he is through with the law forever!

Out of the fifth verse a question arises. "The sinful passions which were through the law" (ASV), Paul says. If the inclination to sin comes from the law, then isn't the law something sinful? Paul answers that question in the second division by affirming that the law is holy. Look at the twelfth verse for a clear statement of this fact.

But another question will emerge right here. If the law is holy, then why cannot the law make the Christian holy? The answer follows logically, "We know that the law is spiritual: but I am carnal" (7:14), and that is why a good and holy law cannot make a person holy. Not because there is anything the matter with the law, but because the person is "carnal."

Thus, an established fact is laid down in the first division; and then the two other sections answer two questions that arise out of that fact.

LAW AND THE CHRISTIAN

"The law hath dominion over a man as long as he lives." This is a generally accepted fact concerning the laws of men, but ignored in relation to the law of God. Paul is talking to those Christians who have failed to account themselves dead back there at the time of faith. Here is a fellow who has said, "No." This man has failed to see it; he is still talking about "I," what "I can do." He still lives as the old self and has not reckoned himself to be dead with Christ. Now Paul says, "Don't you know that the law has dominion over a man as long as he lives?"

Verses 2 and 3 give an illustration from the law itself. Paul takes an illustration from the law to prove that the Christian is not under the law. These two verses teach that the woman who has a husband is bound by law to the husband as long as he lives; but if the husband dies, she is discharged from the law of her husband. If he is not dead, and she marries another, she will be called an adulteress, and that word *called* means publicly branded. But if the husband dies, she is free from the law.

Verses 4 to 6 make the application. A man is bound to the law for life, just as the woman was bound to her husband. But through the death of Christ, the man was made dead to the law. It looks as if Paul has mixed up his illustration. In the first instance it was the husband who died. Now Paul says, "*Ye* are dead." But this is not an analogy, which corresponds in every point; it is an illustration. Paul wanted to establish the fact that the marriage bond cannot be broken except by death. It does not matter who dies. He could not say that the law dies. The law of God never dies. The Jews would have had Paul in a moment, had he said the law died. He says that we were made dead through the death of Christ. We died with Him, and that broke the relationship. That is the application.

But that is not the end. To paraphrase Paul, "You died to the law in order that you should be joined to another, that is, Him who was raised from the dead, so that you might be fruitful to God." And so, while some say this is a dangerous doctrine, that of being dead to the law, do not forget that there are two things that go together: first, freedom from the law; second, union with Christ. And that combination makes it safe! God cuts us loose from the law and then joins us to Jesus Christ; and that union insures that we shall bring forth fruit to God, and not to sin, as before.

"Now we have been discharged [or delivered] from the law, having died to that wherein we were held; so that we serve in newness of the spirit, and not in oldness of the letter" (7:6, ASV). The word *spirit* should be capitalized, for it is the Holy Spirit.

This, then, is the figure Paul draws in the first six verses. First of all, though we were joined to the law, having died in Christ broke that relationship. While joined to the law, you brought forth "fruit unto death," which is the issue of that marriage; but when joined to Him who is raised from the dead, you produced "fruit unto God."

THE LAW AND SIN

The first six verses raise a serious question in that, "The sinful passions . . . were through [or by] the law." Somebody will surely say that the law must be sinful. What is Paul's answer in two words? "God forbid!" (You will notice, if you go back to the sixth chapter, the same response to the three great questions he asked there.)

If the law is not sin, what is it? The first thing the law does is to *reveal sin.* And that is a good thing. Paul says, "I had not known lust" or "coveting" (v. 7). The two words are the same. "I had not known coveting, except the law had said, Thou shalt not covet: but sin, finding occasion, wrought in me through the commandment all manner of coveting: for apart from the law sin is dead" (vv. 7-8). The *law* did not do it, but *sin* (as the Greek has it) took up a base of operation in the law itself and worked the sin of coveting.

Law not only reveals sin, but it *provokes* sin. Law does not cause sin, but law in the carnal mind provokes sin. The moment a man tries to be holy or righteous by keeping the law, the very commandments that came to him will provoke him into acts of sin.

Paul says, "Apart from the law, sin is dead." It does not mean that it does not have existence. It means that it is dormant. The law only exposed his true nature. Sin lies torpid like a serpent in the sun, until stirred up by the law.

Verse 9 declares that *sin produces death.* When was Paul ever "alive without the law"? It was when he was a child. Brought up at his mother's knee, he was taught to trust Jehovah; but there came a time in his life, at the age of twelve, when he was made a "son of the law." Then the whole body of the law was imposed upon him in a regular ceremony as a rule of life. When Paul was a child, he was taught just to trust and believe His promises, "but when the commandment came, sin revived." Sin was there all the time. He was born in sin, but it lay dormant until this moment. "Sin revived and I died." He passed under the doom and curse of the law, and he died spiritually. When we bring our children up, we have a right to teach them that the atonement saves them until they come to the age of accountability, when death comes by sin and they must have the new birth.

Verse 10 goes on with an affirmation concerning "the commandment which was ordained to life." As God had declared, "This do, and thou shalt live!" The law was intended to be unto life. But Paul says, "I found [it] to be unto death, for sin, finding occasion, through the commandment, beguiled me, and through it slew me" (7:10-11, ASV). "Finding occasion" means finding a base of operation. This is a military expression. So sin, taking up a base of operations through the commandment, deceived and slaughtered. In that verse is a picture of the fall. Substitute for the word *sin* the word *serpent*. Every man falls some time in his early life, just like that.

But verse 12 insists again that *"the law is holy."* The law must be holy if it does its work. It is the work of the law to prescribe how man shall live, and if he does not so live, to slay him (or, bring a curse upon him). The law reveals sin, provokes sin, condemns sin, and slays man. So the law is holy, righteous, and good.

Another question arises: "Did then that which is good become death unto me?" (7:13, ASV). Paul's answer: "God forbid." This difficult verse teaches one thing plainly: "But sin, that it might be shown to be sin, by working death to me through that which is good;—that through the commandment, sin might become exceeding sinful" (7:13, ASV). Sin is a terrible thing, whereas the law is good. The nature of sin becomes all the more plain, because it can take a good thing (the law) and work evil through that good thing. The law demonstrates this, so that in the final analysis it reveals how sinful sin is.

LAW AND THE CARNAL MAN

"We know that the law is spiritual." What is the matter then? Why cannot the law, if spiritual, holy, and good, bring holiness? Here is Paul's answer: "But I am carnal." There is the key to it.

A statement in the eighth chapter sheds further light: "What

the law could not do, in that it was weak through the flesh"
(8:3, ASV). It fails to accomplish in your life and mine what
it should, not because there is anything the matter with the law,
but because we are carnal.

Unsaved men are "sold under sin." Therefore Paul is talking about the "I," not the new man. When he talks about the
new man, he says, "I died." But he is now expressing a sup-
position. "Supposing I do not reckon myself to be dead and
recognize I am carnal. I am sold under sin." This poses a
hopeless case. You cannot improve the old man. He is always
what he is.

In this passage are three cycles. In each one of those cycles
Paul states a fact, proves it, and draws a conclusion. Then he
goes over it again.

Verse 14 states the fact: "For we know that the law is
spiritual." Verses 15-16 present the proof: "For that which I
do I know not; for not what I would, that do I practice; but what
I hate, that I do. But if what I would not, that I do, I consent
unto the law that it is good."

Verse 17 marks his conclusion: "So now it is no more I that
do it, but sin which dwelleth in me." He does not do what he
wants to do; he does what he does not want to do.

Is Paul trying to get rid of his responsibility for sin? Paul is
saying, "I gave myself over to sin." We all do it. We did something we liked to do which we know is sin. We did it, and
then sin became the master. While the first time it may have
been something we wanted to do, and enjoyed doing, after sin
becomes our master it compels us to do something we do not
want to do. Paul is saying, "The reason why this conflict is in
my life is that I am under the mastery of sin, and I want to
escape. It is no more I that do it." But Paul remains responsible, because he permitted himself to become a slave to sin.

Paul is not trying to shed responsibility here. He is only
showing that sin has obtained a mastery in his life that he
could not break. He is a slave. Isn't that the experience we
have sometimes, when we lose sight of Jesus. We try "to be
good" by keeping rules and laws?

Now follows the second cycle: Verse 18 states the fact: "For
I know that in me, that is, in my flesh, dwelleth no good thing."

The latter part of verse 18 and verse 19 present the proof: "For to will is present with me, but to do that which is good is not. For the good which I would I do not; but the evil which I would not, that I practise."

Verse 20 is the conclusion: "But if what I would not, that I do, it is no more I that do it, but sin which dwelleth in me." Again this is the same conclusion—"Sin is my master, my lord, my king. I cannot break it." Paul has gone around the cycle twice and comes out the same place: still sinning.

Now the third cycle comes up (each cycle begins with a similar phrase: "We know"; "I know"; "I find"): Verse 21 states the fact: "I find then the law, that, to me who would do good, evil is present." Verse 22 presents the proof: "For I delight in the law of God after the inward man." In the latter part of verse 25 appears the conclusion: "So then I of myself with the mind, indeed, serve the law of God; but with the flesh the law of sin."

Let us face it, the conclusion is the same, isn't it? The sinner never gets anywhere. Obviously, this is not the place to stop. This is not the normal situation for the Christian. God forbid!

If we go back now, do we have anything to do with law? Do we serve law? We are *dead* to law. When a man comes to this last verse, he should go back to the sixth chapter and consider that he is dead to sin, and then to the first part of the seventh chapter and read that he is dead to the law. Reckoning those two things to be true, what is the only way to escape this situation? The answer is to present himself to Christ.

There is a parenthesis in this passage. "O, wretched man that I am! What shall I do?" Does Paul say that? Paul never would have said, *what*. *"Who* shall deliver me from the body of this death?" His answer: "I thank God through Jesus Christ our Lord!" He will deliver me—He *has* delivered me, in fact. "For if we have become united unto Him in the likeness of His death, we shall be also in the likeness of His resurrection, *knowing this,* that our old man was crucified with Him" (6:5-6).

Do you believe that is true today? Are you ready to reckon it to be so? Then you have the deliverance he is talking about here. *He* delivers us! There is deliverance in no other.

May we learn here just what Paul is talking about. It is good for us to be brought into a place like this in order that He may take us on into victory!

16

Preservation: Kept Securely in Christ Jesus

IN A REAL SENSE the eighth chapter of Romans is the conclusion, the consummation, of the apostle Paul's treatise on salvation, answering the question, "how does God save sinners?" The climax is in this chapter.

In chapters 1, 2, and 3 the whole world was shown condemned and lost in sin. In chapters 3, 4, and 5 condemned sinners were seen as justified and declared righteous, if they believe on Jesus Christ. Then, in chapters 6 and 7, the method of sanctification was explained.

Now then, the end of chapter 7 completed the treatment of justification and sanctification. There remains just one more question that can arise: will this divine method of justification and sanctification last? The eighth chapter of Romans was written to answer that question, and the whole burden of the chapter is this: *if you are in Christ Jesus, you are safe!* Justification and sanctification in Christ will endure.

So then, we might say that the theme of Romans 8 is *security,* or to put it broadly, *preservation.*

There is a peculiar phrase which occurs in the opening verse of this chapter and also in the last verse. That phrase is "in Christ Jesus." If those two ideas are put together, "preservation" and "in Christ Jesus," this statement results: "preserved in Christ Jesus." Moreover, this very phrase occurs in the first verse of Jude. Speaking of the saints, he declares, "You are preserved in Christ Jesus."

The roots, so to speak, of the teaching of this chapter may be found in the sayings of our Lord Jesus Christ while He was upon earth. Those who like to criticize God's Word and are

159

not in sympathy with the faith often say that Paul was in conflict with Jesus Christ. They say that Jesus Christ gave us
truth while Paul gave us theology. But the germ of this chapter
can be seen in what Christ taught and said while on earth. At
least three passages from the gospel of John can demonstrate
this. The gospel of John is preeminently the gospel for the
Christian. The Lord says: "He that heareth my word, and
believeth on Him that sent me, hath everlasting life, and shall
not come into condemnation; but is passed from death unto
life" (Jn 5:24).

This chapter of Romans starts out with those two ideas—
first of all that there is no condemnation to those that are in
Christ Jesus. Christ taught this truth, and Paul developed it
under the guidance of the Holy Spirit. The second verse says,
"The law of the Spirit of life in Christ Jesus hath made me free
from the law of sin and death," and that idea is developed
down at least to verse 11, dealing with the passing from death
unto life.

When Christ prayed concerning His own, He said, as He
spoke to His Father, "The glory which thou gavest me I have
given them" (Jn 17:22). He spoke in the past tense, "I have
given them"—not, "I will," but "I have." The whole central
section of Romans 8 (from verses 18 to 30) is permeated with
the idea that Christ expressed in John 17:22. Paul begins with
reckoning "that the sufferings of this present time are not
worthy to be compared to the glory," down to verse 30, where
he says, "whom He called, them He also justified; and whom
He justified, them He also glorified."

One other statement of Jesus, "They shall never perish"
(Jn 10:28) contains a concept worked out in Romans 8.
Practically the whole chapter in germ form, is contained in
what our Lord Jesus Christ taught in the three passages.

Somebody has called Romans 8 the brightest jewel in the
setting of the Bible, and surely it is only as you examine the
diamond closely, as does the expert, that you can comprehend
its beauty and glory! It is impossible to mention, let alone
explain, all the truth that is in this chapter of Romans. That
would be a hopeless task in one chapter. When we come to
form an outline of the chapter, again we almost despair—not

that one cannot find an outline, but the trouble is to find one that is suitable for the study and comprehends all the truth that is in it. I have tried a dozen or two, and all were good, but somehow each outline seemed to leave out about nine tenths of the truth!

I want to suggest four or five and then go more deeply into one I have decided on.

POSSIBLE OUTLINES OF ROMANS 8

SECURITY

First, a simple outline emerges from the viewpoint of *security*. The chapter starts with the phrase, "In Christ Jesus." I want to state it like this: *Jesus Christ is around us.* Of course He would be, if we are *in* Him (vv. 1-4). Next, the Holy Spirit is *in* us (vv. 5-27). God is *for* us (vv. 28 ff). In this chapter is stated very beautifully the relation of the Triune God to the believer.

MINISTRY OF THE HOLY SPIRIT

The second outline can be made from the standpoint of the *ministry of the Holy Spirit:* the Spirit of Life (vv. 1-13); the Spirit of adoption (vv. 14-17); the Spirit of glory (vv. 18-25); and the Spirit of intercession (vv. 26-27). That does not exhaust His ministry by any means, but that is all here in this chapter. However, some of the chapter is thus omitted.

SERIES OF CONTRASTS

Something that enters more deeply into the chapter is a *series of contrasts:*

The first contrast occurs in the second verse: "the law of the Spirit of life" over against "the law of sin and death" (vv. 1-4). "In the flesh" and "in the Spirit" (vv. 5-13) are two further contrasts. Next is "the spirit of bondage" and the "spirit of adoption" (vv. 14-17). *"Present sufferings"* and *"future glory"* are set against one another (vv. 18-25).

What we do not know and *what we do know* (vv. 26-30) are a further contrast. We do *not* know "how to pray as we ought," but we *do* know that "all things work together for

good to them that love God, to them who are the called according to His purpose."

God for us; no one against us (31-39).

IN CHRIST JESUS

But there is still another viewpoint for an outline, and that
is to take the key statement: "No condemnation." View the
chapter as setting forth the theme *"in Christ Jesus,"* and then
we might say that in Christ Jesus:

1. There is no condemnation.
2. There is no defeat.
3. There is no fear.
4. There is no despair.
5. There is no calamity.
6. There is no adversary.
7. There is no separation.

There is no condemnation. Why? Because Christ died for
us!

There is no defeat. Why? Because the Spirit of God in-
dwells!

There is no fear. Why? Because God has become a Father
to us!

There is no despair. Why? Because we know that our very
sufferings reap the glory! How could there be despair?

There is no calamity. Why? There is no calamity that can
overtake us in Christ, because, "We know that all things work
together for good."

There is no adversary. Why? Because God is for us! Nobody can be against us!

Last, there is no separation in Christ. Why? Because God,
in Christ, has set His love upon us!

NEW THINGS

There is a phrase that occurs twice in the first section: "in
Christ Jesus." Our new position is in Christ Jesus, so we will
call the first section "our new position."

Our new life. "For the mind of the flesh is death, but the
mind of the Spirit is life" (v. 6, ASV). Look at verse 10: "If

Christ is in you, the body is dead because of sin; but the spirit is life because of righteousness." The idea of life runs all through this section, so it shall be called "our new life"—the Spirit of God (vv. 6-13).

Our new relation. Verse 14 says that we are sons of God. "The Spirit himself beareth witness with our spirit, that we are children of God" (v. 16, ASV). There, then, we have "our new relation" (vv. 14-17).

Our new hope. Verse 19 speaks of "the earnest expectation." The last word of verse 20 is "hope." That is almost like expectation in thought. Hope is what you look for. "In hope we were saved" (v. 24, ASV). All through this section appears the idea of hope. So verses 18-25 may be entitled "our new hope"—"the hope of glory."

Our new help. Beginning at verse 26: "And in like manner the Spirit also helpeth." Let us call this section "our new help" (26-27).

Our new knowledge. "And we know" (v. 28). We know something. We are going to call this "our new knowledge" (vv. 28-30).

Our new assurance. "What shall we say to these things?" (v. 31). Read also verse 38. We have our new assurance (vv. 31-39).

Paul said in his second letter to the Corinthians, "If any man be in Christ Jesus, he is a new creation; old things are passed away; behold all things are become new" (2 Co 5:17). "In Christ Jesus" everything is new. We have a new position, a new life, a new relation, a new hope, a new help, a new knowledge, and a new assurance.

NEW THINGS

OUR NEW POSITION

Let us consider our new position as set forth in verses 1 to 4: "There is therefore now no condemnation to them that are in Christ Jesus." Be sure to put a period at this point, if one is not there in your Bible. The remainder of that verse does not belong to the original. You may ask, "How did it get in?" Look at the end of verse 4: "Who walk not after the flesh, but after the Spirit." It is the same phrase. Back in the early church, scribes copied the Scriptures by hand. It must be remembered that scribes were subject to error. Perhaps a scribe read the verse as it was in the original and thought to himself, "If I leave it that way, folks are apt to take it that way and live in sin. I must protect God a little bit." And so he may have added that phrase in the margin; and then another scribe concluded that it had been accidentally omitted and placed it in the text. On the other hand, the scribe may have had a wandering eye, and accidentally picked up and repeated the clause in verse 4. Nevertheless, since that time archeologists have found many older manuscripts and not one has that clause in it. It is essential that this clause be excluded, for it is not a part of the Word of God. What God has intended to do in this chapter is to give us assurance, and He points us to Christ Jesus. The moment we look at that last phrase we look inward, and the moment we look inward we lose assurance. The only thing that is necessary is that we be *in Christ Jesus.* If we are in Him we can then say, without the slightest feeling of presumption, "There is therefore now no condemnation."

The little word *is* is not in the Greek. Literally it reads "Therefore now no condemnation." There cannot be now, nor ever, any condemnation. That is the initial proposition he starts out with—"No condemnation." That is our new position.

He passes on quickly to give us the evidence that there is no condemnation. "The law of the spirit of life in Christ Jesus hath made me free from the law of sin and death."

There is a law, just like the law of gravitation that operates all the time, in the spiritual world. Paul says that the law of the spirit of life has freed him from the law of sin and death. He does not say that it freed from sin and death, but from the law of sin and death. That is important, because he is talking about actualities here. Can a believer sin? Can he die? Yes. If the Lord does not come we shall die. But the point is that sin and death can never hold the law as a fixed law (like the law of gravitation that operates all the time). Christ has broken the law of sin and death forever! He has rendered that law inoperative in its final sense. Your body may be separated from your spirit, but God says He will raise that body some day and it will again be joined with your spirit. So the law cannot any longer exercise full authority over you.

That is the evidence of our new position, the evidence that there is no condemnation.

Paul shows us *the cause*, the ground, of our position in verse 3. He is not talking about the law he mentioned in the second verse. The law in verse 3 is the law of Moses. "For what the law could not do." It could not justify us; it could not sanctify us. "It was weak through the flesh." Nothing was the matter with the law—it was holy and good—but our flesh was weak and therefore the law could not justify nor sanctify. So God sent his Son, but did Paul say in sinful flesh? No. The apostle is accurate. He said, "In the *likeness* of sinful flesh." There never was any sin in Him. "And for sin" is a technical phrase from the Old Testament. That little phrase means as a sin offering, so that we might actually read it: "God sending His Son as an offering for sin, condemned sin in the flesh." At the cross He condemned it forever. "Therefore there is no condemnation to them that are in Christ Jesus."

There are some people who teach that Jesus Christ, by His life, condemned sin in the flesh, that He came in the flesh and yet lived without sin and therefore condemned it. But how does that help us? They have ignored that little phrase, "As an offering for sin."

Is the result license? To live as you please? Not by any means, but rather, "that the righteousness of the law might be fulfilled in us." It does not say that we might fulfill the law, but that it might be fulfilled in us. We are passive; God is the actor. The only thing we need to do is "to walk not after the flesh but after the spirit"; and while we are doing that, God fulfills the law in us. There are people (and I have been guilty of it myself) who say that when we are Christians, God gives us the power to overcome sin. He does not. God does not give the Christian power to overcome sin. If He did, you would surely be self-righteous, proud, and self-sufficient. God comes into you and overcomes sin as you yield to Him. The moment you do not yield to Him, you are in the muck and the mire. Why does He do that? He does that to make us cling to him in trust—second by second, moment by moment, hour by hour. This is so that our praise and boasting will not be about ourselves, but about the Lord (1 Co 1:29-31).

OUR NEW LIFE

The Spirit of God has been scarcely mentioned in the book of Romans. Yet our new life is the Spirit of God.

The contrast between those who "walk after the flesh" and those who "walk after the Spirit" is not a contrast between two kinds of Christians. We talk about the Christian who walks after the spirit and the Christian who walks after the flesh. But God never talks that way. The contrast here is between Christians and non-Christians. Christians walk after the spirit; non-Christians walk after the flesh. Look at verse 9: "But ye are not in the flesh, but in the Spirit, if so be the Spirit of God dwell in you." Then, is there a question as to whether the Spirit of God dwells in every Christian?

"If any man have not the Spirit of Christ, he is none of His." Every Christian has the Spirit of God, and if he has the Spirit of God, he is not in the flesh, because to be in the flesh is death, and we have passed from death to life. The Christian is the one who is in the Spirit. No Christian is in the flesh. It is an impossibility.

Many Christians like to pamper themselves, to excuse their sin. They say, "We are not saints. We cannot walk on that high level where we ought." So they try to bring in two classes of Christians. But there is only one. The flesh, however, remains in the Christian, although the Christian is not in the flesh. He may feel that way, when he does not yield to God. But he does not go under a law or fixed rule. In such circumstances God can bring him out.

If Christ is in you, what about you? "The body is dead." The body is not dead because Christ is in you. It is dead in spite of the fact. Because Christ is in you, what about the spirit? "The spirit is life because of righteousness." What is he teaching you? He is simply teaching that the body we have is not redeemed yet in the final sense. It is still subject to sickness and to death. It is true that if Christ is in you, even though the body is dead, the spirit is not: "the spirit is life."

What about the body? Will we lose it? Not at all. "He shall quicken your mortal bodies." We have life in the spirit now; we shall have life in the body at His coming.

OUR NEW RELATION

We are "sons of God," "children," "joint heirs" (vv. 14-17). On the judicial side, God adopted us as a son with every legal right as a son. But He was able to do more than go through a legal ceremony of putting us into His family. He actually gave to us His own Spirit, so that we are in His family by nature, and we are so conscious of this that we call Him "Father."

OUR NEW HOPE

Paul personifies all of nature. He says the whole of nature is looking for just one thing, and that is "the manifestation of the sons of God"!

There are three classes, or three realms, that groan: First, the creation groans, waiting for release from the endless cycle of corruption. Then, "we ourselves groan"; the believer groans because he is still in the body. He groans, waiting for that day. Not only that, but even the Holy Spirit groans (v. 27).

Have you ever noticed that no matter how happy nature may seem to be, there is a kind of minor note that runs through it—the cries of the animals, the moaning of the sea? This is the result of the curse. Someday the curse will be removed. This removal is associated with "the manifestation of the sons of God."

OUR NEW HELP

The word *infirmities* is better read in the singular—"infirmity." We have an infirmity. In the midst of the suffering of this life, we do not know how to pray as we ought. Paul prayed three times for the removal of a thorn. Then the Lord admonished him and said in effect, "Paul, you are praying wrong" (2 Co 12:7-9). But the Spirit of God knows how to pray! He knows what the will of God is: "He maketh intercession for us with groanings which cannot be uttered."

Here is an instance in this connection which illustrates what

Paul is saying. The great Saint Augustine had been a very
wicked man in his youth, but he was later converted. Augustine was greatly loved by his mother, Monica, who was a
Christian and had a heavy burden on her heart for her son.
She learned that he was leaving home and going to Italy, so
she prayed that God would not let him go, because she feared
he would get into worse sin there. That was her special request.
But God did not answer. Augustine went to Italy and he was
converted there. His mother did not know how to pray as she
ought, so God did not answer her *special* request in order that
He might answer her *life-long* request. God knows our aspira-
tions and He answers in His own way.

OUR NEW KNOWLEDGE

There is one thing we *do know:*

> We know that all things work together for good to them
> that love God, to them who are the called according to his pur-
> pose. For whom he did foreknow, he also did predestinate to
> be conformed to the image of His Son, that he might be the
> firstborn among many brethren. Moreover whom he did pre-
> destinate, them he also called: and whom he called, them he
> also justified: and whom he justified, them he also glorified.
> (8:28-30).

God foreknew us, predestinated us, called us, justified us,
glorified us. But earlier, in the verse preceding is a statement
of what we know: "We know that all things work together for
good . . . to them that are called according to His *purpose.*"
His eternal purpose comes first, then foreknowledge, then pre-
destination.

Then God breaks forth in time. God did all the above
before we were created, but then we came. Whom He predestinated, He calls (we are on the earth now), He justifies.
Now he is ready to swing over into another eternity, but instead
of saying He *will* glorify them—"He glorified"—all past. These
six words are the six golden links which bind the believer to
the two eternities—the eternity that is past in the purpose of
God, and the eternity that is future in glory with Him!
Look back in the eighteenth verse, then forward to the

thirtieth. Notice the development of that theme, so that it may be said that Paul has been talking about the glory in contrast with the suffering, until he comes to the last word of the thirtieth verse.

OUR NEW ASSURANCE

The thirty-first verse is a conclusion of the first eight chapters of Romans and not merely of this chapter.

"What shall we say to these things?" He means everything that has gone before—our condemnation, our justification, our sanctification, and our glorification. The last word he used was *glorified*. Now he says, "What are we going to say?" That is a searching question. What are *you* going to say this day to these things? Shall we say, "Well, that is interesting. I am glad that it is that way. But I am going to go on living as I have always lived. Certain things I like to do, and I am going to keep on doing them"? If you do say that, you do not know God! No true Christian can be brought into the presence of these truths without having them grip his heart and lead him in the path of righteousness.

But that is not principally what Paul intends to talk about now. There are four questions here:

"If God be for us, who can be against us?" The answer: "He that spared not his own Son, but delivered him up for us all, how shall he not also with him freely give us all things?" (v. 32).

"Who shall lay anything to the charge of God's elect?" That is to say (and he is issuing the challenge to a universe), "If there is any man, any angel, any demon who can bring forth a charge and lay it at the door of God's elect, let him stand up!" There is no answer. Why? Because "it is God that justifieth" (v. 33). Who is the man then that can bring a charge against God's elect when the very word *elect* shows that you can never do it? This is a foretaste. God has declared them righteous; no other man can undo it.

"Who is he that condemneth?" Anybody can issue a charge, but there is only one who has the authority to condemn. God has committed all judgment into the hand of—whom? The Son of God! (Jn 5:22). There is not a being—not even the

Father nor the Holy Spirit—no angel or archangel—there is only one person who can condemn any man. That is Jesus Christ! The only person in the world who can condemn you died for you! Even right now He is at the right hand of God, making intercession for us. How can He condemn us? It is impossible!

"Who shall separate us?" He is thinking now of those "present sufferings." Some say that present sufferings have a tendency to separate us from God. But these things cannot separate the true believer. Paul is talking about his own personal experience here too. He suffered every one of those things except the sword, and he was yet to suffer that at the hands of Caesar. For we are told that he lost his head on the Appian Way at the hands of the Roman governor. Not only can these things not separate us from Christ, but that is not all. In every one of them "we are more than conquerors." Are *we* that? No, let us finish it—"through Him that loved us." A French translation says, "Nay, we are conquerors *and beyond,* through Him that loved us!"

He goes on to his final paean of praise! A Christian may take those words upon his lips without the least shadow of presumption. "I am persuaded that *nothing* shall be able to separate me from the love of God!" Now he is going to search the universe for anything that could possibly separate us. He goes to the realm of death—he looks at it, he searches it. He says, "There is nothing there that can separate us." He turns then to the realm of life. He finds nothing there. He looks to the angelic or spiritual world. He finds nothing there among the good angels. He regards the other side—the principalities, representing Satan and all his hosts. There is nothing there!

He then begins to examine "things present." In all the vast realm of "things present" he finds nothing! Then he peers out into the future, "things to come." Who knows what those three words comprehend? Judgment—the ages of eternity! But he says, as he looks through the ages of eternity, "There is nothing there!"

But he does not stop. He scans the entire universe—the heights and depths of the universe. He finds nothing there!

One would have thought that Paul had covered everything,

but lest he may have missed something, he says, "There is no creation that is able to separate us from the love of God." Do you know what he means when he says that? He is considering the future, imagining the present creation passed away. He is anticipating that perhaps there will be infinite creations—on and on through the ages of eternity! He says, "They all come up, as far as the prophetic eye can reach, and *there is nothing in it all that can possibly separate us*."

And he closes the passage as it began—"in Christ Jesus!"

17

The Exhibition of Divine Sovereignty in Election

THE EIGHTH CHAPTER ended with that unforgettable hymn of praise. Paul has now finished dealing with the doctrinal points of his letter, that is, in the special sense of dealing with the divine provision for salvation.

The apostle might have gone directly to chapter 12 of Romans, to the exhortation answering the question of how a saved man shall conduct his life. Paul has shown how God saves a sinner. And, as in every other epistle he has written, Paul follows the doctrinal portion with exhortation, as in Ephesians: "I . . . beseech you to walk worthily of the calling wherewith ye were called" (Eph 4:1, ASV).

Notice how nicely chapter 12 would follow. He has finished telling us about the mercies of God. "I beseech you therefore, brethren, by the mercies of God"—that is, on the basis of the mercies as dealt with in the first eight chapters—"that ye present your bodies a living sacrifice." Then Paul tells them how they ought to live their lives. You may wonder why Paul does not go into this discussion immediately—why does he put these three chapters (the ninth through the eleventh) in the middle of the book? Some teachers have even spoken of these three chapters as a parenthetical portion, which is true in a certain sense. In another sense it is not true at all, because this book would not be complete without these three chapters. While the connection might not appear to be logical, it certainly (as one writer puts it) is psychological.

After Paul has treated in general the issues of salvation, a particular problem arises. It is the problem of the Jewish nation and their relation to the gospel that Paul has been setting forth in the first eight chapters.

The Jewish people, as a nation, had not received the gospel. They had rejected the Christ. Paul knew that. Everybody knew it at that time. Only a few Jews were in the church. As a nation, they had rejected the gospel. As time went on, a great deal of opposition had arisen from his "brethren according to the flesh."

The gigantic proportions of this problem now appear. The whole Old Testament was simply packed with promises that God had made to this Jewish nation. They were Messianic promises, promises which went with the Christ, the Messiah. Now notice the paradoxical situation. If the Jewish nation will not accept Jesus as Messiah, then the unbelieving Jew would say that there are two possible conclusions to be drawn. Either the gospel that Paul is preaching is not true, or else, if it is true, then the promises of God to Israel have failed, because the Messiah and blessing to Israel were connected inseparably. The Jew would say in essence that, either Jesus Christ is not the true Messiah or the Word of God has proven false.

That is the problem, and it was a tremendous one! It is still a problem today, with which men are trying to cope. If people would only read these chapters carefully, they would find a clear statement of the problem as well as the ultimate solution. A great many people set aside the Jew entirely. They say the promises have failed as far as the Jews are concerned. But that is not true.

Paul's treatment of this problem is daring! He admits the fact that the Jew as a nation has rejected the gospel, and yet he takes his stand firmly and declares that the nation still has a place in the economy of God. There is nothing in all the Word of God, in logic itself, that can exceed the movement of thought constituting the ninth, tenth, and eleventh chapters of Romans.

With that by way of introduction, let us consider the subject. And that subject is *vindication*. And the question being confronted is this: *why is Israel rejected?* Paul's answer is marvelous! Let's take a quick preview of these three chapters, to paraphrase what they teach in answer to that question.

The ninth chapter admits to the fact that the Jewish nation has not received the gospel, but it also declares that the Word of God has not failed. Why? Because some Jews have believed, and these Jews, says Paul, are a part of that elect remnant that the Old Testament tells about. So the conclusion is that there is always a continuing line of believers, in whom the promises of God are being fulfilled.

The tenth chapter carries the argument further and lays the blame on Israel. The apostle says that if Israel, as a nation, has been set aside, it is through no fault of God. The reason that God has rejected Israel is because Israel rejected the gospel.

Then in the eleventh chapter, the apostle tells that although the nation of Israel has been set aside, and although that rejection of them as a nation has been richly deserved (because they rejected the gospel), the rejection of Israel as a nation is not final. It is temporary only, and through all that (through the election and through the rejection) God is working out a mighty, loving, and gracious purpose. For by the rejection of Israel as a nation, salvation has been brought first of all to the Gentiles. And if Israel's rejection has resulted in the enrichment of the world, how much more blessing will come someday when God receives Israel back in the place where it once was.

Paul vindicates the ways of God in rejecting Israel by three lines of argument (one in each chapter): (1) the absolute sovereignty of God (chapter 9); (2) the moral responsibility of man (chapter 10); (3) the final purpose of God (chapter 11).

God has the right to reject Israel if He wants to; He has the right to choose one man and to reject another. It may not sound right, and to most people probably doesn't seem right. But neither how it sounds to men nor seems to their finite comprehension changes the fact. The doctrine of election is hard to receive, but remember that God has a sovereign right over His creatures.

Notice how inevitably the next follows: you bring a man into the presence of the sovereignty of God and election, and he will say, "Well then, man is not responsible. Man is not free. If God chooses one man and rejects another, then man is not free." But Paul says he is! So in that next chapter he lays the whole responsibility upon the Jews' own shoulders. He says the gospel is free—anybody could believe that wanted to. So moral responsibility is emphasized in the tenth chapter.

Confronted with moral responsibility as running parallel with the sovereignty of God, the human mind shifts its charge against God and says, "God is not good. If God is sovereign, if He chooses one man and not another, then God is not good." Paul is going to answer that God *is* good. Through this exercise of sovereignty, God is going to work out a mighty purpose, through which He will bring the whole world to a knowledge of the gospel!

Back of it all, God has a purpose. It is not like the old pagan conception of the mills of the gods grinding like machines and devouring men. It is not like the Mohammedan idea of men modeled out of clay—this one for hell, that one for heaven! Back of this sovereign election is a God who loves the world, a God, the mystery of whose will no man knows and perhaps no man will know until the end comes. Paul has chosen here in this eleventh chapter to draw back the curtain and show how God, even in the things which appear to be mysteries is going to work out His holy and divine purpose in the end.

So we are confronted with an amazing and beautiful unfolding of the plan of God: chapter 9—election; chapter 10—rejection; chapter 11—reception.

The absolute sovereignty of God is seen in *election*.

The moral responsibility of man is seen in *rejection*.

The final purpose of God is seen in *reception*—that is, the future reception of Israel back into the will of God.

There you have the three things beautifully set forth in those three chapters.

It is necessary to point out one or two other things before we enter into the study. If you have read this chapter you will have noticed how sorrowful is the tone of it (vv. 1-5). "I have great sorrow and unceasing pain in my heart." But he ends the whole section with a note of rejoicing: "O the depth of the riches both of the wisdom and the knowledge of God! how unsearchable are his judgments, and his ways past finding out!"

(11:33). This marks an amazing change. As Paul begins his discussion he faces the problem of Jewish unbelief and sees his own brethren going down to the pit! This strikes at everything he has held dear. As he goes on, step by step, the solution of the problem unfolds, and he is brought into the presence of that God who works all things according to the counsel of His will. Paul is led to utter the most wonderful doxology in the Word of God (11:33-36).

In these three chapters, Paul is writing for the Jew first of all. They may contain things that the Gentile who is out of Christ will reject utterly. For instance, tell the average unbeliever, "Hath not the potter a right over the clay, from the same lump to make one part a vessel unto honor, and another unto dishonor?" The average Gentile will reject that. Take him into the presence of that passage that says that God raised up Pharaoh to show His own glory in the earth, that "God hath mercy on whom He will and He hardeneth whom He will." The average Gentile will reject that, but no orthodox Jew dare reject it, because it is written in his own Scriptures.

Here is our outline for the ninth chapter, as we are dealing with the absolute sovereignty of God as shown forth in election:

1. The problem stated (vv. 1-5). "For I could wish that I myself were anathema from Christ for my brethren's sake, my kinsmen according to the flesh."

2. The explanation offered (vv. 6-13). "But it is not as though the word of God had come to nought. For they are not all Israel, that are of Israel."

3. The objections answered (vv. 14-24). "What shall we say then? Is there unrighteousness with God? . . . Thou wilt say then unto me, Why doth he still find fault? For who withstandeth His will?"

4. The proof given (vv. 25-29). Paul quotes from the Old Testament Scriptures in proof of the statements made.

5. The conclusion drawn (vv. 30-33). "What shall we say then?"

Now we are ready to enter the passage and study it more closely, following the outline suggested.

THE PROBLEM STATED

It is possible for a Christian of redeemed heart to be full of unspeakable joy, and at the same time have sorrow. In chapter 8, Paul is up in the heavens—joy unspeakable—and in the next moment he is telling us that he has great sorrow and heaviness of heart. Every Christian has that experience. It is a paradox. You have unceasing joy in the Lord, and yet in the very midst of your joy there may be unceasing pain and sorrow for some loved one, some "kinsman according to the flesh," who is out of Christ.

The Jew might have brought the charge against Paul that he did not care for his kinsmen. They might have said, "He is so wrapped up in this new gospel that he has forgotten all about his people." So he starts out, "I say the truth in Christ, I lie not, my conscience bearing witness with me in the Holy Spirit, that I have great sorrow and unceasing pain in my heart."

The first verse sets forth the reality of his grief, and the second the intensity of it. The third verse implies that his sorrow was sacrificial. There is a mystery in that verse. "For I could wish that I myself were accursed from Christ." What does the word *accursed* mean? It means utterly *lost forever!* Can you imagine a man who has come to know what it is to be in Christ, wishing that he might be lost forever, if only his kinsmen might be saved? It doesn't seem right, does it?

Recall a similar request back in the Old Testament. There came a time when Moses went up in the mountain to get the Ten Commandments. While he was up there, the people melted their gold ornaments and made a molten calf; and when Moses came down he found the people of God naked, dancing before a molten calf, and saying, "These are the gods that brought us up out of Egypt." Moses broke the tables of stone in his hand and rebuked them. God was going to destroy the whole nation. They deserved to be destroyed. Moses threw himself upon his face before God, as a type of the Lord Jesus Christ. "You have sinned a great sin; and now I will go up unto the LORD. Peradventure I shall make atonement." Can a man make atonement for sin? No. Moses was beyond his depth here. He was wrong, but he says, "Perhaps I can save

you." Moses returned to Jehovah: "Oh, this people have
sinned a great sin and have made them gods of gold. Yet now,
if Thou wilt forgive their sin—" That sentence was never
finished. There is a dash there. "And if not"—what then?
"Blot me, I pray thee, out of thy book which thou hast written."
Moses is asking God to destroy him along with the people, if
forgiveness is not possible. Notice the answer. God rebukes
him: "And the LORD said unto Moses, Whosoever hath sinned
against me, *him* will I blot out of my book."

Moses was ready to perish with his people; Paul now wished
that he too might be accursed for his kinsmen's sake. Only
Paul goes beyond Moses. Moses says, "If this people perish,
then Lord blot me out—let us die together." Paul says, "Let
me die that they might live!" But there is a difference. The
apostle Paul could never have completed that wish. Paul,
knowing what it meant to be in Christ, could never say that as
it is in our version. The translation does not convey the true
sense. Paul himself said, "You are not your own. You are
bought with a price." How then could he have said this in
Romans 9:3? Notice what he did say: "For I *could* wish."
The Greek tense is the imperfect, incomplete. "It was in my
heart to wish it, but I never completed it. That is the way I
feel about my people, but when I come to wish myself accursed
there is something that stops me." It is an uncompleted wish
and was never completed. "I *could* wish, if God would let me,
but He won't. I *could* do it, if it were permissible, but it is not."
No man has a right to say, "Let me be accursed and let this
man be saved," because as Christians we are no longer our
own.

Paul sets forth the position of Israel in verses 4 and 5, and
while his sorrow was deep because these were his own brethren,
yet his sorrow was made more acute by the position of the
nation. He refers to them as "Israelites," not "Jews." "Israelite"
is the theocratic name. "Israel" was the new name given to
Jacob (Gen 32:28). The word means "God striveth through
you." They were the only nation that God ever called a son.

"Whose is the adoption and the glory"—that is, God's manifested presence was with them, the Shekinah glory. "And the
covenants"—God has covenanted with this people as He has

covenanted with no other people on the earth. "Giving of the law"—no other nation had a code of laws that God gave, even though other laws are founded on those laws. "Service of God"—the temple ritual, the sacrificial system—all that service of God that was rendered. *"The promises"*—the Messianic promises were to Israel alone. *"The fathers"*—Abraham, Isaac, Jacob, David—all those great men belonged to Israel, not to the Gentiles.

Now Paul comes to the climax—"of whom is Christ" but he guards the statement with the phrase, "As concerning the flesh." Suppose he had said, "Of whom is Christ." We might have thought of Him just as a human being then. "Of whom is Christ as concerning the flesh." The Holy Spirit is careful to protect the person of our Lord Jesus Christ. Only "according to the flesh" is He of Israel, born of a virgin. His humanity came from Israel, but He was the "bread that came down from heaven."

Now Paul refers to the other side of His nature. "God blessed forever." That is, "according to the flesh" He was a man of Israel, but in His own true inner personality, He "is over all, God blessed forever!" Men who do not believe in the deity of Christ have tried to get around this passage. They have tried to put a period after *flesh* and make the last a doxology, making it refer to God the Father instead of Jesus Christ. It only means a wresting of the Greek language to do it that way. It ought to read as we have it in our version.

The apostle Paul has faced the problem of Israel rejecting the gospel, and yet he declares that there is still the adoption. Israel as a nation still has the promises. That is the problem Paul has summed up here. Israel has rejected the gospel and yet they are still holding their position in the Old Testament.

THE EXPLANATION OFFERED

In the face of this remarkable setting for Israel, somebody will say that the Word of God has not held true. But Paul says that is not so. The Word of God has been driven out of its course as a ship is driven. "They are not all Israel who are of Israel." There is the first hint of election.

In verses 7 and 10, Paul uses Abraham and Isaac, two instances from the Old Testament, to prove that God works on the principle of election.

Abraham had at least two sons, Ishmael and Isaac. The Jew would say the physical descent from Abraham makes him an Israelite. He declared any man born a Jew had a right to the promises of God. In contradistinction to this, Paul demonstrates that God never worked on that principle. What about Abraham himself? And Ishmael was a son by physical birth, he is not an Israelite. God set Ishmael aside and chose Isaac instead. As he says, "In Isaac shall thy seed be called." Here is a clear instance of election.

But someone might say, "Ishmael was not legitimate. He was born of an handmaid," which was true. So Paul takes the case of Jacob. What are the facts in this case? Two boys were born; they were twins. Jacob and Esau were twins; so that the Jew could not say, "Well, the one man had the prior right because he was the older." Here were two sons with the same father and the same mother, born at the same time. Not only so, but Esau was born first, and if there should be any priority on the ground of age, Esau should have had the priority. What did God do? He said, "The older shall serve the younger." Every Jew knew that. This was another instance of election, God working in absolute sovereignty (verse 11).

That is the answer to the Jew. God chooses according to His own sovereign will and sets aside all human ideas of merit and superiority.

Verse 12 states that this act of election was before they were born. Verse 13 declares the basis of that election, namely, "Jacob I loved, but Esau I hated." That is a hard verse, but it need not disturb you if you remember the setting of it. You say, "Is it possible that God said that?" But He did not *say* it before they were born. It is from the book of Malachi, the last book in the Old Testament (Mal 1:2-3). It was only after Jacob and Esau had been born and had made their lives what they were, that God said, "One I loved, the other I hated." There was a reason for it. If there was an election in Israel, every Jew must admit from his own history that God works that way, choosing whom He will.

THE OBJECTIONS ANSWERED

The moment you assert the election in this sense, men begin to object, and so Paul anticipates these objections and answers them.

"What shall we say then?" Is God unrighteous because He takes one man and sets aside another? "God forbid!" Away with the idea! He is going to take two cases—Moses and Pharaoh.

Paul works logically. He states his problem and then proves it from examples in the Old Testament. "For He saith unto Moses, I will have mercy on whom I have mercy, and I will have compassion on whom I have compassion." The incident recorded in Exodus 32 illustrates the same thing. Because of their idolatry at Mt. Sinai, they all deserved to be destroyed. What did God do? He destroyed three thousand and left the rest alive, when they *all* deserved to be destroyed.

Paul says, if you are going to say that God is unrighteous because He chooses one man and not another, then God was unrighteous at Sinai when He let you all live. Everybody should have died then, but God said, "I will have mercy." Grace, mercy, lovingkindness were the only reasons. If you do not like the doctrine of sovereignty and election, just remember that the only reason the nation was not absolutely destroyed then was because of the sovereign mercy of God.

God is also sovereign when it comes to bestowing His judgment. In the case of Pharaoh, God said, "I raised him up for this purpose, that I might show forth my Name." God does not say here that He *made* Pharaoh for this purpose. It means He made him to be in the place he was, He permitted him to be king of Egypt that through his very hardness God might show forth His power. God said, "Let my people go." Pharaoh said, "No!" Pharaoh hardened his heart. God said, "Let them go." Pharaoh said, "I won't let them go!" God poured out plagues upon him, and Pharaoh steeled his heart the more, until finally there came a time when God stepped in and He hardened Pharaoh's heart.

To understand this, let us imagine a man goes to bed and sets an alarm clock. The first morning it goes off, he gets up.

But after a week he says, "I will sleep a little longer." There will come a time when he will not even hear the clock go off. You say, "that is a law of nature," but who is behind nature? In other words, the God-ordained psychological laws take their course, and it may be said that a man hardens himself, and yet in the ultimate sense, God hardens him. And so, the man goes into a church and hears the gospel, and first of all rejects it, then keeps on hardening his heart. Soon he will not need to harden his heart, the heart will just go on hardening. God will finally step in and keep on hardening the man's heart.

But Paul uses it here to show God's sovereign right. To borrow an illustration: here are two men; one takes poison, the other does not. Can a man take poison and escape the consequences? He cannot. Can a man reject God's counsel and expect to escape? He cannot!

The other objection is in verse 19: "Thou wilt say then unto me, Why doth he yet find fault? For who hath resisted His will?" This man will insist, "If all this you say is true, if every man is as God made him, why does God find fault with my sinfulness? I am what I am. God made me this way." There is a subtle lie involved in that statement. God did make man, but He did not make the sinner what he is. However, Paul does not intend to argue that question. But He does give the man what he deserves, a rebuke. "O man, who art thou that repliest against God?" Who are you, to talk that way? A creature of the dust! And the contrast is between man and God. O man, who are you that you should reply against God? What right have you to say anything like that? What right have you to cavil even in the very presence of the sovereignty of God? *None whatever!* "Shall the thing formed say to him that formed it, Why hast thou made me thus?" Is that the way man can talk, for "hath not the potter power over the clay, of the same lump to make one vessel unto honour and another unto dishonour?"

Now perhaps that is the very crux of the problem of this chapter. You say, "That sounds terrible—that God has the right to take the clay and make one man a sinner and another a righteous man!" But he does not say that. God makes no man a sinner. Remember this: God takes the clay as He finds it, and the "clay" here is man who is already a sinner. "Thou art the potter, we are the clay." Paul is not talking about the creation of man. God created him good, holy, and righteous, but the clay that the apostle is talking about here is sinful clay. Out of that clay every man stands alike. Every man is a sinner, every man deserves judgment. God has a right to pick out one man from that mass and have mercy upon him, and let the other man go if He wants to. Paul is not talking here about God creating man in sin. God did no such thing.

After Paul rebukes the objector here, he shows how God acts. What are the actual facts? "He endureth . . . vessels of wrath fitted to destruction." God was merciful even in the case of men who deserved destruction. "That He might make known the riches of His glory on the vessels of mercy, which He had afore prepared unto glory."

Two different classes of vessels are referred to here—one class of vessels is fitted for destruction, the other is fitted for glory. Now, who fits the vessels for destruction? Does it say God did it? No, it does not say that. "Fitted for destruction"— the middle voice of the Greek verb means that *man fits himself* for destruction. God never does that.

Who prepared these vessels for glory? *God did that.* If any man ever goes to hell (and a good many men will go unless they turn) it will be his own fault. It will be because he rejected the mercy and longsuffering of God. He will fit himself for destruction. On the other hand, if any man ever reaches heaven it will not be because he fitted himself for heaven, but because *God* fitted him for heaven!

THE PROOF GIVEN

Paul quotes the Old Testament Scriptures to prove the fact of election. That is his thesis, his proposition. He says this matter of election is nothing new. It is in the Old Testament.

A lot of folks think that this passage refers to the Gentiles. It does not. They think Paul made a mistake and quoted from the Old Testament something that belonged to the Jews and applied it to the Gentiles. He is talking about Israel. "I will call her my people which was not my people." God cast Israel off and then picked her up in mercy.

How many are going to be saved? Just a remnant. So Paul

is saying, "This is just exactly what your own Scripture says. Your own prophets said if anybody was to be saved, it would only be a remnant." "A seed" that is all. "If He had not left us a seed, we had become like Sodom and Gomorrah." They were destroyed utterly.

THE CONCLUSION DRAWN

"What shall we say then?" Here is what he said: "The Gentiles who followed not after righteousness, attained to righteousness." The Gentiles who originally were not interested in it at all and went down into sin—these were the ones who gained righteousness. That is wonderful! They were not looking for righteousness, but they got it, "a righteousness by faith." But Israel "tried to be good" in their own strength, in their own righteousness, and did not arrive there at all. There are the two classes: the Gentiles who did not follow it, but got there; the Jews who tried, but failed. Why was it so? "Because they sought it not by faith, but as it were by works of the law." When a man seeks righteousness by the works of the law, he will never get there. Not if he gives his body to be burned, nor if he makes an ascetic out of himself will he reach righteousness.

"They stumbled at the stone of stumbling, even as it is written" in their own Scriptures. Jesus Christ is the rock—some men stumble over Him, other men build on Him!

It is a solemn possibility to be a member of the visible church and not a member of the invisible church. That is the lesson for us today. It is possible to be humanly numbered among the people of God and yet not to be a true child of God. A second lesson is that spiritual life does not come through physical birth. Your father and your mother, and all your family as far back as you can trace, may be Christians, but that won't make you a Christian any more than it made Ishmael and Esau Israelites because they were born of Abraham and Isaac.

Let us take these things to ourselves and examine ourselves, and find out whether we are really in the Lord Jesus Christ or not.

18

The Exercise of Human Responsibility in Rejection

WHEN YOU BRING unbelieving sinners into the presence of God's sovereignty, there is a frequent common response. Their reasoning follows a similar pattern. They charge God with being responsible for what they are—for their sin and unbelief. As taught in chapter 9 of Romans, and the unbeliever will begin to argue like this: "If God is sovereign—if He is the potter and we are the clay, then I am not responsible for my lost and sinful condition. I am just what God made me."

The apostle, in the tenth chapter, addresses his argument to this response. In the course of the tenth chapter of Romans, the apostle Paul does not apologize in any way for what he has said in the ninth chapter on divine sovereignty. There is not the slightest hint of retreat from what he has taught in the ninth chapter. However, he does demonstrate to the unbelieving sinner that God is not responsible for his lost condition. Man alone is responsible and he cannot hide behind divine sovereignty nor use the doctrine of election as an excuse for his sin.

First of all, Paul has discussed election in chapter 9; divine sovereignty always comes first. After that he talks about human responsibility in chapter 10. Israel has rejected the gospel. God has rejected Israel because the people have rejected the gospel. In this tenth chapter Paul brings out and establishes three main facts, which conform with the ideas of this chapter:

Verse 8 asks, "What saith it? The Word is nigh thee." It is right near you, in your mouth and in your heart. The first fact that the apostle insists upon is that *the gospel is within reach of all.* You see how that may apply in this very objection. The Jew says, "I am what I am because God made me that way." Paul says, "The Word is close to you in your Scriptures. You could have believed if you had wanted to."

Verse 11 declares, "For the Scripture saith, whosoever." Again in verse 13, "whosoever." That word occurs twice. In the twelfth verse the word *all* also occurs twice. "Whosoever" and "all." The second fact is simply this: *the gospel is offered to all.*

"They did not all obey" (v. 16). Look at the last verse— "All day long have I stretched forth my hands unto a disobedient and gainsaying people." But they were disobedient. The third fact is this: *the gospel is not obeyed by all.*

Those three facts form the outline of the chapter:

1. The gospel is within the reach of all
2. The gospel has been offered to all
3. The gospel has not been obeyed by all

That is the answer, very simple but very crushing, to those who hide behind divine sovereignty.

Consider the introduction (vv. 1-4), where several matters come to our attention. There are people who say (and they are Christians, or at least they call themselves Christians)—"God has cast off the Jew. That is the end of it." But Paul did not feel that way. He said, "My heart's desire and my supplication to God is for them, that they may be saved."

A wonderful encouragement emerges in this first verse, in contrast with the preceding chapter. When some people are shown what Paul has taught in the ninth chapter, they are apt to say, "There is no use to pray. If God does as He pleases, if He is a sovereign God, what is the use of praying? You cannot change His mind." Actually, the sovereignty of God should be an incentive, not a discouragement to prayer. The only kind of God who can answer prayer is a sovereign God! If God were not sovereign, we would all be doomed right now. We would not dare pick out a sinner and pray for him. When I see a man that looks absolutely hopeless, I can pray for him exactly because my God is a sovereign God who does not have to give that man what he deserves.

For that reason, the apostle Paul did not show any inconsistency whatever between what he taught in the ninth chapter and what he teaches in the tenth chapter. Those very people God had rejected, he now reaches toward, praying that they might be saved. We get our heads started along one line and can think of nothing else, but the Holy Spirit inspired Paul to present two sides of a truth like this, in order that we might understand and have consolation, and also be encouraged to pray.

Verse 2 bears further witness about these people. They have "a zeal for God." The Jew did have that, didn't he? The apostle himself, before he was converted, went out to kill people because he was zealous for God. The reason the Jews gave for opposing this gospel that Paul preached was because God had given the law. They opposed Jesus of Nazareth because they had a zeal for the name of God, and Jesus claimed to be God. Paul says, "I know them. They have a zeal for God."

But what was the matter with them? This zeal was "not according to knowledge." Did the Jew know anything about God? Oh yes, he did. He knew something about God. He was not totally ignorant about God. The English version does not give the precise meaning of the Greek word. That word *knowledge* means "a full knowledge." The Jew had some knowledge, but here is where he fell short—*he did not know God in Christ Jesus!* He knew Him as He was revealed in the Old Testament, but he did not know Him in Christ Jesus, and so his zeal was a mistaken zeal—"not according to the full knowledge." All religious persecution has been based upon a partial knowledge, a zeal for God growing out of partial knowledge.

In the third verse the apostle states his charge, which forms the theme for the whole chapter: "For they being ignorant of God's righteousness, and going about to establish their own righteousness, have not submitted themselves unto the righteousness of God."

If that ignorance were the usual kind of ignorance, you might conclude that they were excusable. But this was a *willful*

ignorance. So it could be expressed, "Ignoring God's righteousness"—meaning, therefore, willful ignorance.

"Being ignorant of God's righteousness" is the first thing,
then it is affirmed they were "going about." The ASV says
"seeking." Let us use the word *seeking*. Since they were seeking to establish their own righteousness, they did not *submit* to
the righteousness of God. Being willfully ignorant of God's
righteousness, they exerted continuous effort in searching for
a way in their zeal to establish their own righteousness, refusing
to submit to God's righteousness!

That explains the trouble with many people today. They
have enormous zeal for God; they will work their fingers to the
bone for the church, trying to serve God; and yet all the time
they are ignorant of God. And they are actually trying to
establish their own righteousness, unwilling to submit to the
righteousness of God.

God's righteousness is something not only that we *believe*,
but also something to which we should be *submitted*. One of
the primary reasons why more men do not believe the simple
gospel of God is because of human pride and human reason.
They are determined not to *submit*. It is hard for all of us to
submit and yield. The central issue is just submitting ourselves.
That is all we need to do with this righteousness. Just let God
put it on you. In Zechariah 3, the prophet was clothed with
filthy garments. God spoke and said, "Take off those filthy
garments and put clean ones on him." All he did was stand
there and permit it to be done.

According to verse 4, "Christ is the end of the law for righteousness to every one that believeth." You may never hear
another sermon, but in that verse you will have learned all
you need to know to be saved—that Christ is the end when it
comes to righteousness. To illustrate it: there is an old road
that is called the Santa Fe Trail, that runs out to Los Angeles.
If you want to get to Los Angeles you take that road. But
suppose you want to go there, and you could just be lifted up,
transported, and set right down in Los Angeles. Would you,
after you got there, say, "I must go back and come over this
Santa Fe Trail"? You are already there; Los Angeles is the
end.

When you come to Christ, He is the end—He *is* the righteousness. When you are in Christ, you have reached the end as far as righteousness is concerned.

The last word in verse 4 is "believeth." Back a little way, "everyone"; back to the third verse, "They did not submit." There are three ideas: *faith*—believing; *everyone*—universality; *did not submit*—rejection.

Those three things are stated in the introduction and are what Paul discusses in the chapter.

Faith puts the gospel within the reach of everyone, pointing to its accessibility; "everyone" corresponds with the division that teaches that the gospel is for everyone—"whosoever" marks its universality; "did not submit themselves" indicates accountability.

THE GOSPEL IS WITHIN THE REACH OF ALL

Paul first shows that the righteousness of the law was not within the reach of all. What does he say about it? "The man that does these things shall live." The righteousness of the law can be summed up in three words: "Do and live." Nobody ever lived by doing the law. They all died back there. That is what the Lord said, "Your fathers ate manna in the wilderness and they are dead." Every Jew should have known that there was no life in the law, and that it was an impossibility to find it in those ordinances back there. But somehow or other, they did not seem to feel that way.

Verse 6 points to the contrast in "the righteousness which is by faith." "Say not in thy heart, Who shall ascend into heaven? (that is, to bring Christ down from above)." What is he talking about? He is saying that man (humanity) had nothing to do with the coming of the Son of God down from heaven into this world. Man had nothing to do with the incarnation.

According to verse 7, it is clear that just as man had nothing to do with the incarnation, neither had man anything to do with the resurrection—with raising Him up from the dead. God did it! *God did it all!* There is nothing left for man to do in this "righteousness which is by faith." Do not say you have to do something big to be saved. "God sent not His Son into the world to condemn the world, but that the world

through him might be saved" (Jn 3:17). God raised Him from
the dead, too.

According to verse 8, "The word is nigh thee even in thy
mouth, and in thy heart." You cannot get anything much closer
than that. That was literally true back there. This simple
message of salvation, the righteousness that the Apostle Paul
preached, was upon the lips of every Jew of the ancient world.
Every synagogue where they met, whether they believed or
did not believe, they were discussing Paul and what he taught.
They argued hour after hour about this thing, trying to show
how Paul was wrong. They had it in their mouths and in their
hearts.

Let me give you an illustration. Here is a man taking the
name of the Lord Jesus on his lips in vain. He is using profanity. Then he suddenly stops, and under the leading and
energizing of the Holy Spirit, says, "Jesus is my Lord! I confess Him!" This has happened. Two thieves were crucified
with our Lord Jesus Christ—one on each side. When put there,
they both reviled Him. Just a few moments passed and one of
those thieves, with the reviling in his mouth, turned his face
up to the Lord of glory and said, "Lord!" He confessed Him
as Lord right there. More than that, he said, "Remember me
when thou comest into thy kingdom" (Lk 23:42). That dying
thief had the faith to believe that this crucified Lord would be
risen from the dead! This dying thief was nailed to the cross.
He could not do any works of righteousness. There was no
time to talk about obeying the law, doing works of goodness,
and improving his character. All he could do was move his
lips; and with those cracked, swollen, parched lips, he looked
up into the face of the Lord and said, "Lord." With his heart
he believed that this man would arise from the dead, and he
was *saved!* For Jesus turned to him and said, "Verily I say
unto thee, Today shalt thou be with me in Paradise" (Lk
23:43).

That is an illustration of what Paul is talking about in verses
9 and 10. Verse 9 looks as though it were backwards, because
it puts confession before faith. But that is merely the outside
view. Until you confess Jesus as Lord, I do not know whether
you believe or not. If you confess Christ, then I know there is

faith in your heart. In the tenth verse comes the actual order. "For with the heart man believeth unto righteousness; and with the mouth confession is made unto salvation."

The illustration is sufficient to show that the gospel is within the reach of every man. "The Word is nigh thee, in thy mouth and in thy heart"—just receive it and it is done. No Jew can say, "God has made this thing too hard for us, we cannot do it," blaming God for his condition.

THE GOSPEL IS OFFERED TO ALL

What a wonderful thing it is that Paul could go back and quote from their own Scripture to convict the Jews. He says, "Let us have a little of the law now." For the Scripture says that those who wait for Him shall not be put to shame (Is 49:23).

Now Paul extends his argument to the human race. It is evident that God's salvation not only applies to the Jew, but to the Gentile as well. "The same Lord is Lord over all, and is rich unto all that call upon Him." Then he quotes again, this time from the prophet Joel (Joel 2:32). If the Jew had read the book of Joel, he could not have objected to any Gentiles being saved.

Having quoted that, Paul gives in the fourteenth and fifteenth verses a beautiful little discourse, to show the Jews the necessity for taking the gospel, which is intended for all, *to* all. If God provided a righteousness which is for all, if we know anything about it, then the obligation and responsibility for taking it to all lies upon us. In other words, world reconciliation demands world evangelization. He approaches this responsibility in reverse order, but nevertheless in a way that emphasizes the need.

This "sending" has nothing to do with church boards. It is God who sends. Church boards under God may help missionaries to go, but ultimately God sends the men. If they are not sent of God, they ought not go. Jesus Christ insisted, "As my Father hath sent me, so send I you" (Jn 20:21). Recall how Isaiah put it. There were two questions: "Who will go for us?" and "Whom shall I send?" Isaiah could answer either one, but did he say, "Here am I; I will go"? No. He said, "Here am I; *send* me" (Is 6:8).

Now Paul goes to the very heart of his argument with the Jew. Remember now, the two things about this gospel: first of all, it was within the reach of every man; second, God intended it for every man, not merely for the elect. Why had not the Jews been saved? Is it because God elected some men to perdition? Not at all.

But They Have Not All Obeyed the Gospel

God, through Paul, takes the responsibility for Jewish unbelief and places it squarely upon them. Here is the gospel, but they did not submit to it. The proof of it? He quotes again from their own Scripture, "For [Isaiah] saith, Lord, who hath believed our report?" What kind of a report was it they did not believe? The report of a Messiah, who was a man of sorrows and acquainted with grief, bruised for our iniquities—a Christ who was broken upon the cross. That was the report that the prophet brought, looking down through the centuries. But who has believed the report? It was foretold—the very thing that came to pass.

There is a parenthetical clause here. He cannot pass up the opportunity of telling what faith is. The Jew might say, "Faith? That is hard. How can I get faith? If I do not have it, that is not my fault." Paul says, "Here is the way it comes: faith comes by hearing." How does hearing come? "By the Word of God." If you want more faith, do you pray for it? No. Just listen to the Word of God and accept it, and your faith will grow. How can you believe a thing unless you know it? So, if you want a big faith, just feed upon the Word of God.

That word *report* in the sixteenth verse is identically the same word in the Greek as the two words which are translated *hearing* in the next verse. It is a very difficult word to translate, because it means not only a report but that the man who reported it had heard from somebody else. We might paraphrase it: "Lord, who hath believed that which we heard and reported?" It has within its meaning the idea of a message, and therefore in that seventeenth verse the word *hearing* is not a good translation. A better rendering would be, "A message heard."

Faith does not come just by your hearing. That would be human. But faith comes from something heard. Where do you get something heard? From the Word of God. That is where we get the message. Very simple, very plain.

When the apostle says that these Jews have not obeyed the gospel, he expects protests on small points. So he raises two questions. "Did they not hear?" A Jewish listener might say, "Some have heard, but not all." Paul says, "Yes, they have heard." He uses the language of Psalm 19 to remind them of the testimony of heaven and the stars. The apostle was correct; the gospel had gone through the whole Jewish world. It was therefore appropriate for the apostle to refer to this psalm.

Then he anticipated another objection. He would say, "Did Israel really know? Did they understand this? Did not God spring something on the Jews, and without warning?" Then Paul quotes twice in answer to that objection.

First, he takes them to Moses. "But I say, Did not Israel know? First Moses saith, I will provoke you to jealousy with that which is no nation, with a nation void of understanding will I anger you" (Deu 10:19, ASV; see 32:21). So Moses foretold this situation fifteen hundred years before.

Second, Paul says, "[Isaiah] is very bold, and saith, I was found of them that sought me not; I was made manifest unto them that asked not of me" (10:20; see Is 65:1).

Perhaps the Jew said, "This is too hard for me—I would not understand it." God says, "I am taking a nation that has no understanding at all, and they understand. These Gentiles understand this gospel and have received it. Not only that, but I was found of them that sought me not. Here are people that did not even try to seek me—Gentiles that never raised a question about the true God and His righteousness, whereas you Israelites with all the light you have, and all the understanding you have, you cannot understand this simple gospel. You surely ought to."

The truth of the matter is in the last verse, which is the conclusion: "But as to Israel, He saith, All the day long did I stretch out my hands unto a disobedient and gainsaying people" (10:21, ASV; see Is 65:2). Isn't that a startling verse after the ninth chapter? In His sovereignty God had rejected some and elected others, yet He says concerning this nation, "All the day long have I stretched out My arms to this nation!" That is grace, *sovereign grace!*

That word *day* does not mean a twenty-four-hour day. Rather, it refers to the age of the law. All through those centuries, God says, "I had My arms stretched out to this nation, but they were disobedient when I tried to help them." So God has loaded the responsibility for this people's condition squarely upon their own shoulders.

The gospel is within the reach of every man. The only reason men are without Christ, without God, without righteousness and will go out into eternity lost is that they refuse to submit to God.

What a lesson for us! To think that it is possible for us to be zealous for God, to busy ourselves everyday with what we conceive to be God's work, and yet to be utterly blind to the truth of the simplicity of the gospel. To think that we are asked not to do anything big, but merely to submit to the righteousness of God and let Him put it on us as He wants to do.

Then here is another lesson: the Jews studied their Scriptures, and yet they utterly failed to see the truth. There is a possibility of that today. It is possible for a man to study diligently the Word of God, but if he does not see Jesus, it will profit him nothing.

19

The Experience of Merciful Purpose in Reception

THE THEME of the concluding chapter of Paul's discussion of the Jewish nation is stated in the first verse. It is in the form of a question: "Hath God cast away His people?"

The reference is certainly to the nation of Israel and not to the election within Israel. It would be foolish to conclude that this means the election within Israel, for certainly God has not cast away those Jews who believed and composed the election. This fact will be all the more clear if you will look at the last verse of the preceding chapter: "A disobedient and gainsaying people"—the nation of Israel itself. God is speaking of national Israel. Paul has already shown that the church is here now in view. Even though there may be a few Israelites in whom the promises of God can be fulfilled, they are in the church.

Now the Jew would say, "If all Paul has been saying in chapters 9 and 10 is true, then God is through with Israel as a nation." So Paul takes up that question right here and faces it squarely. The whole of this chapter can be summed up in two statements: (1) Paul shows first that the rejection of Israel is not total, but partial; (2) Paul demonstrates that even this partial rejection of Israel is not final, but only temporary.

This question in the first verse suggests the outline of the chapter. Paul asks, "Hath God cast off His people?" and in answering, states and develops three facts here: (1) there is a present election, which proves God has not cast them off (vv. 1-10); (2) there will be a future reception (vv. 11-24); (3) there will be a final salvation of Israel (vv. 25-32).

195

After his answer, Paul concludes with a doxology, which is a conclusion not only to this chapter and this section, but to all that has gone before—the whole eleven chapters. It is perhaps the most wonderful doxology in Scriptures.

Each of these three points has a key verse; and that key verse has a phrase that suggests its contents. In verse 15— "What shall the *receiving* of them be but life from the dead?" The nation that is cast away will someday be received. Look at verses 25 and 26—All Israel shall be saved finally. This will be the final salvation, or the total salvation.

HATH GOD CAST OFF HIS PEOPLE?

What, in two words, is Paul's answer? "God forbid!" For there is a present election (vv. 1-10).

Now, the apostle Paul knew the Old Testament Scriptures. He could have turned back and quoted from the Old Testament a good many times. The issues here are vital. In fact, the interpretation of this eleventh chapter will settle one of two methods of interpretation.

There is a school of thought in Christendom which says that in the church God has fulfilled everything in the Old Testament and there is no future for the Jew as a nation. But the opposing view is that God has set Israel aside for an age, and at some future time (in the next age) God will fulfill to the letter every promise He has made to Israel as a nation.

That second view is the right one, and to show that it is the right view, let us examine some passages from the Old Testament. "If those ordinances depart from before me, saith the LORD, then the seed of Israel also shall cease from being a nation before me for ever" (Jer 31:36). He ties up His promises to Israel with the very stars in the heavens and the planets. "If heaven above can be measured, and the foundations of the earth searched out beneath, I will also cast off all the seed of Israel for all that they have done, saith the LORD." He uses the very words that Paul does, *cast off*. It is not that they have not done enough to be cast off. They have. But God in mercy remembers His promises to their fathers. In Jeremiah 33:24 there is a taunt. Some of the heathen had seen what God had done to His people and here is what they said: "The two families [Judah and Israel] which the LORD hath chosen, He hath even cast them off?" But here is God's answer: "Thus saith the LORD; If my covenant be not with day and night, and if I have not appointed the ordinances of heaven and earth; then will I cast away the seed of Jacob, and David my servant . . . I will cause their captivity to return, and have mercy on them" (Jer 33:26).

But that is not enough, Paul shows some evidence that God has not cast off His people. First he takes his own case. Was Paul cast off? He certainly was not! He was enjoying the promises of God. Paul used his own case to show the Jew that God has not cast off the Jew entirely. Second Paul points to God's foreknowledge. Christians rejoice in the fact that "whom He did foreknow, them He also did predestinate . . . whom He did predestinate, them He also called: and whom He called, them He also justified: and whom He justified, them He also glorified." If God's foreknowledge of us as individuals cannot fail, neither can it fail when it comes to this nation of Israel which He foreknew in ages past. So it is a fact that His foreknowledge does not allow Him to cast them off; they may be set aside, but He will bring them back.

Then he goes for an illustration to the Old Testament— Elijah. In many respects the positions of Paul and Elijah were very similar. You have all read the story of Elijah—how he ran for his life and ended up under a juniper tree, and said, "It is enough; now O LORD, take away my life" (1 Ki 19:4). Paul might have said that, too, but he didn't. The condition that existed under Elijah existed in Paul's time, too, but Elijah pleaded with God against Israel. "Lord, they have killed thy prophets, they have digged down thine altars; and I am left alone, and they seek my life." It was not true. Elijah thought it was true, but here God replied with the truth of the situation: "I have left for myself seven thousand men who have not bowed the knee to Baal." God had reserved these seven thousand for himself, and they had responded by refusing to worship Baal. There is the divine and the human side. They always go together. God chooses men for the purpose of holiness. At the time when Paul was writing to Rome, there probably were more than seven thousand Jews in the church. If the existence of a remnant back in Elijah's day showed that God had not cast off Israel, surely the presence of all those Jewish believers in the church indicated that He has not cast off His people.

In verse 5, with the use of the phrase *even so,* Paul makes the application to Israel. "Even so then at this present time also there is a remnant according to the election of grace." They did not deserve to be saved, but it was grace that saved them! This next verse does not really belong in the argument, but Paul could never lose an opportunity to hammer in the truth of grace. The very fact that this election of Israel, which existed in that present time, was of grace, ought to give hope to the rest of Israel, because if God, who is a sovereign God, can show grace where it is not merited, He can do it to a whole nation.

He sums it up in the seventh verse. Israel did not obtain what it was seeking. What was Israel seeking for? Righteousness. The tenth chapter says they were ignorant of God's righteousness while seeking to establish their own and so did not submit themselves to the righteousness of God. It was their own fault, because they sought it by works and not by faith.

Israel, as a nation, did not obtain this, but the election obtained it, and the rest were "blinded" judicially. The retribution of God fell upon a people who first closed their eyes. If a man says, "I will not," there may come a time when he will say, "I cannot."

So the rest were hardened, "according as it was written." Paul refers to their own Scriptures to show that what he is saying is true. "God gave them the spirit of stupor." Then he moves to Psalm 69, one in which the Jews rejoiced. They placed great confidence in this psalm. Verse 21 depicts the Lord Jesus Christ speaking at the cross. "They persecute Him whom Thou hast smitten." The retribution that God poured out upon them, according to this psalm, was their own fault.

Paul has asked the question first of all, "Hath God cast off His people?" and he shows in answer that there is in Israel a saved election, and that the rest of the nation has been hardened and blinded, not because of any arbitrary decree on God's part, but because of the response in their own hearts. When He sent His Son, they crucified Him.

THERE WILL BE A FUTURE RECEPTION

The Jew might say, "I can admit that there is an election, but what about the rest of the nation? Are they cast off?" Paul now answers in verses 11-24, "I say then, Have they stumbled that they might fall?" He has just been talking about their table being made a stumbling block to them. When the Lord Jesus Christ came as their Messiah, He really was bringing all the benefits of a banquet. He was their table, and their table became a stumbling block to them. But Paul says, "Did they stumble that they might fall and never be brought back? God forbid!" This is the same answer as before.

But why did they stumble and fall? There was an immediate reason: "By their fall, salvation comes to the Gentiles." Isn't that true? "He came unto his own, and his own received him not" (Jn 1:11). They crucified Him, and that opened the door of salvation to the whole world. "Now if their fall is the riches of the world, and their loss the riches of the Gentiles; how much more their fullness!" They lost everything back there—their Messiah, their kingdom, their land, all the millennial blessing that God had promised them—lost them all, and their loss was the benefit of the Gentile world. Notice Paul's argument in verse 12: "How much more shall their fullness be!" If the Gentile world gained through their fall, think what it will gain when God receives the Jews back again! Paul is reasoning from the lesser to the greater.

In Psalm 67:7 Israel says, "God will bless us." Some criticize the selfishness of Israel and their bigotry, "God shall bless *us*," but these critics need to read on—"and all the ends of the earth shall fear him." That is what will happen. When God blesses Israel, then all the ends of the earth will hear of the Lord Jesus Christ in a way that they have never heard before. That is the "fullness" here to which Paul makes reference.

But now a question arises. The church at Rome was a Gentile church. There might have been a few Jews in it. Since Paul was an apostle to the Gentiles, Gentile believers will want to address a question to Paul. "Paul, why are you bothering yourself about the Jews?" He responds to the question. "I magnify my office," that is, make it great. "How do you do it, Paul?" "If by any means I may provoke to jealousy them that are my flesh, and may save some of them." Can you see how he is magnifying his office in trying to save the Jews? The more Jews that are saved, the more Gentiles there will be saved, and the greater will be the ministry to the Gentiles. That is true to this day. Whenever a Jew comes to the Lord, he makes a flaming evangel. So we should not be lifted up with pride. We should not be anti-Semitic. Though Paul knew the future blessing was to come, he was trying to save Jews, which in turn would bring more Gentiles.

Now we come to the great fifteenth verse. Where did the reconciliation of the world take place? At the cross. "For if the casting away of them be the reconciling of the world, what shall the receiving of them be, but life from the dead?" They rejected their Messiah; they took Him to the cross and there He reconciled the world. If reconciliation occurred at the cross, then "What shall the receiving of them be but life from the dead?"

Ezekiel 37 is the vision of the dry bones. God asked the prophet about the bones, and Ezekiel said, "I am not going to speak. They look pretty dry to me." Imagine taking a man out into a valley and asking him to talk to a lot of dry bones! The prophets had some hard things to do. But Ezekiel was obedient and he said, "I prophesied as I was commanded."

There is a stirring in the "bones" in this twentieth century. Many of Israel have gone back, but "there is no breath in them," that is, spiritual life. They are going back to their land unconverted. But even though that is the picture, the word comes to the prophet, "Son of man, these bones are the whole house of Israel." That is the divine interpretation. "What shall the receiving of them be but life from the dead?"

Comparing verse 2 ("God hath not cast away His people") with verse 15 gives the appearance of a contradiction. The best way to explain this seeming contradiction is to look at Jonah. He was cast into the sea, and yet he was not cast into the sea. God cast Israel into the sea of the nations, and yet He has not cast them away. He has cast them away in the nations; but in the nations He has preserved them, just as Jonah was preserved in the whale. Israel was told to preach to the Gentiles just as Jonah was told to go preach to the Ninevites. Jonah was three days in the whale, and "a thousand years are but as one day" in God's sight.

Then Paul discusses the olive tree. You are all familiar with this story of the olive tree. A great many people have said that the olive tree here is the church, or that the olive tree is Jesus Christ, and as the Jews were in the church in the Old Testament and they by their unbelief were cast off, God broke them out as branches and put in the Gentiles. They say, "If you do not behave yourself, God will break you out." They use this figure to argue against the doctrine of eternal security.

Anyone who is a Bible student and also a horticulturist, ought to know better than to interpret this passage this way. As I happen to be the latter, you will pardon me if I tell you something about grafting. When you take a scion and graft it into another tree—for instance, take a pear and graft it on the apple tree—will this scion change its identity? Will this bit of pear grow into an apple? Certainly not. It will remain a pear. The moment the sap passes that little place, it begins to bear pears, though right below it the tree will bear apples. In other words, if in this olive tree Jews are put, they are still Jews. When Gentiles are put in, they are still Gentiles. But this is not true of the church, for in the body of Christ there is neither Jew nor Gentile. If the men who studied this passage and misinterpreted it only had known a little about horticulture, they would not have made that mistake.

What is this olive tree? It represents the place of favor or privilege. Abraham is the root, for "salvation is of the Jews" (Jn 4:22). God first brought into favor the Jew, then He cast him out of favor and put in the Gentile. It does not save anyone to be in this olive tree. When you are saved, your nature is changed; but Paul is talking about "the wild branches." Gentiles are Gentiles, Jews are Jews in this olive tree. The apostle is saying that because the Jew did not live up to his privileges and the light God gave him, he has been cut out and the wild branches were grafted into the place of favor. Of course, the whole church is here too—all the professing members of the church—because all the Gentiles are here. Some are really believers and some are not. Those that are not will be broken off. They will be taken out. The great lesson of the passage is certainly this: that just as the Jew in the Old Testament became bigoted, proud, and exclusive, and thought that God knew him only, now that very same thing is happening in Christendom to the Gentiles. There is only one thing that can retain favor in the eyes of God, and that is faith (verse 20). When Christendom begins to manifest unbelief and apostasy, the time is coming that God will take the Gentile out of his place and put the Jew back in.

Paul's argument is very good here (verse 21). The Jew is the stalk. It is much easier to put the natural branch back in than it is to take a different branch and put it in.

THERE WILL BE A FINAL SALVATION

In this last movement of thought is a tremendous lesson for Gentile Christendom! There are so many Gentile believers who are "ignorant of this mystery." It is God who has mercy, but because of "A hardening in part" He cannot leave out the necessity of election. There will only be a remnant saved "until the fullness of the Gentiles be come in."

What is "the fullness of the Gentiles?" In this present age, according to Acts 15:14, God is visiting the Gentiles to take out a people for His Name. God is visiting the Gentile nations, through the ministry of Gentile believers, and is taking out a man here and there for the Bride of Christ. When the body of Christ is complete, the Lord will come; Gentile times will finish and Israel shall be put in again.

Isn't that exactly what we have when our Lord says that "Jerusalem shall be trodden down of the Gentiles, until the times of the Gentiles be fulfilled?" (Lk 21:24). Until the full number that God has chosen out of the Gentiles shall be saved, the fullness of the Gentiles in the position of favor with God will continue. When that happens, "All Israel shall be saved." At that time the Israel that is on the earth is going to be saved. Paul proves his point through the Jewish Scriptures (verses 26 and 27).

Verses 28-29 summarize Paul's argument. "As concerning

the gospel, they are enemies for our sakes." The Jewish nation has become an enemy to the gospel. "But as touching the election" what are they? The believing remnant is "beloved." For our sakes? No! "For the fathers' sakes." God says, "I promised Abraham; I promised Isaac; I promised Jacob"; and God keeps His promises. "The gifts and calling of God are without repentance." God might repent that He had made man, but He will never repent of the promises He made to Abraham.

Verses 30-31 speak to the Gentiles in the word *ye*. The Gentiles were disobedient to God. Paul had talked about the Gentiles being disobedient in the beginning of the book. If God has shown us mercy, who are we to say that God cannot show mercy to the Jew?

Verse 32 is vivid in the ASV: "God hath shut up all unto disobedience." The Greek suggests a man shutting up an animal in a trap. They went into the trap, "that He might have mercy on them all." That statement is the closest that the Bible ever comes to relating the sin of man to the mercy of God. "God hath shut them up unto disobedience that He might have mercy."

God could not have mercy upon us as long as there were certain people on the earth who had certain privileges which they deserved. Not until all human merit had been swept aside could God do anything for us. Every last man had to be "shut up unto disobedience" before He could show mercy. Every mouth had to be stopped. The whole world had to become guilty before God. And then Paul says, "Now the righteousness of God without the law is manifested."

The doxology, as set forth in verses 33-36, constitutes the concluding paragraph. Paul has been like an Alpine mountain climber. Now he has reached the peak, and he does just what anyone else would do—he turns around and looks back to see how far he has come, to know the path by which he has wound around to reach this height!

The person who has mastered the first eleven chapters of the book of Romans knows more about the philosophy of history than all the wisest historians that the world has ever seen. There is a philosophy of history here that is unmatched! It makes the historians of the earth appear like children playing with their toys. In these eleven chapters, Paul shows us the original human race. The race is split into two segments: Jew and Gentile. Then came the promises. But the Jew failed to receive the promises by crucifying the Messiah, resulting in the expansion of the promises to all. Then the two segments of the race come together again, God having mercy upon all.

Paul employs two emphatic words to describe God's wisdom: *unsearchable* and *untrackable* (past tracing out)—as if there were a great deep. God's decisions and judgments are like that; nobody has been able to go down to the bottom and search them out. His ways are so unfathomable that no man will ever be able to follow them.

Who has ever known God's mind, or who ever gave God any advice in this great plan of His? Paul cannot refrain in this verse 35 from going back to grace once more. "Who hath first given to him, and it shall be recompensed unto him again?" It is grace! What man in all the earth ever gave God anything so that God should be compelled to give him something in return? No man! That disposes of salvation by works!

The picture now expands until it encompasses all things. Out of God all things come—He is the origin. Through God all things exist—He is the sustainer of all things. Unto God— back to God—He is the goal. There is the circle of eternity: *out, through, back.*

Someone has pointed out that there is a hint here of the Triune God. The Father is the source of all things—out of Him come all things. The Son—through Him were all things made. He is the one who carries out the purposes that originate in the Father. The Holy Spirit takes the things that exist and so manipulates them and moves them that they move back to God as the goal.

"To him be the glory forever! Amen!"

20

The Christian Life as Exhibited in Transformation

IN THE BROAD SENSE chapter 12 deals with the theme of the Christian and his manner of life.

Some scholars who do not have a very great regard for God's Word and have rather loose ideas about inspiration, have made a severe attack upon this chapter, declaring that it has neither head nor tail, no systematic arrangement, and that it is just a mass or collection of exhortations. Not only does this criticism show the unspirituality of these men but also their lack of ability to decide in literary matters. Most certainly there is a very beautiful and logical order in this chapter if men have eyes to see it.

Here are the three main ideas in this chapter: (1) consecration (v. 1), (2) humility (v. 3), and (3) love (v. 9).

We are going to make our outline with those three ideas in view. First of all, the Christian life should be *a life of consecration* (vv. 1-2). Second, the Christian life should be *a life of humility* (vv. 3-8). Third, the Christian life should be *a life of love* (vv. 9-21).

Those three ideas in those three sections also present three different attitudes of the Christian. Consecration is the attitude of the Christian toward God. We are to present ourselves *to God*. Humility describes our attitude *toward ourselves*. Love describes our attitude *to others*.

A LIFE OF CONSECRATION

"I beseech you." That is the method of the gospel! What would the law say? "I *command* you." We are now out from under the law. For "Christ is the end of the law." We are outside the law entirely. So Paul says, rather, "I beseech you." In your attitude toward others, use the beseeching manner rather than the one of command, for that is pleasing in the eyes of God.

"I beseech you therefore." There are three *therefore's* in the book of Romans, and they mark three great divisions in the book. *"Therefore,* being justified by faith, we have peace with God through our Lord Jesus Christ" (5:1). "There is *therefore* now no condemnation to them that are in Christ Jesus" (8:1). "I beseech you *therefore"* (12:1). Of course, when he uses the word *therefore,* it points back to what has gone before. In the twelfth chapter, where he says, "I beseech you therefore," he is pointing back to all that was said before.

The word *brethren* identifies the group to whom these words are addressed. This word indicates that this chapter is for Christians. When you go out and try to get other men to steer their lives according to this chapter, you will encounter difficulty. If you go to a man who is not a Christian and say, "If thine enemy hunger, feed him," he resents this and rebels. This appeal is directed to the *brethren.* It is most essential that we remember that. This is for the Christian and you cannot take the Christian rule of life and apply it to the man who is not a Christian. It is a spiritual impossibility.

"I beseech you therefore, brethren." What does he beseech them by? "By the mercies of God." Shut your eyes and think back through all those eleven chapters. Mercies! That word sums up all that is contained in those chapters, just mercies upon sinners who did not deserve any mercies. Paul does not talk about what *we* did. He is just talking about what *God* did for us. He uses those mercies as a great moral dynamic and spiritual incentive.

When you have not revealed to people the mercies of God, you have ignored the most powerful moral factor that the world has ever seen. There is the great mistake of modernism. Assuming that we may give them credit for sincerity, and giving them credit for a desire to see the church live on a higher plane of life, still like the blind leaders that they are, they have lost the one motive, the one factor that is powerful enough to get hold of the hearts of men and raise them up to that plane of righteousness where they ought to be. Until sinners have experienced God's mercies, you will get no place. The mercies of God are the basis of all living that is really holy.

Let us consider now the meaning of the word *present*. Remember we are dealing with that same word appearing in chapter 6 back where Paul said we died with Christ, we rose with Him, we are to reckon it to be so, and we are to "yield." Paul did not develop it in the sixth chapter, but here he develops it. "Present your bodies" as an act of consecration.

You may wonder why he mentions the body in the exhortation *Present your bodies*. There is a reason in that. The body, at the present time, is the instrument of the soul and spirit, and God gets no service except it be manifested through the body: the hands, the feet, the mouth, the tongue. Therefore, he speaks of the body, and that includes the soul and spirit, everything, the whole man. In fact the word *body* is a way of describing an organism in its entirety.

"Present your bodies," but what kind of a sacrifice should it be? The answer is clear. It should be "a *living* sacrifice." Very often we have thought of this word *sacrifice* altogether wrongly, as simply giving up something that we would rather not part with. This sacrifice is not only giving up something, but it is giving it up to God with eagerness and joy—presenting it to Him; and furthermore, in contradistinction to the sacrifices of the Old Testament which were dead, these are *living* sacrifices. He died for our sins; we are not called upon to die— we are called upon to *live* for Him! We might die in a moment of time, but to live for Him will require a lifetime.

Concerning this sacrifice, Paul says three wonderful things:

First of all, he tells us what kind of a sacrifice it should be, namely, *holy*. You are a sinner, and you come now in His merit, in His blood, and the sacrifice is considered holy.

Second, it is *acceptable*. He will receive it, because it is well-pleasing (ASV margin). It is attractive to and excites the pleasure of a holy and loving God.

Third, it is *reasonable*. "Your reasonable service." There are two ideas in the word, perhaps three. Basically the word means logical, in the sense that it is the response of a man who recognizes that he was bought with a price and therefore belongs to the one who bought him (1 Co 6:19). It is reasonable in the sense that it is the response of a moral creature made in the image of God and unlike a beast or a mere chattel (2 Pe 2:12). It is spiritual in the sense that it is the response of a creature who now rises to the highest point of priestly service under the direction of the Spirit of God (Heb 9:1, 6). Obviously all three of these ideas go together.

The exhortation continues: "Be not conformed [fashioned] to this world, but be ye transformed." There are two words in the original Greek that deserve special attention, the words *conformed* and *transformed.* The first one, translated *conformed,* is the word from which we get our English word *scheme.* It means a conformation that is outward, without any necessary connection with inner essence, and it is like the world that passes away.

The word *transformed,* however, reaches deeper. This refers to an external form that clearly represents inner essence. To be transformed means that inner essence will make an external manifestation. It is the same root word that is used in Philippians: "Who existing in the *form* of God." The inner reality of Christ, which was essential deity, made itself known in outward manifestation.

Consider first the appeal: Do not be *conformed* to the age. There is nothing so hateful and abominable in the eyes of God as for the Christian to conform himself according to the present age, an outward age which does not truly represent the new nature in purity nor permanence. This age is an evil one and a passing order of things. If you conform yourself to this age, you will pass away with it. Of course, Paul must use a word that describes transience, not permanence.

Consider finally the result, and compare the word *transformed* in 2 Corinthians 3:18 with the phrase "Be ye *transformed*" in this verse. This is not something that *you* are to do, according to the Scriptures. If you present yourself to God as a living sacrifice and "behold the glories of the Lord" in His Word, you will be transformed progressively. This is the Spirit's work, but it also calls for cooperation on the part of the believer.

The end result is "that you may *prove*," that is, test out to discover and approve as the assayer tests the ore to discover and approve it. The issue is the will of God described in three of its aspects: "good," that is pure; "acceptable," that is, meeting the pleasure of God; and "perfect," that is, lacking in no respect. Surely nothing can stand in higher priority in the activity of a saved man than this.

A man who sees the mercies of God will then present himself to God as a living sacrifice. The issue of such consecration will be to *know* by proof and test what is the will of God. The unbeliever does not know, he *cannot* know, and therefore he must falteringly grope his way through the darkness.

That "will of God" is here described by three words which deserve further explanation:

1. *Good.* God's will is always good. It may be hard, but it is always good.
2. *Acceptable.* It ought to be acceptable to you, because it is acceptable to Him.
3. *Perfect.* Sometimes the will of God leads you into places that you cannot see the reason for, and it seems that everything is going wrong. But remember that *His* will is perfect. No matter how devious the way may be, His will is perfect because "He knows the end from the beginning."

We can sum up the meaning of the first two verses of this chapter in three statements: (1) The basis of holy living is *revelation;* (2) The method of holy living is *consecration;* (3) The result, or the outcome, of holy living is *transformation.*

A LIFE OF HUMILITY

The Christian life should be a life of humility.

Verse 3 introduces the general thought, "I say, through the grace given unto me, to every man that is among you." This is for all of you folks who are being confronted with this message, every man and woman. *Man* is a generic term and includes both. He insists that each believer is "Not to think of himself [or herself] more highly than he [or she] ought to think, but to think soberly according as God hath dealt to each man a measure of faith."

A man should not aspire to be something that is not in the will of God for him, because God has made him what he is and has a particular place for him as a Christian. How often we find people who do have some real gift, but who are dissatisfied with the gift they have, a gift which may be lowly but worthy, not spectacular but useful; and so they are desiring to be something else other than what they are and what God has purposed.

There is a rule of measure. God has provided this for each man. You may question God's will in dealing with you in this way, but remember that His will is good, acceptable, and perfect. The measure of His dealing with you is according to your faith. You may depend upon it that if you are His child, He has given you just as great a gift, just as high a position as your faith could stand. It would be a terrible thing to be judged as if we were standing in other peoples' shoes. We could not discharge that responsibility. He knows what we can stand. He knows the capacity of our faith, because He has given us our faith.

Paul moves on from that idea to the fourth verse: "For as we have many members in one body, and all members have not the same office; so we, being many, are one body in Christ." There are many members in the body of Christ. Each one has its place. God, in His eternal sovereign foresight, has apportioned to you just the proper place for *you*. I have heard men say, "If I could only be a D. L. Moody." God knows you better than you know yourself, and it takes a man who is completely open to God to stand where Moody stood, and to give what Moody did. Men also say, "Look at the need of the world today. Why does not God give me a fortune?" Well, He knows whether you could stand a million dollars, whether it would be good for you.

So, be satisfied with the place God has given you. That would be *true* humility. To deprecate yourself is false humility. But use that place God has given you—*occupy* it.

Paul passes on from the idea of membership in the church to the actual gift given each member. Are all the gifts the same? No, they are different. How do they differ? "According to the grace that is given us." And then he names seven gifts. Prophecy, ministry, teaching, and exhortation are the four major gifts. Then follow three minor gifts: *giving, ruling, showing mercy.* That is a beautiful sevenfold presentation of the gifts of the Spirit. There are other catalogues in the Bible that are more specific, but these are inclusive.

PROPHECY

That gift was given to the men who wrote God's Word. We do not have that gift today. They spoke for God directly, and when they did, they prophesied "according to the measure of faith"; they spoke in harmony with what had been spoken already. Men who come today and prophesy not according to this Word are not prophets—according to the marked out proportion that God has already given. Even when the men wrote the New Testament, they remained in accord with what had already been written.

MINISTRY

This is that great, broad ministry within the church that ought to be performed by the deacons. In fact, that is the word used: "Let us give ourselves to deaconing." The office of deacon is a very broad office and may cover almost any kind of service in the church. They are really the closest assistants to the pastor, to help him in every duty and to help the church. It should be a place of service, not a position of power.

TEACHING

Teaching is a gift always. The teacher is a gift; let him give attention to his teaching. Teaching is the art of making the unchanging divine message understandable to the unlearned.

EXHORTATION

Exhortation is sometimes "run into the ground," but it is necessary for those who have been given this gift to exercise it. Prayer meeting is a good place for it. Exhort those Christians that are growing weak. Strengthen them, encourage them.

GIVING

"He that giveth" refers to a gift that is seldom regarded as one. Every one of us has that gift to a certain extent. This exhortation is for those who have some degree of material wealth. God has granted to some laymen in the church the ability to acquire and dispense wealth. He has prospered such men in order that they might use their money for God.

RULING

"He that ruleth" applies to those in the place of authority. The church is not, in the absolute sense, a democracy. We read in other places in the New Testament of the elders who *rule*. They are to rule under God, of course. They are the shepherds. But there is a gift for those who are elders. The boards of the church come in at this point, men who have the ability to exercise oversight. "Let them give diligence."

MERCY

"He that showeth mercy" undoubtedly has wide application. This may be in relation to the poor, taking care of them. The church has always had a ministry there. Down through the ages it has been the church that has led the way. Men never started a hospital until the church started one. Men generally did not show mercy to the sick. Within the church there are folks who go about their business in an unspectacular way, and yet they have a wonderful ministry visiting the poor and the aged. If God has called you to this, you ought to be using that gift and not be trying to exercise the more spectacular gift of teaching.

When God has called a man and given him a certain gift, he is not to do something other than that for which God has called him.

A LIFE OF LOVE

Now we come to the flower of the Christian life. There is the further appeal in the words, "Let love be without dissimulation is actually the word *hypocrisy*. It is a tragic thing that the greatest grace of the Christian life is sometimes made a cloak for hypocrisy. No wonder Paul admonishes against it.

The remainder of chapter 12 explains how love should manifest itself.

This covers an area that is twofold: first, love within the church, and then, in the latter part of the section, love outside of the church.

Verse 13 identifies love within the church: "distributing to the necessities of the saints"—that is in the church. Notice also verse 10. What kind of love is mentioned? "Brotherly love," that is, in the church.

Verse 17 identifies love outside the church: "recompense to no man." Now you are including everybody. Verse 18 strengthens the idea: "live peaceably with *all* men." So, first it is love in the church, and then love outside the church.

In verse 9 the word *cleave* in the Greek, means "to be glued." "Glue yourself fast to the good thing." It is the same word used in the eighth chapter of Acts, where the Spirit said to Philip, "Go near, and join [glue] thyself to this chariot" (Ac 8:29).

Verse 10 in the ASV reads somewhat differently: "In love of the brethren," and the word is in *Philadelphia*. That is what it is literally—brother love, not *"brotherly* love." It is the love that ought to exist between brothers. Anybody could have "brotherly" love, love *like* a brother loves; but what God wants us to have is brother love itself.

In verse 11 Paul touches on a delicate matter when he says, "not slothful in business." Business in the church dare not be neglected. The church ought to be run as businesslike as any other organization. Paul is still talking about love when he says this, for love in business is not slothful.

The expression *fervent in spirit* in another version has been translated beautifully: "in enthusiasm be at the boiling point." The figure in the Greek actually indicates something that is about ready to boil over! The Lord help the church that is dead and has no enthusiasm! Be fervent! Do not be afraid to say "amen" once in a while, if the Spirit so moves you.

"Rejoicing in hope; patient in tribulation; continuing instant in prayer; distributing to the necessities of the saints" (vv. 12, 13). If you see a Christian that is in need, you ought to share with him. "Given to hospitality." The word *given* literally means "pursuing." Do not merely be ready to entertain folks when they come in on you, but *pursue* hospitality! Paul said in Hebrews, "Some entertained angels unawares." And in the Old Testament account, Abraham ran after the three strangers and said in effect, "You must come in and eat" (see Gen 18:2-3).

Verse 14 sounds like the Sermon on the Mount. Verse 15 continues, "Rejoice with them that do rejoice; weep with them that weep." Do you remember how the Lord Jesus Christ beautifully exemplified those two things? He went to the marriage feast and rejoiced with them that rejoiced. Then a little later, He stood beside the grave of Lazarus and He wept.

Verse 16 points to another aspect of love. "Mind not high things, but condescend to men of low estate." He brings in the matter of humility again. Love will not manifest itself in refusing to associate with those of a lower class. But love condescends. What a lesson in condescension we have in the example of our Lord and Saviour! "Who, being in the form of God thought it not robbery to be equal with God: but made himself of no reputation" (Phil 2:6, 7). He didn't hang onto His high position, but He condescended to take on Him our flesh and blood and walk in the midst of sinners. Paul is saying, "Do you see what I am doing now? I am beseeching you by the mercies of God, because it was by the mercy of God that He came down."

Verse 17 reaches beyond the church and takes in the outsiders. When a man does evil, do not pay him back that way. The word *honest* means honorable or beautiful; so, "take thought for the things honorable in the sight of all men." Whenever you see a Christian who says, "I do right and I don't care what people think about me," he is not paying heed to Paul's exhortations. We ought to have some regard for the sight of men. Of course we are not to be slaves to public opinion; yet it is wrong to have this attitude: "I do as I think God leads me, and let the chips fall where they may." Rather, let us take thought for the things that are beautiful, and then there will be no reproach upon the church of God.

Verse 18 confronts believers with a most difficult task, and only by the grace of God can we do it. "If it be possible"—

there he is talking not about you, but the other fellow. The second phrase talks about you: "As much as in you lies"—the emphasis on *you*—"live at peace with all men." That does not mean peace at the expense of righteousness, but the point is this: you are never to be the one to break the peace. If the other fellow breaks it, even then you are to do all you can to keep the peace. When the peace is broken, don't look at the other fellow, but look at yourself and see if you have done all you can do.

We are not to use this exhortation for simply giving in to everything that comes. For instance, when it concerns me individually, then it is right for me to give, give, give to the last drop, and never break the peace! But I also have a duty to others in my life, and when, by permitting somebody to run over me, I fail in my duty to others, then that is a different matter.

Verse 19 explains the underlying reason for saying this. Paul begins, "Dearly beloved." He knows he is uttering a hard thing. The people of his time were accustomed to taking revenge, perhaps even more than today. "Do not avenge yourselves, but *give place to wrath,*" that is, the wrath of God. Let us not imagine this means the wrath of other men or even the wrath of ourselves. It means the wrath of God. The word *God* ought to be supplied at this point, for He is involved. Apparently the translators of the ASV thought it meant that, for they rendered it that way into English. "Give place to wrath." Why? "Because it is written, Vengeance is mine; I will repay, saith the Lord." It is not our business to repay men for what they do to us. Any effort on our part to administer justice will fall far short of the true situation.

But if the believer is not satisfied with that and feels that he *must* do something in repayment, then there is a way to do it. This is set forth in the twentieth verse: "If thine enemy hunger, feed him; if he thirst, give him to drink." That is the only kind of repayment that is permitted the Christian. In doing that, what will you do to him? "Heap coals of fire on his head." What do you think that means? A lot of folks are at sea and do not know just exactly what it does mean. Here is my best judgment in the matter, as God has given me grace to understand: "In so doing, thou shalt heap coals of fire upon his head." If you actually heap coals of fire on his head, you will destroy him in the sense that you will destroy him as your enemy. That is the kind of repayment to make. Or, if you want to look at it as some others do: Very often there is nothing that burns and brings greater remorse than for a man who has done you damage to realize that you have forgiven him for all of it, and that you have treated him kindly. In that sense, it would be a revenge and would destroy him as your enemy.

Paul sums it all up in the twenty-first verse: "Overcome evil with good." Paul had begun his exhortations by saying, "Be not conformed . . . but be ye transformed." The word *good* ought to be the dominant word in the Christian life, from one end to the other. God's people who have been listening to the mercies of God ought to be very prayerful in the presence of these exhortations to holy living. We ought to have regard for the exhortation that says, "I beseech you by the mercies of God, that ye present your bodies a living sacrifice!"

21

The Christian Life as One in Subjection to the State

THE SUBJECT OF THIS CHAPTER is clearly indicated in the first verse: "Let every soul be subject unto the higher powers." In the third verse appears the word *rulers*. There seems to be no question that the subject is the Christian and his relation to the state.

There was need for instruction on this topic in the early church, as there is need for it today. The church at that time was undoubtedly made up to a large extent of Jewish members, and the Jews had a peculiar feeling when it came to bending the knee to a Gentile ruler. Notice the account in Mark of Jesus being questioned by Jewish leaders concerning His attitude toward the Roman government. The Pharisees declared it was wrong to acknowledge a Gentile ruler; the Herodians, being politicians, thought the best policy was to acknowledge Caesar and Herod. The same question was in the minds of the early church members.

An instance of the attitude of the Roman government toward the Jews appears in Acts 18:2: "Claudius had commanded all Jews to depart from Rome." One of the reasons why the Jews were told to get out of Rome was undoubtedly because of their attitude toward the Roman government.

The church was at this time filled with Jews, and the church held the doctrine of the kingship of Jesus. Whether a man was a Jew or a Gentile in the church, he believed that Jesus Christ was King of kings and Lord of lords—and he was right. In Acts 17:7 is a little hint of this. This is an accusation brought against Christians: "These all do contrary to the decrees of

217

Caesar, saying that there is another king, one Jesus." They held to the doctrine of the kingship of Jesus, and they deserve every bit of credit for doing so.

But unfortunately, some men had difficulty in reconciling the doctrine of the kingship of Jesus with the Gentile rule on earth. The doctrine might not pose difficulties to the actual Christians, but tempt those who were professing Christians, who might desire to use this doctrine as a pretext to license the exercise of human passion. Therefore it was very essential that Paul deal with this subject.

There is a connection betwen this chapter and the one preceding. There are some who have denied any connection. Verses 19 and 20 had taught the avoidance of vengeance and the exercise of mercy toward an offender. When Paul taught that, people might respond, "If we act upon that rule, the world will be plunged into a veritable chaos, for wicked men will take advantage of us." For our Lord Jesus Christ, when he was struck, turned the other cheek; when He was insulted, did not give back insults; He did not fight evil; and He did not conquer His enemies either. They put Him to death upon the cross. There are sometimes men who have no regard for your kindness. Thus, the charge is that if we treat men on this basis, the very foundations of human government will be swept away.

Now we come to the thirteenth chapter. The twelfth chapter is the rule for those who are Christians, those who belong to the church. But the state is different. The state is a divine institution with its own definite duties. It is not our business as a church to see that the world is not plunged into lawlessness, but it is easy for the believer to conclude this.

Now for the outline. Here is the key to the outline: Verse 1 presents the "higher powers," which can be summed up in one word, the *state*. Verse 8 proposes another idea, "Owe no man anything save to love one another: for he that loveth his neighbor hath fulfilled the law" (ASV). After referring to the state itself, Paul goes down to the individuals in the state, so we will see that this section in the outline deals with the *citizens of the state*. Verse 11 points to "the day." What day is that? There is only one day, the *day of the Lord's coming* is always in mind when Paul talks that way.

All three of these topics are linked together very closely. Perhaps the outline and its exposition will help to illuminate this relationship. The outline is threefold:

1. The Christian's duty to the state (vv. 1-7)
2. The Christian's duty to the citizens of the state (vv. 8-10)
3. The Christian's duty in view of the near approach of the coming of the Lord (vv. 11-14).

There are in these three sections of the outline, three words which sum up and describe the duties which are set forth in each section: verse 1—subjection; verse 8—love; verse 11—wakefulness. The Christian's duty to the state is subjection. The Christian's duty to the citizens of the state is love. The Christian's duty in view of the closeness of Christ's coming is wakefulness.

There is a harmony between the twelfth chapter and the thirteenth. Look at those two chapters as one single section. In 12:1 is stated the basis of Christian duty, the mercies of God. The last few verses in the thirteenth chapter present the great incentive to the Christian's duty, the Coming of the Lord. Paul starts out with the mercies of the Lord; and he closes with the coming of the Lord!

In between the basis and incentive, Paul sets forth Christian duty in two distinct realms. In 12:4 he shows that every member is set in his proper place in the church. So first there is the Christian's duty in the realm of the church. Then, in the thirteenth chapter, Paul shows the Christian's duty in the realm of the state. The Christian's duty in the church and in the state should be enforced and performed in just one way, in love. Compare 12:9 and 13:8.

The apostle Paul here teaches what is dogmatic as to the realm of the church and the state, and therefore the first seven verses of chapter 13 constitute a passage without parallel in the whole Bible. Paul carefully avoids two errors concerning the realm of the church and the state. The first error is that view which would confuse the church and the state, uniting them, as Roman Catholic doctrine likes to do, or as is seen in the Church of England.

On the other hand, Paul avoids the other extreme of setting them in opposition to one another. He steers his course very skillfully, keeping them separate—one spiritual, the other temporal—and yet he shows that there is no essential opposition between the two. He does not oppose them; neither does he confuse them.

THE CHRISTIAN'S DUTY TO THE STATE

As to the scope of subjection, he declares it extends to "every soul." Not every church member, but *"every soul* be in subjection to the higher powers." That is the rule. When Paul speaks in the twelfth chapter about our relation to God, he says that is our "spiritual service." We render our service to God in the spirit; but in the thirteenth chapter we come to a different sphere. Our service to the state is not a spiritual thing; it involves "every *soul"* being "subject to the higher powers." In place of the word *powers,* the word *authorities* would be more exact.

The next phrase, *"There is no power but of God,"* is significant. There is no governmental authority except through God. That is exactly what Daniel teaches. He says that God establishes kings and He dethrones kings. What happened to King Nebuchadnezzar was for the purpose that people might know that "the most High ruleth in the kingdom of men, and giveth it to whomsoever He will" (Dan 4:17).

Our Lord pointed out this truth when He stood in the presence of Pilate. Pilate said in his anger, "I have power . . . to release thee" (Jn 19:10). Then our Lord said, "Thou couldest have no power . . . except it were given thee from above" (Jn 19:11). Even that profession of authority was authority that God Himself had invested in the man. This applies to the Premier of Russia, the Prime Minister of Great Britain, and the President of the United States—all power comes through God.

No ruler can hold his place except by permission of the God of heaven, and in that sense every power that exists is of God, as Paul says, "And the powers that be," whatever they are, "are ordained of God." That is a solemn statement which is needed in these days of lawlessness. We ought to teach people that they have no right to flaunt the authority of existing powers in governmental reign.

Paul draws the conclusion that opposition to government is opposition to God. The word *damnation* in verse 2 is too strong; *judgment* is better. That is all it is. "They shall receive to themselves judgment." If you withstand the properly constituted authorities, you receive judgment from them. Not only that, but God will call you to account, for we know we must all stand before the judgment seat of Christ and give an account (Ro 14:10-12). God will take a Christian to task if he rebels against the authorities.

Paul himself experienced judgment during a trial before the Sanhedrin. He said something that was just a little bit rebellious, and he was slapped by the high priest. Not knowing the identity of the man, Paul rebuked him. He in turn was rebuked, "Revilest thou God's high priest?" (Ac 23:4). The priests, in a sense, were rulers. Paul apologized. His eyesight was poor, so he explained, "I did not know it was the high priest" (Ac 23:5). That is the Christian attitude. Paul stopped immediately. That absolutely shuts out the Christian's participation in all rebellion against existing forms of government. You may say that is difficult. Whenever a government becomes established, it is not your duty to ask, "Why?" but to submit. That is the true Christian's attitude, and it will accomplish more than all the rebellion in the world. That does not mean that we are not to try to improve a form of government; but we are not to use physical force in attempting to accomplish this result.

In verse 3 the government is described as "a terror to the evil." Paul is speaking generally. As a rule, governments reward the good and punish the evil. Sometimes they get things mixed up, but even so, the mixup is often from right motives. Even in those terrible persecutions in the early church, when the Roman emperors put thousands of Christians to death, the emperor acted on what he considered the best interests of the state, because he thought the Christians were a danger to the state. That does not justify him, but it does illustrate the fact that the state exists for the good of its subjects.

In verse 4 Paul discusses the officer of the state—"For he is a minister of God." Pastors are ministers of God. But let us not forget that the United States government is a minister of God, only in a different sphere. The pastor ministers in the spiritual; the state ministers in the temporal or the material sphere.

Moreover, the government is established "for good." The apostle Paul learned that in the course of many experiences. At Jerusalem the Jews were about to kill him, and he said, "I appeal to Caesar," Nero probably. And yet that monster of iniquity, that man who is held up as the very acme of cruelty, saved the life of the apostle Paul because he was the state. Since the apostle's life had been saved through the existing authorities, he could say this.

"For he beareth not the sword in vain: for he is the minister of God, a revenger to execute wrath upon him that doeth evil." This verse undoubtedly justifies capital punishment. God's commision to the state is absolute! He has given the sword to the state and "he beareth not the sword in vain." It is the business of government to punish evildoers, and when a government seeks the extradition of a criminal in a foreign country, it is executing a divine commission. This will often require the exercise of physical force. The government is therefore discharging its divine commission. This divine directive was established immediately after the flood, as recorded in Genesis, "Whoso sheddeth man's blood, by man shall his blood be shed" (Gen 9:6). This does not mean in the sense of venting individual passion, but *man* in the sense of constituted government.

We often think that we ought to leave vengeance to God, and He will take care of it at the judgment day. That is true in the ultimate sense, but God has another way and that is through the state. That is exactly what Paul means. To take a concrete illustration, if a man enters my house and steals something, it is not my duty to retaliate by stealing something from his house. I am not to avenge myself; that is not my duty. It is the state's duty to lay hold upon him and make him restore in corresponding value. It is God who is doing it, but He is using the state as a means to the end. That takes vengeance out of the individual man's hands and places it in the hands of constituted authority. There is infinite wisdom in what the apostle teaches.

Verse 5 unveils the external and internal coercion to submission. We submit to avoid God's wrath, and in reality it is God's wrath, because He executes it through the government. That is the *external* pressure. But there is an *internal* reason why the Christian should obey, namely, "for conscience sake." This becomes valid because God, here in His Word, has told us to do that. The last phrase, "For conscience sake," limits us in our obedience to the state. Someone may ask, "Is there no limit to my subjection to the state?" Of course there is a limit. If the state asks you to steal, would you steal? Certainly you would not. If the state asks you to bear false witness, would you do it? Of course you would not. If the state asks you to commit some immorality, would you do it? If the state asks you to kill another man, would you do it? The state is limited to the extent that the commands of the state agree with the duty that God lays down for you as an individual. There are several instances in the book of Acts. The apostles were arrested for preaching in the name of Jesus, beaten and released with the charge that they should speak no more in that name. They answered, "We must obey God rather than man" (Ac 5:29). It was the regular constituted authorities that spoke, but Peter did not allow any man to stop him from preaching. God has the prior right over the soul, and this was recognized by Paul. Who is over the state? God is! God will not contradict Himself in the expectations He reveals. If He has laid down something for me, and the state tells me to do something else, there is a conflict between God and the state. In a situation such as this there is no question as to what the choice should be for the Christian.

Verse 6 brings us to a practical reminder. *Tribute* is the word meaning "taxes." Believers are to pay taxes, "for they [the government] are ministers of God's service." Remember that. It is supposed to be a fine indoor sport to beat the government, by "putting one over" on the tax collector. When the tax collector comes, he is a minister of God. The state cannot exist without taxes. When we turn in our income tax, we are not to take away anything that belongs to the government.

Paul outlines the different angles of the situation. *Tribute* has to do with personal tax and property tax. Render your personal and property taxes when they are due. *Custom* means the tax that is put on imports and export. Often people come into the country and try to smuggle something across the boundary. They think they have accomplished something. "Pay custom to whom custom is due."

"Fear to whom fear," as a phrase, has to do with our attitude toward the high officials of the land. Fear means respect, the recognition of position and the honor that should be paid to it.

"Honor to whom honor" means it is never right for a Christian to speak in a disrespectful way about any officer of the state. One day I heard a man standing on a soap box berating the President. He referred to him as "that old stiff." Everybody laughed, and I laughed too because I was not in sympathy with the administration. Yet that is forbidden here. No matter what the character of a man may be, we are to respect his office because he holds that office by divine commission, and we are to uphold the regular, divinely constituted authorities and not to help the world in its chaos of lawlessness. We are to uphold the authorities. There was never such a need for this as now. The utter disrespect that men have today for the voice of the law and of the government is appalling. It is the Christian's business to be the salt of the earth in everything.

THE CHRISTIAN'S DUTY TO THE CITIZENS OF THE STATE

Mere submission to the government is not the best way to discharge our duty to the citizens of the state. There is a better way which is described by the little word *love*. It is not enough to be simply subject. We are to perform our duty in love.

Verse 9 exhorts believers to "owe no man anything." That almost sounds as if we are not to borrow money. Some people hold it to be so. There are some saints who never permit themselves or their mission to borrow a cent. There is a great deal of wisdom in this attitude, for there has been more trouble through the borrowing of money than almost anything else in the world. Someone has said if you have a friend and want to get rid of him, lend him some money.

Perhaps we should not take Paul's statement so strictly, but rather in this sense: we ought to owe nothing that we cannot pay upon demand. A man should never assume an obligation that he cannot be reasonably sure he can pay. There are exceptions, and these must be handled on their own merits. But relations between men would be much sweeter and kinder if this were the principle that prevailed universally in the business world.

The previous statement provides Paul with a basis for a greater responsibility. There is one debt that you can never pay, and that is the debt of love. The more you pay that debt, the more you owe.

The principle of love has various aspects to the sphere of its display. These are introduced in verse 9, "Thou shalt not commit adultery; thou shalt not kill; thou shalt not steal; thou shalt not covet." If the state orders you to do any of those things, you have a right to refuse. "Thou shalt not bear false witness" is not in the best manuscripts, but the principle is there. Adultery, murder, theft, and coveting form the basis of all human law. You cannot think of a single statute that does not deal with some form of these things.

You may wonder why Paul does not say, "Thou shalt love the Lord thy God." Why does he confine himself to mere human relationships? Paul is here discussing the state. Certainly, in a limited sense, the state has nothing to do with our relation to God. But it has everything to do with our relation to our fellowman. Paul keeps out the name of God entirely and confines himself to only human relationships.

Verse 10 defines more clearly to whom love should be shown. This is toward the "neighbor" in the state, any man who exists along with us as citizens of the state.

THE CHRISTIAN'S DUTY IN VIEW OF CHRIST'S COMING

Paul comes last of all to the great incentive to do all these things. Do all this "knowing the time" or "the season." You are to work hard at this, and be diligent and zealous in these things he has been talking about, because you are aware of the spiritual situation of the age.

What about the time? "It is high time to awake out of

sleep" because "now is our salvation nearer to us than when we believed." Do not get the idea that we are not saved. There are three tenses to salvation: past (we have been saved); present (we are being saved); future (we shall be saved at the coming of the Lord, when He redeems our bodies).

Be wakeful, be watchful, because the Lord is coming. When He comes, what is He going to do? He is going to set up His kingdom. If there are imperfections in the government of today, in *that* day there will be no imperfections. The very closeness of His coming ought to make us more diligent in doing the things He lays down in this chapter.

The "night" of sin on this earth is far spent. It has extended ever since Adam. If it was "far spent" nineteen hundred years ago, what is it today? The Morning Star had already appeared. The first coming of Christ was His coming as the Morning Star, the precursor of the day. When He comes the second time, He will come as the "sun of righteousness"; the sun will rise and the day will break!

Verse 12 declares that we have a duty: "Cast off the works of darkness," those things that men do in darkness and in secret. We live in the night, but we are sons of the day, therefore let us put off those things. Perhaps there may be a reference here to plotting against human government in secret, for in the days when Paul wrote, the realm was full of secret societies (from which some of the societies today claim descent). These societies were plotting to take the government from the hands of those in authority. Instead of the works of darkness, we are to wear "the armour of light." This armor is described at some length in the sixth chapter of Ephesians.

In verse 13 Paul says, "Let us walk honestly"—honorably, becomingly, decently, beautifully, attractively, is what the word suggests. This means "not in revelling and drunkenness," signifying intemperance, "not in chambering and wantonness," pointing to immorality. These are the sins of men in relation to men.

Verse 14 brings us to the final exhortation—"But put ye on the Lord Jesus Christ, and make not provision for the flesh." Conduct yourself as though there were no flesh. Do not make provision for it, because it is supposed to be dead in the sight of God. In what respect do we "put on" Jesus Christ? In everything, of course. Our attitude toward God, toward our fellowmen, and toward the state should be what His attitude was.

Three passages illustrate what will be our attitude if we "put on" Him:

The Pharisees asked Jesus if it was right to pay taxes to Caesar, a Gentile power (Lk 20:19-26). His answer: "Render therefore unto Caesar the things which be Caesar's, and unto God the things which be God's." If you put on the Lord Jesus Christ in your attitude toward the government, you obey the powers that be in the things where they have a right to command you, but obey God in the areas that belong to Him. Peter was asked if the Lord paid tribute money (Mt 17:24-27). Peter did not know, when they asked him if his Master paid tribute, but he said "Yes," in his impulsive fashion. He knew his Lord was right, whatever He did. When he came into the house, the Lord asked him, "What thinkest thou, Simon? The kings of the earth, from whom do they receive toll or tribute. From their sons or from strangers?" Peter answered, "Strangers," to which Jesus replied, "Therefore, the sons are free." We are free from all human government, in a sense, because we are the sons of God, and our allegiance we owe to Him. But Jesus didn't wish to mislead anyone in exercising His freedom from the state, so He requested that Peter go to the sea and catch a fish. In the mouth of the fish was the coin to pay the taxes for Christ and Peter. Perhaps Peter was thinking about that incident as he wrote in 1 Peter 2:13-17, "Submit yourselves to every ordinance . . . Honour the king."

The supreme example of our Lord's attitude toward human government is seen when He submitted to the men who came to arrest Him. Peter saw his Lord going into the hands of the authorities and, pulling his sword, said, "I am going to defend Him, even though these men came from the government itself." But listen to what the Lord said: "Put up thy sword into the sheath" (Jn 18:11). "All they that take the sword shall perish with the sword" (Mt 26:52). "The cup which my Father hath given me, shall I not drink it?" (Jn 18:11). Men may talk about injustice, but never in all the history of human government has there been such an awful miscarriage of justice as in the arrest, trial, and crucifixion of our Lord, but He submitted! He did it because He was the Lamb slain from the foundation of the world, but there is also a second consideration: He respected human government. It was His hour of submission. He knew the government was wrong, and so He committed Himself not into their hands, but into the hands of the Father, the righteous judge, who shall in His good time set all things right.

22

The Christian Life as One of Consideration for Weaker Brethren

THE FIRST THING TO ASCERTAIN is the subject of this chapter. Look at the first verse: "Him that is weak." Then look at the first verse in the fifteenth chapter: "We then that are strong." Do you see the contrast?

All through this chapter, Paul considers these weaker brethren in the church. Obviously the subject is this: "The Christian and his weaker brethren." You may ask (and this is the proper place to ask the question), "Who are these weaker brethren, and what are they like?" First of all, these men are not men who are *morally* weak. That is the frequent misinterpretation. We think immediately of some man that is weak morally, who, if he does not look out, will fall into some popular sin of the day, such as a taste for liquor. Such a man is weak, but he is not among the weak brethren talked about in this chapter. These men about whom Paul is speaking were exceedingly sensitive to sin. They were so sensitive to sin that they picked out indifferent things, things that were neither moral nor immoral. If these men had been men who were morally weak, Paul would never have asked the consideration for them that he did, for to the mind of the apostle Paul, sin is never a thing to be coddled or babied.

In what way are they weak? "Him that is weak in *the* faith," not merely "weak in *faith*." What does that mean? Those who are weak in the faith are Christians who have not laid hold by faith upon these wonderful things that have been unfolded in the book of Romans. They are the men who have not yet been able to apprehend and grasp full and free salvation as it is

229

230 Romans: The Gospel of God's Grace

revealed in the Lord Jesus Christ. They have not grasped entirely that wonderful proposition in Romans 8:1 which says that in the Son of God there can be *no condemnation whatever!* They have not grasped the fact that salvation is apart from all works and the Christian, when he enters into Christ, leaves legalism and ceremonialism and all other "isms" behind him and is free! That is their weakness. They were incapable of comprehending the system of truth.

The believers of whom Paul was now speaking, namely, the weak Christians, were probably Jewish Christians. Their weakness is understandable. Contrast them with the Gentile who has come into the church and has become a Christian. He was an idolator before he came in. His religion was a pagan religion. He has been taught now that his religion was nothing but idolatry and must be put away. The Jew who became a Christian had a different situation. He had been taught, and correctly so, that his religion was of God. Therefore, when Christian faith, the proper unfolding of Judaism, came into his life it was very difficult for him to divorce himself from that which he had before. He had a tendency to cling to some of the legalism and the ceremonialism of the Old Testament—the eating of meats and the observance of days—because God gave that originally.

That was the Jewish viewpoint. But we might say, "Of what value can this possibly be to us?" But it has a value. We have some of these very same weak Christians in Christendom today. Who are they? They are the ones who are afraid to eat pork on religious grounds, saying the Bible forbids it. They are the people who won't eat meat at all, on so-called religious grounds. (There may be a good sound reason for refusing to eat pork on the grounds of health which is a different matter.) They are the individuals who will not take communion if the bread of the communion is not unleavened. The unleavened bread is a better symbol, but if you do not have unleavened bread, couldn't you take communion without it? If not, you belong to this class. You are as weak as those belonging to this class. There is also that great class in Christendom which sees virtue in keeping Lent. They, too, are weak in the faith. You may ask, "Who are the strong?" for we refer to them in the fifteenth chapter, and they are in view all through the fourteenth chapter. The strong are those who have laid hold of the great faith. They have fully grasped the wondrous things that Christ has done for the world, which Paul has been revealing in the book of Romans. They are the men who have entered completely into the rest of Jesus Christ. They know that justification is apart from works; they have realized that liberty Christ has given us and are done with rules of legalism and ceremonialism forever! They are the strong in the sense of comprehending the meaning of the Christian faith.

You may ask, "Which of these two groups is right?" Doctrinally, the strong are right, for they understand the significance of the faith, and the apostle Paul would take his stand with them unequivocally. But the issues involved are broader than merely a correct view of the Christian faith. The issues involve people, those who in all sincerity have endorsed the Christian faith, even though they do not fully comprehend it. In this situation both groups need correction in areas involving attitude and conduct.

The weak brethren need correction because their position is wrong; and they condemn other folks who do not agree with them. They engage in censorious judgment. On these points Paul corrects them lovingly. But the strong also need correction because, while their principle is right, they have misused it in their attitude toward the weaker brethren. This chapter unfolds in amazing beauty that principle of consideration and conduct for preserving the harmony and perpetuating the Christian fellowship.

The first verse introduces the theme which is to be discussed; then the three main divisions in the chapter progressively emerge: (1) the concrete examples cited (2-5); (2) the divine principles laid down (6-12); (3) the practical exhortations given (13-23).

A concrete example occurs in verse 2: "One believeth that he may eat all things." The question of food is an example of a nonmoral issue. Another one is mentioned in verse 5—"One man esteemeth one day." The observance of special days raises problems for some people.

In the next section the apostle Paul lays down some *divine principles* by which these issues may be viewed. There are three principles. The first principle involves keeping God in mind as we live. "Unto the Lord" says Paul in verse 6. He does his actions because the glory of the Lord is his aim. The second principle is set forth in verse 8: "Whether we live, we live unto the Lord; and whether we die, we die unto the Lord; whether we live therefore, or die, we are the Lord's." We all have one Lord, regardless of whether we are weak or strong. The third principle reminds us of one common judgment seat. "We shall all stand before the judgment seat of Christ" (v. 10).

Thus, there are three different principles common to all Christians: the same aim, the same Lord, the same judgment seat.

Several exhortations grow out of those principles: "Let us not therefore judge" (v. 13); "But if thy brother be grieved" (v. 15); "For meat destroy not the work of God" (v. 20).

Think of those three words: judge, grieve, destroy. Paul is saying, "Don't *judge;* don't *grieve* your brother; don't *destroy* the work of God." Notice how this arrangement of exhortations develops. The first ("judge not") is addressed to the weaker brethren. The second ("grieve not") is addressed to the strong brethren. The third ("destroy not") is addressed to both groups.

Look at verse 14 of the thirteenth chapter. This speaks of making no provision for the flesh. Surely there is a connection between this verse and the next chapter. What were these strong people very likely to do? Perhaps their very liberty would lead them into a careless attitude, which could issue in provision for the flesh. Acting on the conviction that he is free, how easily and unconsciously the strong brother could "make . . . provision for the flesh, to fulfill the lusts thereof."

INTRODUCTION

Verse 1 provides the proper introduction to the problem. "He that is weak in the faith": What attitude should we take toward him? Should we kick him out? The answer is no! We are to *"receive"* him, bring him right in, just as long as he holds the faith. We are to receive him, but we are not to receive him "to doubtful disputations." That is rather an astonishing expression and does not mean very much to us perhaps. This means, "Do not receive him just because you want to criticize his scruples." We see someone who is a stickler on things that do not matter one way or the other, and our first reaction is to criticize him. Paul says, "Don't do that."

CONCRETE EXAMPLES

In his approach to the problem, Paul takes two concrete examples. "One believeth that he may eat all things; another . . . eateth herbs." Now which is right? The first is right doctrinally, because God has given us everything in Christ, and if we give thanks to God we have a right to eat them. All those distinctions in eating and drinking were swept away in Christ.

Verse 3 is addressed to both groups. First, he addressed the strong: "Let not him that eateth despise him that eateth not." We are so likely to do that very thing. You may think, "Oh, what is the matter with him! Can't he see the truth?" Now he is going to turn to the weak: "Let not him which eateth judge." Why? "God hath received him" and what right have you to judge a man whom God has received? That is to violate the very principle laid down in the eighth chapter. "If God justifies, who is he that condemns?" Who am I to judge, even if he should eat something I did not think he should?

Verse 4 continues the admonition to the weak. "Who art thou that judgest another man's servant? to his own master he standeth or falleth. Yea, he shall be holden up, for God is able to make him stand!" By the way, that is the only security of the saints. The strength of the strong is not of himself, because it is God who makes him stand. Unless you are a true Christian and have the help of God and His strength, you don't dare to throw aside all law. You will go down! It is a dangerous thing to attempt to enter into the liberty of Christ without Him, because there is nothing to hold you. The only restraining power in this world for those who are not converted is law; and it is only when a man enters into the Lord Jesus Christ that he is free.

In the fifth verse, he goes to another concrete example: "One man esteemeth one day above another" (this is the weak man); "Another man esteemeth every day" (the word *alike* is in italics, so let us omit it). The man that is weak picks out one day and says, "This day is holy. It is more holy than the other days." The other man takes every day in the week and in the month and says, "They are all holy." That is quite different from "esteeming them all alike." *Esteemeth* means "gives honor to." One man picks out a certain day and gives honor to it. The other man says, "They are all holy." That is the true Christian attitude. You will not find one place in the New Testament commanding us to keep the first day of the week. That would be to go back to the Old Testament, imposing the sabbatic law on us, which is contrary to the spirit of Christianity. As far as Christianity is concerned, every day of your life is holy—every dollar that you earn is holy, not just one-tenth.

When we move into the day of the Lord, when all the earth will know what enlightened Christians know today, then the very bells on the horses are going to be "Holiness unto the Lord." But before that day comes, however, let us remember that we are all Christians, both weak and strong. In this present time we are not to live according to specific rule, but according to the principle with which Christ has made us free. This only makes us more devoted in our obedience to Him.

DIVINE PRINCIPLES

"He that regardeth the day, regardeth it unto the Lord." Let us turn to the other fellow who does not esteem it above other days. How does he regard it? "Unto the Lord." What is the motive of the two men? Each is seeking the honor of the Lord Jesus Christ. That is his motive. It is not the motive of either that he may go out and do as he pleases on the Lord's Day. Though their actions are different, their motive is the same.

"He that eateth," how does he eat? "Unto the Lord," and he gives thanks too. But here is the man who would not eat meat. Why? That he might honor the Lord. The motive is the same in both cases. But beware of confusion on this point. You cannot commit sin unto the glory of the Lord. That is a wholly different matter.

Paul elaborates that principle in the seventh verse: "For

none of us liveth to himself, and no man dieth to himself." This verse has been very much misapplied and misinterpreted. We have taken it like this: we do not live unto ourselves; every action affects everyone else. That is true, but that is *not* taught in this verse. Paul is carrying out the thought of the sixth verse. He is saying that no true Christian lives unto himself. He lives unto the Lord, and that is the aim of every true Christian, whether he is weak or strong. It is not an exhortation; it is a fact. No man lives just for himself if he is a Christian. God is in view all the time. Not only does he live to the glory of God in this life, but even when he dies, he dies unto the Lord because the Lord appoints the time when he goes. The non-Christians do not do that. The mere professing Christian does not do that. Whether we live or die, it is for His glory. Everything is for His glory!

We have lived for His glory, now we are His! We have the same Lord, whether we are weak or whether we are strong. Verse 9 further amplifies this point. "For to this end Christ both died and lived again, that He might be the Lord of the dead and the living."

Then Paul launches into an exhortation. "Why dost thou judge thy brother?" In this question he is addressing the weak. But immediately he turns and addresses the strong: "Why dost thou set at nought thy brother?" Then he addresses both: "For we shall all stand before the judgment seat of Christ." The man who is not a Christian will never stand there. There is just one class of people who stand there before the judgment seat of Christ, true Christians. Those who are not Christians will stand before the great white throne (see Rev 20:11-15).

Verse 12 makes it clear that "every one of us shall give account of himself to God." I will not give an account for you, nor will you give an account for me. The strong will not have to defend the weak, neither will the weak have to speak for the strong.

We are all going to stand before the judgment seat of Christ. But there is not a word said in this passage, nor any other passage, saying that we shall suffer penal judgment. We shall stand there and give an account of ourselves. Every deed done in the body will be exposed and an explanation given to Him who loved us and gave Himself for us.

In summary, we have one aim—to glorify the Lord. We have one Lord—Jesus Christ. We shall all stand before one common judgment seat—both the weak and the strong.

Practical Exhortations

In concluding the argument, Paul gives some practical exhortations (vv. 13-23). He is saying first to the weak, "Let us not therefore judge one another anymore: but judge this rather," (if you want to judge anything) "that no man put a stumblingblock or occasion to fall in his brother's way." That is where judgment ought to begin.

In the fourteenth verse Paul sides with the strong: "I know, and am persuaded by the Lord Jesus, that there is nothing unclean of itself." There is not any food on earth that is inherently defiling. The distinctions between foods were demolished when Christ died on the cross. We must even recognize that not even alcoholic liquor is unclean in itself. (It only becomes unclean when it is wrongly used.) But that is not what Paul is talking about here. If a man regards a thing as unclean (even though it be so little a thing as eating pork), his conscience will condemn him for eating it. Even though his conscience may be wrong, if he eats it, he violates his conscience and that is an awful thing to do. The man who violates his conscience on a little thing will soon be violating it on a big thing.

So in verse 15 Paul admonishes the strong. "Destroy not him with thy meat." Think of it! For a piece of meat a man will start a process going which might, if it were not for the power of God, end in the eternal perishing of a soul. Is this against the security of the saints? Can a Christian be destroyed? No. But you can (present tense) *be destroying* him. This passage does not teach what God will do, that is, how He will step in and rescue the brother. Paul is talking about what a Christian may produce by his actions. By exercising his own freedom, he may start something which could result in moral disaster (if uninterrupted) and bring ruin to another brother.

In verse 16 Paul says to the strong: "Your position is good.

You are free; you can do anything. Just don't let what is good to you become the object of criticism and misunderstanding."

Verse 17 records the great principle. The kingdom of God is not founded upon the distinctions between what you eat and what you do not eat. The kingdom of God is not a set of rules and legalistic ceremonies. In their differences and irritations, the weaker brother and the stronger brother have violated the very spirit of Christianity, because the kingdom of God is not a thing of eating and drinking. What is it? It is "righteousness, and peace, and joy." And where is it? "In the Holy Ghost."

This is just a summary of earlier portions of Romans. You may ask, "What are righteousness, joy, peace—subjective feelings?" Not altogether. "Therefore being justified" (being declared *righteous*) "by faith, we have *peace*" (5:1). That statement covers the first two items of the kingdom of God: righteousness and peace. Joy comes next: "We . . . rejoice in hope of the glory of God" (5:2). Paul has already explained, in that fifth chapter, what is the source of peace with God and joy. The love of God is shed abroad . . . by the Holy Ghost" (5:5).

This verse 17 of the fourteenth chapter is a summary of the truth in the fifth chapter. Paul says, "This is the Kingdom of God. It is not meat and drink at all. It is a question of righteousness, peace, and joy." Verse 18 makes meaningful application of the truth in verse 17. If you want to do any teaching, for instance, do not go out and teach about meats and rules. What are you to teach? You are to teach and preach righteousness. If you do this, you are acceptable to God, and not only so, but you will be approved of men. If there is anything the world resents, it is these little irritating rules that appear to have no meaning. The world can approve some things, such as righteousness, peace, and joy, even without knowing their full significance.

Verse 19 concludes this section which is addressed to the strong. The word *edify* means "to build up." Paul says to both classes, "For meat destroy not the work of God." What is the work of God? The church. God is building the church today. He is putting in members; some are weak and some are strong. Paul is saying, "For the sake of a little meat; do not pull down the work of God." I heard of a church being nearly broken up over a cake that a woman baked. Because some sort of controversy came up over a cake, it nearly broke up the church! "For the sake of meat, do not destroy [or pull down] the work of God."

Verse 21 is a wonderful verse! That word *good* might be translated "beautiful." It is a beautiful thing neither to eat meat nor to drink wine, nor anything by which your brother might be offended or caused to stumble or made weak. You may have a right to all these things. There may not be a thing wrong with doing it, but it is a beautiful thing for the Christian voluntarily to forego the thing, if by taking it he makes his brother to stumble. That is for the strong, and they ought to remember it.

Paul closes now by talking to both parties: first to the strong in verse 22. Are you proud that you know the liberty that is in Christ, as we have been teaching it here? "Have it to thyself"; do not go around displaying how much you can do and how far you can go because of your faith. Lay your faith before God and not before other people. Suppose you could go to the theater and prove that you have faith strong enough. Do not display it. You may allow things in your life because you are free, but there is a danger that you may upset another's faith.

Then Paul turns to the weak: "He that doubteth is condemned." His conscience condemns him because what he is doing is not with the faith that it is acceptable. Then he adds: "Whatsoever is not of faith is sin."

Three lessons can be drawn from this chapter: The first is a lesson for the strong. Do not despise the weaker brother. The second is for those who are weak: Don't judge your brother if he takes more liberty than you on matters indifferent to the faith. The third is for *both*. The supreme teaching of this chapter is that the voice of conscience must not be ignored. You may ask, "Isn't the Word of God above the conscience?" Certainly. Your conscience may be wrong and may need to be corrected by the Word of God, but even then, it is your conscience. Here is a man who is weak, and his conscience says, "Don't eat that piece of meat. It is wrong to do it." If he eats that meat he violates his conscience which is a dangerous thing to do. The man has started upon a road that can theoretically wreck his whole moral universe. He needs to be taken kindly and patiently to the Word of God and have his conscience corrected.

There are three guiding lights for the Christian life in this chapter. We ought to live our lives, first, in the light of the Lordship of Christ. Second, we ought to live our lives in the light of the judgment seat of Christ. Last of all, we ought to live our lives in the light of the cross of Christ. We must heed the admonition, "Destroy not thy brother for whom Christ died."

These principles ought to be the dominating motives in the life of every true child of God.

23

The Christian Life as One of Exemplification in Ministry

THIS CHAPTER is closely connected with the previous one: "We then that are strong ought to bear the infirmities of the weak, and not to please ourselves. Let every one of us please his neighbour for his good to edification."

The subject of this chapter could be exemplification. "For even Christ pleased not Himself." Paul holds up Christ as an example. We are to act like Him. But there is a better word, though the idea of exemplification is certainly here, which could be considered the key word.

Look at the eighth verse: "Jesus Christ was a minister." Verse 16: "That I should be the minister of Jesus Christ . . . ministering." Look at the twenty-fifth verse: "To minister." Look at the thirty-first verse: "That I may be delivered from them that do not believe in Judaea, and that my service." (That last word actually means "ministration" and comes from the same Greek word as minister.)

Now for the outline. In verse 8, who is the minister? Jesus Christ. The first point in the outline shall be the Ministration of Jesus Christ (vv. 1-13).

In verse 16, who is the minister? Paul, the writer. The second point in the outline is the Ministration of the Apostle Paul (vv. 14-32).

There are two aspects of Christ's ministry that are emphasized here: "Even Christ pleased not himself," but pleased others. His ministry was *sacrificial* (vv. 1-7). "The promises made unto the fathers," that is, the Jew. In the ninth verse: "And that the Gentiles might glorify God for his mercy." Christ

240

was a minister both to the Jews and to the Gentiles. The ministry of Christ was *impartial* (vv. 8-13).

There are four aspects to Paul's ministry: In the first place, in verse 16 is stated "That I should be the minister of Jesus Christ." His ministry was a *personal ministry* (vv. 14-17). In the second place, verse 19 reads, "Through mighty signs and wonders, by the power of the Spirit of God." The ministry in the second place was a *powerful ministry* (18-21). In the third place, Paul is making plans. He says, "I intend to go to Spain: I will go up to Rome, but first of all I must go to Jerusalem." In other words, his ministry was a *purposeful ministry* (22-29). In the fourth place, he asserts in verse 30, "That ye strive together in your prayers." His ministry was a *prayerful ministry* (vv. 30-33).

Christ's ministry was sacrificial and impartial.

Paul's ministry was personal, powerful, purposeful, prayerful.

THE MINISTRY OF CHRIST

Paul begins by saying, "We then that are strong ought to bear the infirmities of the weak, and not to please ourselves."

"The reproaches of them that reproached thee are fallen upon me" (Ps 69:9). The bitter criticisms that were leveled against God fell on Jesus Christ. Paul is holding Christ up now as an example to the weak and to the strong, that they should not reproach one another.

Then he calls attention to the Old Testament: "For whatsoever things were written aforetime were written for our learning, that we through patience and comfort of the scriptures might have hope." The article *the* is before that word *hope* in the original. "That we might have *the* hope," and "the hope" means just one thing: the hope of the coming of the Lord which carries hope of the glory of God, as mentioned in 5:2. Paul next speaks of "the God of patience"; he had talked about patience in chapter 5. *Consolation* means "comfort." "The God of comfort grant you to be likeminded." He is talking about these two classes, the strong and the weak, in their dealings one with the other. "Be likeminded toward one another, according to Jesus Christ." Just as His mind was when He took upon Himself the reproaches of sinners, which reproaches were aimed at God, so these men ought to be willing to suffer and to bear with one another.

The *wherefore* of verse 7 means, "what are you to do?" The answer is "receive." Look back at the first verse of the fourteenth chapter: "Him that is weak in the faith, receive." So he is going back to that idea: you are not to receive one another for the sake of arguments and criticisms of each other's scruples, but you are to receive one another "as Christ also received you." He received us freely, forgave us all our sins, all our reproaches, never reminds us of what we did and where we were wrong, but "justified us freely." God receives us in Him. If God has received us that way, we should receive the weaker brother that way, and also the stronger brother that way.

He says, "As it is written, For this cause I will confess to thee among the Gentiles, and sing unto thy name" (see Ps 18:49). Paul continues, "And again he saith, Rejoice ye Gentiles, with his people!" (see Deu 32:43). Jews and Gentiles, should not break into two separate groups in the body of Christ (where there is neither Jew nor Gentile). Paul points back to the Old Testament where they are exhorted to rejoice together.

Verse 12 introduces a passage from Isaiah. Jesse was a Jew, the father of David. "He that shall rise to reign over the Gentiles" (he extends beyond the Jewish race) "in Him shall the Gentiles trust" (see Is 11:1, 10).

Verse 13 sums up the ministry of Christ and sums up everything that Paul has written before in this epistle, because this is the end of the doctrinal part of the book of Romans.

Let us look at the first phrase of this verse: "The God of hope." What is hope in the abstract? Nothing! It may mean anything. But the Christian hope is a definite thing; it is *the hope!*

"That you may abound in the hope," that your hearts and your lives may be filled with this hope. And there will not be any trouble with your weaker or stronger brother. This is not because your mind will not be different from other minds, but because your mind will yield to that mind which is above all other minds, the mind of Christ as represented in this book.

There is no other place where joy and peace and fellowship and unity can be had. No other place exists where people who are diverse in mind, method, characteristics, nature and make-up can find unity and peace. That place is the mind of Jesus Christ, which is revealed in the Bible; and once we reject any part of His mind, as revealed here, it is impossible for us to have peace and unity.

THE MINISTRY OF PAUL

Paul says, "I myself also am persuaded of you, my brethren, that ye also are full of goodness, filled with all knowledge, able also to admonish one another." He is very courteous. "I know you are full of knowledge; I know that you are able to exhort one another." But he says, "As putting you in mind." Why? "Because of the grace that is given to me of God." What was that grace? "That I should be a minister of Jesus Christ unto the Gentiles"; and the Roman church was mostly a Gentile church.

A good many of us think of ministry as something hard and unpleasant. Paul says it comes by *grace*. Shipwrecked, stoned, beaten with rods, in prison, hungry, weary, and naked; and yet he says, "It was given me by the grace of God." If we could only view every task in relation to the church of God as the apostle Paul did, not a duty to be borne, but as a gift!

"Ministering the gospel" of verse 16 means to minister as a priest ministers. "That the offering up of the Gentiles might be acceptable, being sanctified by the Holy Ghost." The same figure occurs in Numbers 8, where Aaron took the Levites, sanctified them (in the Old Testament sense), and then offered them up to God. The apostle Paul was a priest ministering "in the gospel," that is, sanctifying the Gentiles, as the Levites were offered up by Aaron to God. Paul was offering up all those "trophies" he gathered in his travels.

Verses 18-19 indicate that Paul would take no credit for what others did. In verse 20 he gives the reason, "Lest I should build on another man's foundation." Paul had a great ambition. He wanted to go out where nobody had ever been. In verse 22 Paul comes to the point of telling his plans. A ministry should not be a haphazard ministry. It should have a plan to it and a purpose.

"My journey into Spain" provided Paul's occasion for coming to Rome. Whether Paul ever got to Spain or not, we do not know, but possibly he did. At the time of that journey, he says, "I will come to you," because Rome was on his way. He says with anticipation, "If I may be somewhat filled with your company," refreshed as a man is filled when he sits down to a feast of good things. Paul longed for their fellowship, but of these people, only a few had he ever seen.

In verse 25 the word *minister* means not to minister as a priest, but to minister as a deacon. This gives the office of deacon a holy aspect. Verse 27 indicates that the Gentiles owe a great deal to the Jews. Paul cannot refrain from reminding them of that. Go back to the eleventh chapter where he said, "The casting away of them was the reconciling of the world." So, Paul concludes, we should share with them our bodily or "carnal" things such as food, clothing, and money.

Verse 29 presents an amazing collection of words: "In the fulness of the blessing of the gospel of Christ." Paul did not know then how he was going to come. He went to Rome as a prisoner with a chain upon his wrist and was shipwrecked on the way. Yet he came "in the fullness of the blessing of the gospel of Christ"; for he wrote, after he was in Rome and placed in a cell, to the Philippians, "I would ye should understand, brethren, that the things which happened unto me have fallen out rather unto the furtherance of the gospel." This was another way of saying that he came "in the fullness of the blessing of the gospel of Christ."

He closes this discussion with a plea: "Now I beseech you, brethren, for the Lord Jesus Christ's sake, and for the love of the Spirit, that ye strive together with me in your prayers to God for me." The minister of God needs the ministry of prayer on his behalf. It is a ministry that the world does not take much account of, yet there is nothing greater than a prayer ministry.

Paul tells them three things that he wants them to pray about. He is very specific. *Pray that I may be delivered from them that do not believe.* He is going down to Jerusalem, where the unbelieving Jews tried to kill him. They hated him! He was delivered from them, but not in the way he expected. He was delivered into the hands of Rome and so escaped with his life.

Pray that my ministry might be acceptable. There were some Jewish Christians who did not like Paul. A message is sometimes accepted from one person, but not accepted from another. These Jews felt that way about Paul. Paul's attitude could have been, "If they won't take it from me, they won't get it." But instead Paul said, "Pray that they will accept it." What a beautiful spirit that is!

Pray that I may come to you with joy. He went up as a prisoner, and when the brethren met him, they kissed and greeted him. This was a great encouragement to him. For two whole years he was permitted to dwell in his own hired house, where he preached the gospel to every one who came. So this prayer was answered, too.

In verse 32 Paul insists that his visit must be "by the will of God." In other words, "I want to come to Rome, but I am not going to tell God how to do it." The purpose of his visit: "that you may be refreshed."

Then he closes with that beautiful benediction, addressed to those two groups of Christians who had been engaged in strife: "Now the God of peace be with you all. Amen."

May the Lord help each one of us, that our ministry may be fashioned after the ministry of the Lord Jesus and the ministry of Paul: sacrificial, impartial, personal, powerful, purposeful, prayerful!

24

The Heartwarming Conclusion to a Great Revelation

WHILE TO SOME the final chapter of Romans may not look very interesting, often those portions of the Word of God which appear at first sight to be the least interesting are simply packed with precious things! Not many, in reading the Bible devotionally, will turn to a genealogical list or catalogue of names. This doubtless includes the sixteenth chapter of Romans. Yet there are items in this sixteenth chapter that make it worthwhile to spend a time with it.

As to general subject, there is none. It is simply a conclusion to the whole book. There is, however, a key phrase:

Verse 2—"That ye receive her *in the Lord.*"
Verse 3—"My helpers *in Christ Jesus.*"
Verse 7—"Who are of note among the apostles, who also were *in Christ.*"
Verse 8—"My beloved *in the Lord.*"
Verse 9—"Our helper *in Christ.*"
Verse 10—"Salute Apelles approved *in Christ.*"
Verse 11—"Which are *in the Lord.*"
Verse 12—"Who labour *in the Lord* . . . which laboured much *in the Lord.*"
Verse 13—"Rufus chosen *in the Lord.*"
Verse 22—"I Tertius . . . salute you *in the Lord.*"

That phrase occurs eleven times in this chapter, which contains only twenty-seven verses.

Although this section is not tightly structured, an outline can be placed on it: (1) commendation (vv. 1-2); (2) greetings

(vv. 3-6); (3) a warning (vv. 17-20); (4) salutations (vv. 21-24); and (5) the doxology (vv. 25-27).

The second point and the fourth point appear to be the same: "greetings" and "salutations." In the second division Paul mentions people to whom the greeting is sent, while in the fourth division he mentions those with him who are sending greetings.

COMMENDATION

This woman, Phoebe, undoubtedly carried the Roman epistle up to Rome. The early church was under the impression that this letter was carried up to Rome by Phoebe. She has three credentials that he mentions: "Our sister . . . a servant of the church . . . a succourer [or helper] of many and of myself also." The word *servant* in the Greek means deaconess. Phoebe was a deaconess. It is such that he recommends her to the church at Rome.

Here is perhaps the first instance of a church letter, for it really was Phoebe's church letter, in which Paul recommends her from the church at Cenchrea to the church at Rome; and he asks them, "as becometh saints, and that ye assist her in whatsoever business she hath need of you." Paul is referring to business that the woman had in Rome to attend to. She may have been a wealthy woman and owned property, or perhaps she was a merchant. But Paul is saying, "Give her all the assistance you can." Here is a beautiful lesson for us! We should always give our brethren all the assistance we can.

GREETINGS

He singles out Priscilla and Aquila as having done something: "Greet Priscilla and Aquila, my helpers in Christ Jesus." Then he adds, "Who have for my life laid down their own necks."

They were Jews, apparently a man and his wife, perhaps of some means, who made it their business to go to different places and help Paul with his work. First they were at Rome; then, driven out of Rome, they went to Ephesus. What a wonderful thing for a man and his wife: having sufficient means to provide for themselves, they could go to a mission field and stand by an evangelist and provide for his need. The wife is named first, and not the man; this was the couple who took Apollos aside and taught him "the way of God more perfectly" (Ac 18:2, 18, 26).

"Likewise," Paul says, "greet the church in their house." For two centuries the Christian church did not build temples nor special buildings in which to hold their services. All their means and effort went to the preaching of the gospel; and they met in the homes. Naturally, this man and wife who were tent-makers would have a large chamber in their house where they made the tents; and that room evidently provided a meeting place for the church. And so Paul says, "Greet the church that is in their house."

There is a beautiful story that comes down to us from the record of Justin Martyr He was killed by the Roman government in the third century. When he was on trial before the Roman prefect the prefect said to Justin Martyr, "Where do you Christians assemble?" Justin Martyr said, "We do not, as you suppose, meet in one place; for our God, the God of the Christians, fills heaven and earth and therefore He is present anywhere. We can meet anyplace and have communion and fellowship with Him. When I go to Rome, I have a home, where I go and remain; and those Christians who desire to hear me teach come into that home."

In the fifth verse "Salute Epaenetus, my beloved, who is the firstfruits in Achaia unto Christ" (or in Asia, as it no doubt should be). In verse 6 Paul urges them to "greet Mary" (a Jewish name) "who bestowed much labor on us." According to verse 7, Paul remembers certain "kinsmen." They were probably Jews; and he would speak of every Benjaminite as a kinsman of his. Referring to them as "my fellowprisoners" must indicate that they were in some way associated with his prison experience.

Another little personal detail appears in this verse, "Who also were in Christ before me." They were Christians before Paul became a Christian.

Verses 8 and 9 record two names, Amplia and Urbane, both very common slave names, found in the archeological inscriptions of the city of Rome and Corinth. The church at Rome had in its company many of the slaves.

He mentions "Stachys, my beloved." Then he salutes "Apelles, the approved in Christ," and the word *approved* means tested. Evidently this man had at some time or other passed through some affliction, and having been tested, was found approved.

Verse 10 urges them to "salute them which are of Aristobulus' household." Aristobulus was not a Christian. He was probably the grandson of Herod the Great, a friend of the Roman emperor. When one of these subkings died, his slaves automatically became the property of the Roman emperor. Evidently these slaves, the household of this man, at his death had been transferred to Rome and were there in the household of the Roman emperor. They evidently had become Christians.

We learn from verse 11 that this man Herodian had been given his name from the fact that he was part of Herod's household. Paul singles him out as worthy of salutation with them that are "in the Lord." We know very little about Narcissus. But he had been a notoriously wicked man. He was put to death about three years before this epistle was written. While Paul is not sending greetings to the man himself, he is sending greetings to the man's household.

Verse 12 introduces Tryphena and Tryphosa who were sisters. They may have been twins. The names mean "those who live voluptuously." Though the names are pagan, Paul turns his attention to the fact that in reality these two sisters were laboring very much in the Lord.

In the next part of the verse he says, "Salute the beloved Persis," a woman, for the name was feminine. This shows some of the beautiful delicacy of the apostle Paul. In the eighth verse, Ampliatus is "my beloved"; and in the ninth verse Stachys is also "my beloved." Those are men, but when Paul mentions the name of a woman, he leaves out the pronoun. He was careful in the courtesies and delicacies that a man ought to have, never stepping across the line that would bring reproach upon his name. Persis may have been an elderly woman because Paul refers to the labor of this woman as something of the past. "She labored much in the Lord."

Then, the thirteenth verse says, "Rufus, chosen in the Lord."
Mark 15:21 records that Simon the Cyrenian (who carried the
cross of Christ after the Lord fell under its weight) was the
father of Rufus. Up at Rome is the son of the man who bore
the cross of Christ. Evidently the father had gone to be with
the Lord, but the mother still remains. Paul refers to her as
"his mother and mine." This woman has evidently treated
Paul as a son, and he refers to that event in the past.

A WARNING

When you meet people who cause divisions and who become
stumbling blocks (division has to do with arguments over doctrine; stumbling blocks consist of offenses to a Christian's
sensitivity), you are not to argue with them. You are to "mark
them and avoid them," get as far away from them as possible.

In these modern times we are told we must have unity above
all else. The idea of being united has been exalted to the very
skies, and very often at the price of truth and purity. In this
verse, the apostle Paul does not talk about divisions and offenses in the abstract sense, but they are "divisions and offences
contrary to the doctrine which ye have learned." This is a very
plain commandment that the Christian is never to surrender,
even for the sake of unity, to any man or woman who brings
some teaching contrary to the doctrine we have learned in this
book. In other words, the truth is exalted above unity. If it is
possible for us to have truth and unity, we will praise the Lord!
But if it is impossible, hold to the truth!

We are not to split over trivialities, yet when it comes to
fundamental truth, we are to cling to that truth as we would
cling to life itself.

According to verse 18 these divisive people think of nothing
but themselves. It is all selfish. "By good words and fair
speeches they deceive the hearts of the simple." Christendom
is filled today with men who are teachers, who use the very
same language we do—who talk about the Lord Jesus Christ,
the atonement, the resurrection, the coming of the Lord, inspiration—but they do not mean at all what you and I mean
when we speak of these things. They use the very phraseology
of the Bible, but they do not mean what the Bible means.

Why did the apostle Paul warn the church at Rome, if they had no false teachers? The reason is given in the nineteenth verse. All over the Roman Empire, people had heard of this wonderful church—how willing the Christians were to work, how easily led by any man who wanted to teach them. Paul knew that it would not be long before false teachers would converge on this church. Here was a wonderful church, a church where a man could make a name for himself.

He gives them a little note here in the nineteenth verse: I rejoice therefore over you; but I would have you wise unto that which is good, and simple unto that which is evil." The moralists say today, "Just turn that around—be wise about the evil and simple about the good." That is not Christianity. We hear a great deal about the sophistication of youth. The young men and the young women know everything about evil. They tell us that it is a good thing for a young man to sow his wild oats. That is a lie of Satan! God, in His Holy Word, declares that we should be simple, guileless, in ignorance of evil.

Verse 20 has reference to the first prophecy in the Bible of the coming of the Messiah (Gen 3:15). The God of peace is in contrast to these false teachers, who always stir up strife. "Shortly" does not mean that the time is near, but it means when God starts in, the work will be done quickly—very shortly.

SALUTATIONS

Verse 22 reveals a beautiful aspect to Paul. Who wrote this epistle? The apostle Paul did, but he did it by dictation. He had a secretary, and that man's name was Tertius. When he came to Tertius, he could have said, "Tertius sends his greetings," but the apostle Paul is so gracious and thoughtful that he said, "Tertius, you send your greetings yourself." So we have the personal greetings: "I Tertius, who wrote the epistle, salute you in the Lord."

Verse 23 continues, "Gaius mine host"; he is the man that Paul baptized at Corinth (1 Cor 1:14). He was probably a wealthy man, because he was not only Paul's host, but the host of the whole church which met in his home.

Then Paul says, "Erastus, the chamberlain of the city,

saluteth you." Corinth was no mean city. We might compare it favorably with Philadelphia. You know how great a man a treasurer of Philadelphia would be. This man, who was the treasurer of the city, and Gaius were probably wealthy men.

THE DOXOLOGY

There follows another benediction. "The grace of our Lord Jesus Christ be with you all. Amen" Then comes the doxology. I want to refer back to the first chapter. Those of you who have followed the studies will remember that Paul says, "I long to see you that I may impart to you some spiritual gift, to the end *that you may be established."* That is the reason Paul wanted to go to Rome and why he wrote this epistle. After he wrote this and looked back over the epistle, Paul realized that only God can establish. Paul could not in any final sense do it, and so now this doxology:

> Now to him that is of power to establish you according to my gospel and the preaching of Jesus Christ, according to the revelation of the mystery, which was kept secret since the world began but now is made manifest, and by the scriptures of the prophets, according to the commandment of the everlasting God, made known to all nations for the obedience of faith: to God only wise, be glory through Jesus Christ forever. Amen.

The mystery is not developed. Paul develops it in Ephesians. But it was no mystery that God had some promise for the Gentile world. That was promised in the Old Testament. The mystery was that God was going to receive Jew and Gentile into the same body, the church of Jesus Christ. He is saying that "my gospel and the preaching of Jesus Christ is according to the mystery," that the Jew and the Gentile shall be received together.

The scriptures of the New Testament prophets, not the Old Testament, is here meant.

Then he closes: "To the only wise God, through Jesus Christ, to whom be the glory forever. Amen."

That will be a wonderful day. As we have passed through the book of Romans there have been many things not easy to explain, and perhaps never fully understandable in this life, but it will be wonderful to sit down with Paul and with Gaius, Erastus, Priscilla, Aquila in that day to come. Someday we are going to meet them all! and at last we shall know something of the details that we have been trying to point out in this book.

It has been a great privilege for me to study the book. But we have not finished with it; we have just begun. The many times you read Romans in the future will only give an opportunity for the Holy Spirit to open up new truths.

Our Father, we thank Thee for the book of Romans. We ask Thee, our Father, as we come to the conclusion of this study, that somehow the doctrines of this book may be experienced in our lives, and that in some small way we shall walk more worthy of the calling wherewith Thou hast called us. In the name of our Lord Jesus we ask it. Amen.